Culturally Competent
Family Therapy

CULTURALLY COMPETENT FAMILY THERAPY

A General Model

SHLOMO ARIEL

Foreword by Florence Kaslow

Westport, Connecticut
London

The Library of Congress has cataloged the hardcover edition as follows:

Ariel, Shlomo.
   Culturally competent family therapy : a general model / Shlomo
Ariel ; foreword by Florence Kaslow
      p.   cm.—(Contributions in psychology, ISSN 0736-2714 ; no.
37)
   Includes bibliographical references and index.
   ISBN 0-313-31079-3 (alk. paper)
   1. Family psychotherapy—Cross-cultural studies—Handbooks,
manuals, etc.   2. Psychiatry, Transcultural—Handbooks, manuals,
etc.   3. Cultural psychiatry—Handbooks, manuals, etc.
4. Psychoanalysis and culture—Handbooks, manuals, etc.   5. Cross-
cultural counseling—Handbooks, manuals, etc.   6. Family—Mental
health—Handbooks, manuals, etc.   I. Title.   II. Series.
RC455.4.E8A76   1999
616.89'156—dc21   99-11269

British Library Cataloguing in Publication Data is available.

A hardcover edition of *Culturally Competent Family Therapy* is available from
Greenwood Press, an imprint of Greenwood Publishing Group, Inc.
(Contributions in Psychology, Number 37; ISBN 0-313-31079-3).

Library of Congress Catalog Card Number: 99-11269
ISBN: 0-275-96655-0

First published in 1999

Praeger Publishers, 88 Post Road West, Westport, CT 06881
An imprint of Greenwood Publishing Group, Inc.
www.praeger.com

Printed in the United States of America

The paper used in this book complies with the
Permanent Paper Standard issued by the National
Information Standards Organization (Z39.48-1984).

10 9 8 7 6 5 4 3 2 1

Contents

Foreword

In the past decade and a half there has been an increasing emphasis on the fact that all therapy should be sensitive to the patient's cultural, ethnic and religious identity and what part these background factors play in the problems perceived and presented by the patients in therapy. With the rapid and mounting influx of large numbers of immigrants to many host countries, the need to attend to issues emanating from relocation and displacement like acculturation versus cultural pluralism; different legal and social expectations; different languages, customs and mores; new intergenerational conflicts as children take on the values and behaviors of their adopted country more quickly than their parents do; and sometimes the residuals of multiple traumas, including having witnessed genocide and political repression, has escalated.

In this book Ariel has promulgated a fascinating and clinically useful model for conducting culturally competent family therapy. Much sensitivity is conveyed as he articulates his paradigm; his theoretical discussions are further illuminated in well-selected case illustrations. This comprehensive volume could well become essential reading for those engaged in treating bicultural couples; couples who have adopted children from other countries, or other racial and ethnic groups within their own country; patients from very different cultural backgrounds and with very different life experiences from one's own, as well as for those teaching, supervising and conducting research about this seminal issue in today's society.

This enlightening treatise has relevance to the thinking and practice of mental health professionals across national borders; it is both timely and universal in its depth, breadth and scope.

Florence Kaslow, Ph.D.

Acknowledgments

I feel especially fortunate to have had Dr. Florence Kaslow as my sponsor. Her excitement about my work, her generous involvement with my ideas and her supportive direction and feedback have constituted a continuous source of encouragement during my work on this book. I am particularly grateful to Dr. Kaslow for having taken the time to write about the case of the Hernandez family (see chapter 10) especially for this book.

I would also like to express my gratitude to Professor Paul Pedersen, Series Adviser for the Greenwood Press series Contributions in Psychology for his help and support during the last stages of this work. His warm, friendly attitude has been a continuous source of energy in moments of weakness and doubt, which are an inevitable part of any ambitious endeavor.

I owe a special gratitude to my colleagues Galeela Oren Tabachnikov and Odeda Peled. For many years I have been sharing my ideas with them. I could always count on their careful scrutiny, and their comments have invariably been extremely valuable.

I would also like to thank my students Reena Amar, Shosh Aragon, Orly Bakshy, Malka Hazan, Dinah Mannheim and Sarah Silber, who participated in a course on culturally competent family therapy for social workers I conducted in 1994. Many of the exciting discussions and intriguing case analyses cited in this book are taken from this course.

Finally, many thanks to my wife Ruthie for her support and encouragement during the years of hard work spent on preparing this book.

Introduction

This book is an introduction to a general integrative model of culturally competent family therapy. In this model, concepts, methods and findings borrowed from heterogeneous sources have been incorporated into a synthesis of various current theories of family therapy. The main sources tapped have been social and cultural anthropology, sociology, cross-cultural social psychology, cross-cultural psychiatry and linguistics. All these materials have been explicated, systematized and formalized within the conceptual and terminological framework of information processing and semiotics.

This book is designed as a complete guide to culturally competent family therapy with any family of any sociocultural background. The need for such a guide is self-evident considering the social reality faced by most family therapists these days. Due to the current global trends of rapid immigration, international migration of refugees and workers, formation of multicultural families and social mobility, fewer and fewer clinicians find themselves working within a unicultural context. Most practitioners nowadays work with families of heterogeneous cultural, social, religious and linguistic backgrounds or with culturally mixed families. Furthermore, clinicians very often work together with colleagues whose sociocultural backgrounds are different from their own.

A clinician using this book is not required to have prior intimate acquaintance with, or expert knowledge of, any specific social group. The assumption underlying the model proposed in this book is that every family has its own specific culture, which is partly shared by the various communities to which the family belongs and partly unique to the particular family. The following citation from Schwartzman (1983) is relevant here:

Just as the individual develops a unique personality, learned within the context of the family, each family integrates its socio-cultural context into a unique family culture. . . . The level of abstraction implicit in a [general] cultural perspective . . . may be a misguided way for clinicians to use culture, because it is an inappropriate level of abstraction. Rather, the clinicians should learn about the family's culture by interacting with the family. . . . The therapist must be sensitive to the family's choice of modes or codes, the contents of its interactions and its values and beliefs, all of which compose the "family culture." (P. 183)

A therapist who approaches a family in this manner assimilates parts of the family's culture by means of informal, incidental learning processes, for example, latent inferences, guess, trial and error or sporadic questioning. To become really culturally competent, however, therapists need more than that. Their work should be guided by a general theory and a systematic methodology. The model proposed in this book consists of both such a theory and such a methodology.

A leading hypothesis informing the construction of the theory and the methodology had been that family culture is not a directly observable entity. It is a system of codes learned by family members since birth and somehow represented in their minds. They, consciously or unconsciously, interpret their reality and react to it according to these codes. In this book, such codes are termed *programs*, since they function in a manner analogous to computer programs. When a computer scientist attempts to construct a simulation of a certain type of activity (e.g., English speech, a boxing match or volcano eruptions), she does not attempt to describe this activity directly. She tries to decipher the activity and unravel the hidden codes, the unseen laws that make it tick. And then she tries to formulate programs representing these codes or laws. The set of programs is an information-processing system. *Family culture* is explicated in this book as such an information-processing system. Learning the culture of a particular family amounts to unearthing and formulating the programs constituting its cultural information-processing system.

Cultural family programs are classified in our model into the following four types: *axioms, categories, explanations* and *rules*. Each of these types includes various subtypes, covering heterogeneous content areas. (1) Axioms include, for instance, general ontological and epistemological premises such as "the world as we know it is unreal" and "knowledge of the world is acquired through divine inspiration." (2) Categories subsumes classifications such as brothers versus enemies, sacred versus profane, pure versus impure. (3) Explanations are "natural disasters are punishments for our sins" and "Death is caused by magic." (4) Rules include subtypes such as sexual behavior codes, etiquette, prohibitions and taboos.

In the above classification, programs are grouped according to their functions. Our model includes another classification of cultural family programs in which programs are grouped according to their contents. This latter classification yields the following types of programs:

Existential: pertaining to fundamental existential problems, such as the purpose and meaning of human life and the nature of existence.

Ecological: related to the relationships between the family and its human and non-human environment.

Family identity: referring to the family's subjective representation of itself—its self-concept, narratives by which it describes its past and its future, its subjective emotional experiences, etc.

Family structural: pertaining to proximity and control relations among family members.

Family functioning: related to marriage and family life, for example, rules defining the limits of personal autonomy within the family as a collective body, categories defining significant transitional stages, explanations of children's behavior and rules prescribing mutual obligations.

Communication: pertaining to verbal and nonverbal communication among family members and between the family and outsiders.

Coping and problem-solving: applying to family problems and crises; crisis-management techniques and coping styles.

All these types of family programs are defined and discussed in detail and illustrated by cases and examples in part II of this book (chapters 3 through 6). See also chapter 2.

The programs described above are phrased in ordinary English. Still, they are considered information-processing programs because they structure and regulate the ways in which families process information. A more detailed and precise formulation of programs requires the use of a specialized technical language, which has its own vocabulary and grammatical rules. The technical language of information processing developed for this model is discussed in part III of this book (chapters 7 and 8). See also chapter 2.

There are circumstances in which some cultural family programs become *dysfunctional*. Characteristically, this happens when the family is in a state of *cultural shock*, that is, when the family is overwhelmed by unfamiliar information its available programs are incapable of processing. Typical situations in which cultural shock is likely to occur are immigration, industrialization, military occupation, economic recession and Westernization. Most families do not become dysfunctional in such circumstances, but some do. Families of the nondysfunctional sort adapt themselves to the new situation by changing their cultural information-processing programs. They abandon programs no longer suited to the changed environment, modify old programs or develop new ones. Families of the dysfunctional sort are unable to accommodate their programs to the requirements of the new situation. Their cultural information-processing system becomes dysfunctional. Characteristic "bugs" often formed in such conditions are: blinders (processing only a portion of the input and ignoring the rest), extreme ambivalence or fluctuations (unstable interpretations of the input and unstable output), cultural fixation or regression and cultural naivete (naive, erroneous interpretations of the input).

When a cultural information-processing system is "bugged," it is in a state of stress. The outward manifestations of such stress ("symptoms") often bring the family to therapy. The hypotheses concerning culturally induced family dysfunction are discussed in detail in chapter 8. See also chapter 2.

A culturally competent family diagnosis requires identifying and formulating the dysfunctional cultural family programs, pinpointing and naming the bugs and explaining the presenting symptoms as external manifestations of these bugs. A full culturally competent diagnostic evaluation of the family involves, however, more than that. To establish a good therapeutic alliance with the family and win its trust and respect, the therapist has to at least partly assimilate its culture. Therapists are advised to obtain information not only about the family's current situation but also about its history.

Part IV of this book offers a variety of instruments serving the therapist in the process of diagnostic evaluation. The presenting-problems interview (see pp. 125–126) is designed to structure the process of obtaining information about the family's difficulties. The case-history interview (see pp. 127–130) is an instrument for eliciting data about the family's cultural past and present. A semiotic technique of recording, transcribing and microanalyzing naturalistic observations of family interactions is proposed in chapter 10. The procedures of macroscopic semantic and pragmatic analysis (chapter 10) are designed to assist the therapist in analyzing and organizing data already obtained by interviews and observations. Finally, heuristic procedures are offered, which show the therapist how to scrutinize the semantically and pragmatically macroanalyzed data and ferret out the wanted entities: cultural family programs and bugs.

The main goal of culturally competent family therapy is to solve the problems brought to therapy by removing or weakening the bugs in the family's cultural information-processing system. Since, as claimed above, bugs result from the system's inability to cope with a great amount of unfamiliar, bewildering information, the therapist's role is to help the family digest such information. The therapist's dual position of being both an insider and an outsider makes her fit for this role. She mediates between the family and its new environment. She interprets the unfamiliar information to the family in a way that makes it more comprehensible, more consistent with its own repertoire of programs and therefore less threatening. Such therapeutic moves are expected to soften the cultural shock by reducing the distance between the family's own culture and its new cultural environment. The therapist encourages the family to remove its *blinders* by showing it positive aspects of those parts of the picture it has been afraid to look at. He stabilizes the family's interpretations of their new reality and their reactions to it by showing the logic underlying seeming inconsistencies. He helps them become less naive about their new cultural environment by explaining subtleties that have escaped their notice or have been misunderstood.

Once the bugs in the family's cultural information-processing system have been weakened or removed, the information-processing system regains its adaptability. It accommodates itself spontaneously to the new environment in the ways specified above. Consequently, the presenting problems evaporate and the family is cured. The principles guiding culturally competent family therapeutic interventions are discussed and illustrated in chapters 2, 8 and 12.

The therapeutic alliance in cross-cultural family therapy has some distinctive features, which set it apart from alliance in other forms of therapy. This is due mainly to the fact that the shared cultural common ground between therapist and family is narrower in this form of therapy than in other forms. This obliges the cross-cultural family therapist to adhere strictly to principles such as: Know your own culture. Avoid an ethnocentric attitude. Achieve an insider status. Use intermediaries. Share your own self and life with the family. These and other principles are discussed and illustrated in chapter 11.

Culturally competent family therapy is technically eclectic. It makes liberal use of therapeutic techniques developed within other schools of psychotherapy and family therapy. It also borrows traditional curing and healing techniques employed in folk psychotherapy and medicine in numerous societies all over the world. Every borrowed technique, however, should be varied, modified and adapted to the cultural make up of each family with which it is to be used.

Chapter 12 of this book is devoted to therapeutic strategies and techniques. It includes a typology of therapeutic techniques—considerations for choosing techniques serving particular therapeutic goals and principles—for adapting traditional and modern techniques to the needs of culturally competent family therapy.

Many of the concepts and methods introduced in this book are found in other theories of family therapy or in the culturally competent family therapy literature (see the appendix for a review of the literature). The differential contribution of this book lies in the following:

1. This book includes concepts and methods relevant to the analysis of culture and therapy found in cultural anthropology, sociology, cross-cultural social psychology, cross-cultural psychiatry and linguistics, but so far largely ignored by family therapists.

2. Many concepts and methods proposed in major theories of family therapy have been treated Eurocentrically, with their essential cultural relativity being ignored.

In the model and methodology proposed in this book, the cultural relativity of the same concepts and methods is built into their definitions and uses.

3. To the best of my knowledge, this work offers the first attempt at constructing a general, comprehensive, integrative and systematic model and methodology of culturally competent family therapy to date.

Part I of this book includes a critical review of the current state of the art and a series of arguments why a model such as the one proposed in this book is required. This book is intended to be international in perspective. The model presented in it may be applied to any family in any country. Most of the case descriptions are drawn from the author's own clinical experience with families in Israel, or from the experience of some of his colleagues, students and trainees in Israel, the United States and some European countries. The examples illustrating the theory and methodology are taken from various cultures all over the world.

This book is designed to be a handbook for clinicians and a textbook for researchers, students and trainees. It can be used as a guide for a complete independent method of family therapy. It can also be used as a source of ideas and techniques, which can be selectively incorporated into other forms of therapy.

PART I

CULTURE AND FAMILY THERAPY: AN OVERVIEW

This part is a general introduction to the model presented in this book. It includes a critical review of the current state of the art, a series of arguments why a model such as the one proposed in this book is required and a succinct description of the model—its sources, its main contents and its structure.

1

The Necessity to Incorporate Culture into the Theory and Practice of Family Therapy

CULTURE-BLIND FAMILY THERAPY: WHY?

Until the early eighties, theory and methodology in the field of family therapy had been cultivated in a test tube, as if families lived in a sociocultural vacuum. In the major schools of family therapy, difficulties presented by individuals had been explained as manifestations of certain dysfunctional constellations characterizing their families. Cultural relatively had been consistently ignored in this explanatory format. In each of the family therapy schools, methods of intervention have been directly or indirectly derived from this form of explanation. Again, none of these methods had been differentiated with respect to sociocultural diversity.

This theoretical and methodological lacuna stands in striking contrast to reality in the field. Most countries in which family therapy has been actually practiced are ethnically and culturally heterogeneous. In immigration countries such as the United States and Israel the whole of society consists of numerous ethnocultural communities in various stages of acculturation and mutual assimilation. Most family therapists in private practice, and even more so in public practice, regularly see families of varied homogeneous or mixed cultural backgrounds, which are often different from the therapist's. Furthermore, supervisors, other staff members and the therapist frequently all come from different ethnocultural communities.

Many family therapists have realized that this cultural diversity offers challenges that have not yet been fully met by current theories and methods. They have apprehended that it is impossible to understand fully the family and its problems, communicate with it meaningfully, secure its cooperation and really help it unless one possesses intimate knowledge of the culturally prescribed rules underlying its ways of thinking and behavior. Due to the lack of a systematic basis for approaching this aspect of their work, such therapists have relied on their own common sense, intuition and experience.

One can only speculate why culture had until recently been a neglected area in our field. Until the eighties, one of the main reasons was a social taboo against discussing cultural differences openly. McGoldrick (1982), a leading figure and pioneer in the emerging cross-cultural family therapy movement, writes: "It seems so natural that an interest in families should lead to an interest in ethnicity, that it is surprising that this area has been so widely ignored. Ethnicity is deeply tied to the family. . . . The two concepts are so intertwined that it is hard to study one without the other. . . . However, the subject of ethnicity evokes deep feelings, and discussion frequently becomes polarized or judgmental." (P. 3)

Culture Is Rapidly Coming to the Fore

Fortunately, this taboo has been lifted partly. Since the early eighties the field has been enriched with a steadily increasing number of books and articles dealing with cultural diversity in relation to family therapy. This development has been one manifestation of a rapidly growing public interest, in the whole of the Western world and even more so in the United States, in multiculturalism and its sociopolitical implications. In immigration countries such as the United States, Canada, Australia and Israel the "melting pot" ideology had given way to a "roots" ideology. Racism and openly expressed intolerance are viewed by the mainstream public as politically incorrect attitudes. Acknowledgment of minority rights and encouragement of sociocultural diversity are becoming the accepted norm. Naturally, this new Zeitgeist has been inspiring both theory and practice in the helping professions in general and in family therapy in particular.

THE CURRENT STATE OF THE ART

The culturally oriented family therapy literature since the early eighties may be classified into the following types:

1. Programmatic works: outlining a general plan for culturally competent family therapy
2. Theoretical works: introducing and discussing general conceptual constructs for a culturally minded theory of family systems and therapy
3. Methodological works: proposing various methods and techniques for doing culturally competent family diagnosis and therapy
4. Generalizations: about families of specific sociocultural groups, followed by practical recommendations

5. Discussions: from a cultural perspective, of particular types of families or specific kinds of family problems, often followed, again, by practical recommendations

6. Empirical research

7. Training issues

A list of some of the major contributions in each of these categories since 1980 is presented in the appendix.

A quick look at this classified list reveals that the vast majority of published works belong to categories 4 and 5. There are relatively few theoretical works (Category 2) or methodological works (Category 3) and still fewer empirical research studies (Category 6).

The theoretical and methodological works cover various segments of the whole field. The studies dealing with particular groups or specific problem areas include numerous isolated theoretical and methodological ideas and suggestions. Cumulatively, however, they fall far short of being a comprehensive, systematic model of culturally competent family therapy that can serve as a complete guide for workers in this field.

Publications of Category 4 (specific groups) and 5 (specific problems) have been criticized on various grounds. Here is a summary of the main arguments, both mine and others:

Speculative Generalizations Can Legitimize Stereotypes

The generalizations made in these works have been derived from diverse sources: The writers' own clinical experiences, in some cases their intuitions and perceptions as native members of the groups they wrote about, history books, works of fiction, official statistics, ethnographies, sociological studies and so forth. Sources reporting the results of methodologically sound, appropriately controlled empirical research are the exception rather than the rule. This has apparently been unavoidable given the paucity of research in this field. Furthermore, such diversity is characteristic of a new field in its embryonic stage. Bearing in mind, however, the above-mentioned public sensitivity, one cannot avoid feeling a little uneasy reading some of the statements made in these works. Take, for instance, the following citations: "An Italian-American wife-mother is first mate to her husband, the captain" (Yaccarino, 1993); "Jews tend to be on their guard, anticipating attack, while privately reassuring themselves that they are 'God's Chosen people' " (Herz and Rosen, 1982); "The emphasis in African-American culture is on doing rather than thinking, feeling or talking" (McGoldrick et al., 1991). Such statements look more like the stereotypes all too often used to justify racial prejudices than valid ethnological generalizations. In default of appropriate scientific methodological safeguards, the authors of such propositions are in danger of inadvertently falling victims to their own preconceived ideas about their own or other groups.

Ethnic Groups Are Not Homogeneous

There are other pitfalls. I am doubtful whether groups such as African Americans, Italian Americans and so forth, constitute ethnologically or sociologically researchable entities. These groups are far from being homogeneous. Due to forces such as acculturation, intermarriage and social and geographical mobility, most communities in the United States and other multicultural countries have gone through changes leading to differentiation and mutual assimilation with other groups. Furthermore, in our modern world, social changes are sometimes so rapid that any given generalization about a cultural community can lose its validity by the time the work including this generalization has been published. Processes such as industrialization and urbanization, economic recessions and periods of boom, as well as deliberate governmental social policy interventions can change the sociocultural map beyond recognition within a relatively short period of time.

No Differentiation between the Synchronic and the Diachronic Perspectives

McGoldrick (1982) asserts: "There is increasing evidence that ethnic identifications . . . are retained for many generations after immigration and play a significant role in family life and personal development throughout the life cycle."

This claim warrants closer examination. In what sense may cultural characteristics be said to be "retained" or "conserved"? Do they really remain unchanged? Do they keep the same meanings and functions as they used to have in the past? Ferdinand de Sauassure (1959), the founder of modern structural linguistics, insisted that a *synchronic* description of a language (its structure at a given time) should not be confused with its *diachronic* description (changes in this structure through time). This principle has become one of the methodological cornerstones of twentieth-century social science. Many anthropologists, notably adherents of the structuralistic and functionalistic approaches, have argued that the continuity of a culture over time is more apparent than real. Culture, like language, may be viewed synchronically as a system of interrelations among conceptual units. Each unit derives its meanings and functions from its structural relations with the other units. Every unit is relative, not absolute and dependent on the meanings and functions of the other units. None of them can be understood in isolation. Therefore, cultural continuity is apparent rather than real. What is retained over time are the units, not their functional interrelations.

Another view that casts doubt on the notion of the continuity of culture is the idea that each generation creates its own new version of its groups' traditional culture. Every new generation uses what has been transmitted to it by the older generation as raw materials for this new creation. According to this conception too, elements that superficially look like relics of former states of the culture are new elements in an old disguise because they have acquired new and different functions and meanings relevant to the current context. In this view, the past does not live in the present. It is just a source of myths and symbols harnessed to present needs and purposes (see Rosaldo, 1993).

Lee (1988) describes the zeal with which Serbian Americans preserve the family tradition of *krsna slava*, a yearly whole-day ritual. A close analysis of the informants' motives for maintaining this tradition reveals the new meanings and functions it has acquired. The historical, nationalistic meanings related to past wars and persecution by the Turks, as well as the religious connotations, are hardly mentioned by these informants. On the other hand, they emphasize the ritual's functions of strengthening family cohesion and preventing intermarriage and cultural assimilation. This is understandable in the present American context of cross-cultural integration and family disintegration.

These considerations call into question the historical explanations offered in the ethnicity and family therapy literature. These explanations are based on the assumption that the past creates the present. In view of what has been said above, this assumption seems methodologically questionable.

Prevalent Trends Are Not Necessarily True of Particular Families

Finally, one fails to see much practical gain in works devoted to family therapy with particular problems of specific ethnic communities. Let me explain why: There is a fundamental difference between generalizations that may be called *prevalent trends* and those that may be termed *obligatory codes*.

An example of a generalization of a prevalent trend is: "Blacks place a strong value on being strong." If this generalization is valid at all, its validity is statistically weak. It is based on the assumption that there are significantly more African Americans than non–African Americans who value strength. An example of a generalization of an obligatory code is the rule forbidding unmarried women to lose their virginity in some Muslim communities. This generalization is not of a probabilistic nature. It is a prescriptive law that, in the minds of all the members of a particular community, has an absolute, universal and binding validity.

It is essential for family therapists to be aware of obligatory codes. Generalizations concerning prevalent trends can be misleading, however, because they do not necessarily apply to each specific case.

Suppose, for instance, that you were asked to do therapy with a male-dominated Italian American family. Is this family male-dominated because it is Italian American or simply because it happens to be a male-dominated family? No general description of prevalent trends can provide the answer to this question. However, would any specific answer make any practicable difference? Would you work differently with this family one way or the other? Suppose, further, that you met a female-dominated Italian American family. Is it a deviant family or a normal family that just happens not to conform to the alleged dominant attitude? Would you approach it in the same way as you would a male-dominated Italian family just because both happened to be Italian? Should you design different therapeutic strategies for a male-dominated Italian American family and for a male-dominated Irish American family? A therapist has to interact with real families, not with general statistical trends in the population.

PUTTING CULTURE INTO THE EQUATION

What a family therapist most needs is not a how-to-do-it book describing "blacks," "Jews" or "Hispanics" and their particular problems plus some practical suggestions, but general theories and methodologies of family therapy that take culture into account. Such general theories and methodologies will allow the therapist to approach any family of any sociocultural background in a culturally sensitive way.

Most of the existing systemic theories of family therapy have attempted to explain individual complaints by tracing them to dysfunctions in the family system to which this individual belongs. The same theories have attempted to devise mechanisms for repairing family systems, ridding them of their dysfunctions. The assumption has been that once this has been accomplished, the difficulties presented by members of the family would disappear spontaneously and without any need for further intervention on the level of individuals.

In all these theories, so-called individual psychopathology is treated as the dependent variable [D] and dysfunctions in the family system as the independent variable [I]. The functional relation Fid includes no third variable [C] referring to cultural differences. I suggest adding [C] to this functional relation; that is, to turn it into the function Fidc, which means "individual psychopathology is explained by dysfunctional family systems in particular cultural contexts."

The concept of *culture* is notoriously difficult to define. For our present purposes, it will be defined as a system possessing the same properties and obeying the same laws as the family system. According to this definition, the family is a subsystem of culture. Each family may be viewed as a miniculture. It has its own unique characteristics, but it shares many with the culture of which it is a member.

Why should it be considered so essential to make culture an integral part of family systems theory? Because this theory is lacking in explanatory power without this component. Let me specify the considerations that have led to this conclusion.

Culture Creates Both Order and Disorder

Most family systems theories attribute disorders in the individual to the family system's dynamics of coping with stress caused by external or internal changes. There are good grounds for believing that the coping mechanisms employed by families are at least partly dictated by the specific cultures to which they belong. Behind the scenes, culture plays important roles in the creation of family-mediated distress in the individual. Culture also partly dictates the attempted solutions. Families and individuals learn culturally acceptable and unacceptable ways of becoming "sick" and how to recover or be cured. Emotional or behavioral disorders in the individual are defined as such by the culture. The culture takes its toll of family-mediated individual "pathology." Such pathology serves homeostatic functions for the culture. The family is the vehicle by which the culture preserves its own equilibrium. If all these observations are correct, then culture must be made a part and parcel of family therapy theory and methodology.

Evidence from Culture-Bound Syndromes

The so-called *culture-bound syndromes* studied by anthropologists and psychiatrists are "exotic" disturbances found only in specific cultural groups. Such syndromes clearly attest to the homeostatic function of psychopathology for cultures. Here is an example:

Grisi Siknis is a condition occurring only among the Miskito, a racially mixed group dwelling in a string of villages lining the Atlantic coasts of Nicaragua and Honduras. Sufferers are mainly unmarried teen-age girls. Dennis (1985) describes the symptoms and the cure as follows:

An attack begins when the devil appears to carry his chosen victim away. The individual loses consciousness. She attempts to run away through the village and off into the bush. (P. 291)

The attacks have a sexual basis, according to the Miskito. The devils who appear want young women for sex, and they come particularly for the ones they find most attractive. Attacks were sometimes used to seduce young men. (P. 292)

When a Grisi Siknis attack occurs, groups of men and boys run after the victim, catch her, disarm her if necessary and bring her back to the house. Back inside the house, victims are tied with ropes. (P. 291)

The sociocultural background is described by Dennis as follows:

[In Miskito society] women are dependent on men for financial support and for certain kinds of work in the village. Women realize they must use their charm and sexual appeal to attract a man, but they are also keenly aware of men's unreliability.

When a man finds a pretty younger woman, or a job elsewhere away from the village, he is likely to leave, women say.

Household relationships are still based around groups of mothers and their grown daughters. Girls are strictly chaperoned by their mothers and other relatives while they are living at home. They are not allowed to wander through the village in the evening looking for entertainment.

Having attacks seems to guarantee a great deal of attention to the young victim. In having an attack, a woman seems to be saying something like: "I may be young and subordinate but I am also sexual, aggressive, self-assertive person." It is interesting that the social response to this assertiveness is additional restraint. Going beyond the bounds of proper behavior evokes a counter-response, which re-establishes the subordinate position of the victims.

Dennis' analysis of Grisi Siknis is strikingly similar to the way systemically oriented family therapists explain disturbances in individuals. A young woman reaches a transitional life stage in which she is ready to leave home and mate. This change threatens to shake the current family homeostasis, characterized by mutual overinvolvement between the young woman and her mother and excessive control of the latter over the former. This bond between them is fueled by a shared mistrust of both the girl's father and her prospective husband. These men are viewed as unable to make a long-term commitment to their wives and children. The syndrome may be viewed as a safety valve. The girl, pressed by her age-appropriate needs, partly fulfills her wishes, but may not be held accountable for her deeds, because she is "possessed by the devil." The symptoms also serve as feedback devices, because they trigger a series of curative activities that restore the status quo ante.

The unit of analysis in Dennis' study however is not the family but the culture. It is the culture, as defined above, that creates the syndrome, and it is the very same culture that prescribes the therapy. Both the disorder and the restored order are produced by the culture. Both serve homeostatic functions. To accommodate culture-bound syndromes, a theory of family therapy must include culture as an independent variable.

Culturally Naive Family Therapy Can Lead to Errors of Judgment

The following *imaginary* scenario can serve as an example of the kind of pitfalls a family therapist whose work is not guided by a culturally sophisticated theory and methodology can fall into.

A victim of Grisi Siknis was brought to a psychiatric hospital in the city instead of being treated within the community by the traditional methods described above. The case was taken by a family therapist who had read Haley's book *Leaving Home* (1980). Following Haley's strategy, the therapist joined the parents and put them in charge of restoring the girl to normalcy. She predicted, with Haley, that the parents would paradoxically lead the girl toward more independence, since in her own culture "normalcy" in a young woman necessarily involved some degree of independence. She was very pleased with the results of this intervention. Not only did the symptoms disappear, but the whole family seemed happy. They congratulated her for her "magical" cure. The therapist read in Haley's book that after "normalcy" had been achieved and the youngster had become more independent, the family should be expected to experience considerable stress and the youngster to relapse. But, to her pleasant surprise, this did not seem to have happened in this case. What she failed to realize was that when she had commissioned the parents to restore the girl to normalcy, they did not lead her to independence but reinforced her overdependency on her mother. She did not know that in Miskito culture normalcy in a young woman meant dependence. Her intervention failed to cause stress and relapse because it reinforced the family's previous homeostasis.

If our imaginary therapist had a culturally sophisticated theory and methodology of family therapy at her disposal, she would be less likely to misjudge the process and outcomes of her therapy with this family. She would realize, for instance, how normal this young woman's "abnormal" dependence was in her culture and how abnormal it would be for her to be independent. She would be more sharply aware of the cultural relativity of family dynamics.

Let us examine a number of current theories of family therapy. The purpose is to show that the Eurocentrism and lack of cultural relativity of these theories are apt to limit the therapist's perspective in working with families of non-Western cultures.

Bowen's Family Therapy and Contextual Family Therapy

One of the major concepts in Bowen's theory and therapy is *differentiation*. It has been defined as "the capacity to . . . say 'I' when others are demanding 'we' . . . knowing when one ends and another begins" (Friedman, 1991).

Boszormenyi-Nagy's Contextual Family Therapy is akin to Bowen's. According to this theory, the well functioning family is characterized by flexibility and balance in mutual rights and obligations. Role definitions are arrived at through a sensitive engagement in the intrinsic fairness of relationship. There is no hidden ledger of unpaid debts, real or imaginary, that keeps some family members in bondage to others. Genuine autonomy can be reached through consideration of relational equitability. Dependencies are reciprocal and not exploitative. Therapy is a route to the autonomy and satisfaction for the person (Boszormenyi-Nagy and Ulrich, 1981).

Bowen and his followers explicitly claim that their theory is universally applicable. But this is not so. Both Bowen and Boszormenyi-Nagy's theories are based on traditions characteristic of Western dominant culture. Their ideal of the well-functioning family seems to be derived from White, Anglo-Saxon, Protestant values such as individualism and personal autonomy, flexibility, democracy, fair play, honesty, trust, open negotiations and equality.

These values are not espoused, however, by many non-Western cultures where prevalent values are collectivism, rigid family role structures, no personal autonomy, no equality between men and women and between generations, rigid behavioral codes, hierarchical decision structure, duties and obligations prescribed by religion, family honor and no free negotiations.

Some years ago, a Muslim Bedouin member of the Knesset (the Israeli parliament) was assassinated by the two sons of a Druze Knesset member. (The Druze are a religious sect whose members live mainly in Syria, Lebanon and Israel.) The two Knesset members had a gentlemen's rotation agreement. This agreement was breached by the Bedouin Knesset member, who refused to give up his Knesset membership when his half-term expired. It was the sons' unnegotiable duty to avenge their father's injured honor and assassinate the offender. They had to sacrifice their own freedom and well-being to save their father's, their family's and their religious sect's honor. In Druze culture ideals such as personal autonomy, loosening loyalty chains and balance of fairness in intergenerational relationships are considered objectionable.

The author has recently been studying, with some colleagues and students, some cases of suicide in the Ethiopian Jewish community in Israel. Annual data of the Israeli Central Bureau of Statistics show that the rate of suicide in the Ethiopian community ranges two to six times higher than among the general Israeli population.

Analysis of these and other cases led us to the conclusion that suicide in the Ethiopic community was motivated, first and foremost, by a combination of guilt and a sense that life has lost its meaning. The guilt stems from the following circumstances. In many cases, before immigration to Israel, the head of the family deputized some of the sons to prepare the ground for the immigration. Most of these vanguards failed in their mission due to conditions out of their control. To join their sons, the families had to walk hundreds of miles through the desert. Most lost at least 50 percent of their members to hunger, disease, robbers or murder by Christians and Muslims. The vanguards felt guilty for their families' plight, however unjustifiably. This, according to their own internalized codes, denied them the right to go on living. Suicide was considered desirable, but some were prevented from committing suicide if they still had other familial obligations.

For these people, the sense of loss of life's meaning was related to their inability to fulfill their familial duties. One's self was collective. There was no such cultural concept as an independent individual self unrelated to family, community and religious duties. Due to circumstances described above, as well as the absorption into Israeli individualistic, competitive, achievement-oriented culture, these people lost their collective self. They did not have, however, a differentiated individual, private self to replace it. They had no identity any longer and therefore no reason to go on living.

One may argue that Bowen's theory can be used to partly explain the plight of these people. But, can Bowen's therapy be applied usefully to such cases? Is the goal of universal, culture-independent movement toward individual differentiation a valid goal for family or individual therapy in this community? Can therapists prevent suicide in this community by helping the clients toward greater differentiation? The answer is "no." The concept of differentiation, as defined by Bowen and his followers, has no meaning for them. Furthermore, this concept is bound to be perceived by them as something totally objectionable and unacceptable. The only way therapy can succeed with Ethiopian Jews is by reinforcing their undifferentiated self and reducing their guilt. One way to achieve this might be to show them that, according to their own set of beliefs, they are mistaken in thinking they betrayed their own people. Their religious beliefs should be reconfirmed and their collective identity restored.

Structural Family Therapy

The basic assumption behind this approach is that dysfunction is the result of the inability of the family structure to adapt itself to external or internal (developmental) tasks and stresses. One should have no quarrel with either the assumption or the techniques based upon it. Both, however, fail to take into account the following consideration: The same structural properties (e.g., enmeshment, disengagement, triangulation) in the same environment can be functional in one culture and dysfunctional in another culture, depending on many other variables. Falicov and Brunder-White (1983) assert that the same types of family triangles can be functional and normative or dysfunctional and nonnormative in different cultures. The same applies to parentification, hierarchical reversal or incongruity.

In immigration countries such as Israel and the United States, there are many intermarriages in which the wife comes from a Western individualistic cultural community and the husband from a traditional collectivistic cultural community. Such marriages are often characterized by a coalition of the parents and their son against the wife and blurred boundaries between the husband and his family of origin. According to the theory of structural family therapy these features are dysfunctional. They are normative, however, in the husband's culture. It is impossible to fix these marriages just by applying structuralistic techniques.

Strategic Schools

These are based on the same general systemic and structural premises as structural family therapy, but differ in techniques. Prescribing family rituals, one of the major techniques of the Milan school (see Campbell, Draper and Crutchley, 1991) is a very useful intervention, because rituals are one of the major forms of therapy in many cultures. This technique should be applied with extreme caution, however, in families of other cultures. In many cultures, rituals are prescribed by religion and tradition. They are conducted according to strict rules of ceremony. They have sacred and mystical connotations.

One of the family therapeutic techniques proposed and illustrated by Campbell, Draper and Crutchley is a mock funeral of the dead sister's clothes. In many cultures, such a procedure would be viewed as a terrible act of profanity.

Other techniques, such as reframing, should also not be used unless one has acquired a deep understanding of the symbolic meanings of certain words or acts in the culture. For example, an Orthodox Jew abstained from intercourse with his wife to punish himself for having breached the law forbidding intercourse during the wife's period. A strategic marital therapist, a gentile, who was ignorant of these cultural connotations, reframed the husband's abstention by attributing to him the motivation of protecting his wife against any disruption of her career. This reframing was offensive to both wife and husband.

Narrative Family Therapy

Story-telling and fables are very common therapeutic devices in many cultures. Narrative Family Therapy can, therefore, be a useful culturally competent technique. Here again, however, therapists should be alert to culturally prescribed traditions concerning the nature of stories and fables. In many cultures, the histories of the community and of each family are considered sacred truths, not to be tampered with. In other cultures, there are strict rules as to how the past and stories about it should or should not be interpreted and who does or does not have the right to interpret. In some cultures stories about the past protect secrets that should never be revealed or create a subjective reality that must not be changed. People in some cultures believe that one's fate and life history have been predetermined by deities and must not be changed or retold.

Symbolic-Experiential Family Therapy

The symbolic-experiential techniques developed by Carl Whitaker and his followers (see Giat Roberto, 1991) throw the family into confusion and create a shock effect that is supposed to shake rigid patterns. There are, however, cultures in which the rigidity of family structure and rules is a culturally prescribed norm.

Psychoanalytic Techniques

Psychoanalytic dream interpretation is based on the assumption that dreams represent a person's unconscious thoughts, feelings and wishes. This, however, is not a universal assumption. In some cultures, dreams are conceived as messages from deities, or other supernatural beings or from the dead, serving as warnings, omens, prophesies or requests. Bilu and Witztum (1993) describe a number of cases in which dreams were interpreted in such manners by ultra-Orthodox Jewish patients in Jerusalem (see chapter 12).

Cognitive-behavioral Techniques

Such techniques attempt to change erroneous cognitions underlying emotional problems and symptoms. An example is Beck's approach to the treatment of depression. Adherents of such techniques are advised to take into account the fact that emotional experiences and the accompanying ideations are not invariant across cultures. For example, there are cultures in which the very subjective experience of depression and its characteristic underlying cognitions do not exist or have a radically different nature (see Kleinman and Good, 1976).

Functional and Educational Approaches

Often such techniques are based on ethnocentric notions. Methods geared toward training immigrants or low-income families in child-rearing techniques, hygiene practices and using existing services are often based on a deficit model. They ignore the culture's traditional child-rearing norms and practices, lifestyle and indigenous problem-solving agencies and methods or consider these inferior.

Families Have a Cultural Face

The prevalent view among students of culture-bound syndromes in recent years has been that it is a mistake, based on an ethnocentric fallacy, to regard these as exceptional, exotic conditions. In their opinion, most psychiatric conditions, if not all, are culture bound, including the diagnostic categories listed in DSM-IV and ICD-9CM. "Western" syndromes such as anorexia nervosa, elective mutism and encompresis are also produced by the local cultures in which they are found, as are the cures. Both syndromes and therapy are functional within these cultures.

Culture was defined above as a system of the same genre as the family. It was claimed that the family is a subsystem of culture, a miniculture. Elaborating on this idea, it may be argued that a description of a family system in the context of family therapy is incomplete if it fails to include certain identifying cultural features. Thus, it is not enough to say, in a diagnostic evaluation of a clinic-referred family: "This nuclear family includes a father, a mother, a son and a daughter" and describe the rules by which they interact. One should also have a notion, for instance, of the culturally prescribed rules of descent applying to this family. That is to say, one should specify whether this nuclear family is *patrilinial, matrilineal* or *bilineal*. A patrilineal family is one in which one is affiliated with kin of both genders through men only. If the affiliation is through women only, it is matrilineal. In a society where the latter rule of affiliation prevails, I would feel closer to my mother's than to my father's sister. In a bilineal family, affiliation is through parents of both genders (Murdock, 1949). A runaway adolescent of a matrilineal family is more likely to obey an aunt on his mother's side who is urging him to go back home than an aunt on his father's side, even if the latter is more friendly toward him. Members of the same lineage clan share obligatory codes regulating their mutual duties. A patrilineal family is likely to respond with fury, sometimes with violence, if an uncle on the father's side refuses to serve as a guarantor for a bank loan taken by the father. They will not feel as insulted if the offender was an uncle on the mother's side. A family member who breached an obligatory code regarding his duties to his lineage clan is likely to feel extremely guilty. This guilt can be manifested by symptoms such as anxiety, insomnia or attempted suicide. To be effective, family therapists should acquire the theoretical basis for understanding such distinctions and reactions.

Family Problems Are Related to Cultural Change

The observation that family-mediated disorders and their cures are regulated by culturally determined homeostatic mechanisms has been set forth above as grounds for integrating culture into family systems theory and therapy. This line of reasoning is fully justified on the theoretical and methodological level. It is flawed, however, on the practical level. If culture provides the cure, why family therapy? Indeed, professional family therapy is not usually summoned for action when the problems that require solution are confounded within the bounds of a single culture. In such cases, the community usually resorts to its own traditional problem-solving routines. In the majority of cases, family therapy comes into the picture only when the family's dysfunction is related to its difficulties in coping with unfamiliar ecological and social conditions. Such situations characteristically force the family to deal with a foreign culture, different from its own. Transitional stages of this kind often result from war, revolution, immigration, demographic changes or technological changes. The processes of ecological accommodation and syncretism, or cultural synthesis, require adjustment strategies that are not always provided by the family's own cultural resources. Family therapy has the task of helping the family derive such new, effective, coping strategies. Therefore, general theory and methodology of family therapy should provide therapists with the conceptual and methodological tools for understanding such social change processes and for mediating successfully between the family and its new environment.

THE DISTINCTIVE APPROACH PROPOSED IN THIS BOOK

The approach proposed here is different from the ethnicity and family therapy approach in the following ways:

In the model proposed below, the source of knowledge about the culture is the family itself. The therapist speaks with the family about itself, not about social generalizations. He does not come to the family with the attitude: "You blacks feel victimized, isn't that so?" "You Irish drink a lot. What about your husband?" He approaches the cultural aspects of the family dynamics—as well as all the other aspects of its dynamics—as the family's own, not as derivatives of some abstract communal characteristics. His observations, questions and actions are, however, informed by general theoretical hypotheses concerning wider cultural aspects of families' functioning.

In the ethnicity and family therapy literature, cultural characteristics are often presented as lists of discrete traits. Therapeutic implications are also offered as disconnected pieces of advice. In the approach proposed here, on the other hand, specifics are systematically related to the general theory. The general theory contains sets of interconnected hypotheses concerning dynamically interacting therapy-relevant aspects of culture and family.

The ethnicity and family therapy literature lists numerous categories that should also be included in a general culturally sensitive theory and methodology of family therapy, for example, kinship systems, extended versus nuclear family, belief systems, stages of acculturation, and so forth. Some writers have gone further and proposed general, coherent classification systems including such categories, for example, Karrer (1989) and Spiegel (1982). DiNicola (1997) has gone even further than that. His book is to the best of my knowledge the first attempt to construct a general integrative model of family therapy. Other interesting attempts at integration are Fish (1996) and Gopaul-McNicol (1997). These are steps in the right direction. As noted, however, general theoretical and methodological works of the latter kind have so far been the exception rather than the rule. In most of the existing studies, the relevant categories are presented in a very uneconomical manner. The same categories are introduced repeatedly in many specific descriptions of particular communities. The prospective state of the art will include attempts at constructing general culturally sophisticated integrative models and methodologies of family systems and therapy, which can be applied to any family of any sociocultural background.

SUMMARY

The purpose of this chapter is to show why any theory of family therapy should be culturally sophisticated to be adequate. In most theories of family therapy, symptoms in the individual are explained by family dysfunction. Culture is not considered an inherent part of this explanatory framework. The following reasons are proposed as to why culture should be incorporated into the independent variable of this function: Culture creates both order and disorder. That is, psychological symptoms serve an homeostatic function, not just for the family as a system, but also for the family as a carrier of culture and for the cultural community to which the family belongs. Culture also provides the means to cure such disorders. Both the deviations and their correction protect the culture's equilibrium. This mechanism manifests itself very clearly in the culture-bound syndromes.

This thesis is true of situations in which the family belongs to a single, relatively homogeneous culture. However, most situations in which family therapy is sought involve fusion of different cultures. In such situations, symptoms serve not just an homeostatic function with respect to one's own culture. They also protect the culture against the stresses produced by the encounter with a different, strange and often hostile culture.

It follows from these considerations that family therapy should be culturally sophisticated. Family therapists cannot afford to be ignorant of those aspects of the family's structure, subjective experience and functioning that are determined by the specific culture to which it belongs. A complete understanding of the dynamics that produce psychological distress requires a great deal of information about the family as a cultural unit. Otherwise, fatal errors of judgment can be committed in the course of the treatment.

No therapist, however, can be expected to be an expert in many cultures or, for that matter, in any single culture. The approach adopted in this work is therefore to provide therapists with a systematic body of concepts and terms that define the main cultural traits and processes found in families of many societies that have been studied so far. The therapist can study each particular family taken to therapy and decide which of these traits and processes are characteristic of it and which are not. Our model also includes a repertoire of culturally sensitive treatment techniques. On the basis of this diagnostic evaluation the therapist can choose appropriate techniques from this repertoire and apply them to the specific family at hand.

2

The General Model of Culturally Competent Family Therapy: A Brief Outline

The line of reasoning presented above has led to developing a general, integrative model of culturally competent family therapy. This book constitutes an introduction to this model. The following is a brief summary of its main sources, its chief contents and the conceptual-terminological framework within which these contents have been explicated and systematized.

MAIN SOURCES

As explained in chapter 1, culturally competent family therapy requires the therapist to attend to culture-bound characteristics of the family's thinking and behavior throughout the therapeutic process. Many such characteristics are discussed in the culturally sensitive family therapy literature, surveyed in appendix 1. This literature, however, has not taken into account numerous relevant ideas and observations studied intensively in other fields. A wealth of pertinent materials had been waiting to be discovered in such fields as social and cultural anthropology, sociology of the family, cross-cultural social psychology, cross-cultural psychiatry, communication and linguistics.

A major area of research in social and cultural anthropology is family ecology. Studies in this area investigate culture-specific modes adopted by families in their attempts to adapt themselves to the environment in which they live. A subarea of studies of this category is coping with ecological change. Culture-bound modes of reacting to changes in the physical and social environment are described and explained. Works of this kind have adopted an *ecological perspective* (see Bell, 1992; Geertz, 1983, 1995; Harris, 1983).

Another relevant area of anthropological research is family structure, as related to the organization of the society to which the family belongs. In these studies, structure and functioning—manifested by lifestyles, rituals and customs—are viewed as two sides of the same coin. Functioning is determined by structure, and structure is determined by functioning. Such works look at culture and society from a *structuralistic-functionalistic* standpoint (see Murdock, 1949).

The anthropological literature holds a wealth of information concerning the subjective experiences of people of various cultures: belief systems (ideologies and religions), values and myths. Studies concentrating on these have adopted the *constructivistic-semantic* perspective.

Anthropological studies that attempt to integrate the ecological, the structuralistic-functionalistic and the constructivistic-semantic perspectives are particularly interesting. In such works, the physical and social environment of a social unit, its structure, functioning and subjective experiences are described as mutually interacting parts of a single system (see Barot, 1988; Geertz, 1995; Harris, 1983). The model proposed in this book comprises such an integration, with respect to the family as a sociocultural unit.

Admittedly, various theories of family therapy view the family from these standpoints and refer to the same characteristics. For instance, in structural family therapy, the problems brought to therapy are explained as responses to ecological changes affecting the family's structure and functioning. This theory describes various structural properties of families that are relevant to their functioning, for example, *triangulation, enmeshment, disengagement* and *hierarchy* (see Minuchin, 1974). Current narrative theories and techniques profess adherence to the constructivistic-semantic perspective. However, each of the current family therapy theories reveals only a part of the picture and presents a sketch from which many details have been omitted. Anthropology can offer both a whole picture and many of the missing details.

Some culture-bound characteristics of families investigated by anthropologists are discussed in chapter 1, for example, patrilineal and matrilineal descent. Many others are included in part II of this book. Their clinical relevance is explained and illustrated by case analyses.

Sociology of the family has been another primary source. Concepts and findings have been borrowed from this field, which are related to socioeconomic, demographic and ecological forces influencing the structure and functioning of families (see Adams, 1971; Anderson, 1971; Cuff et al., 1990).

Cross-cultural social psychology has provided valuable ideas and comparative research data about values, attitudes, cognitive styles and patterns of functioning characteristic of individuals and families of various cultures (see Kleinman and Good, 1985; McGill, 1987; Smith and Bond, 1993; Triandis and Berry, 1980).

The field of cross-cultural psychiatry has provided a rich source of information about psychopathology and culture. One fascinating area of cross-culture psychiatric research, referred to frequently in this book, are culture-bound syndromes (Lebra, 1976; Simons and Hughes, 1985). The relevance of this area to family therapy is demonstrated in the analysis of Grisi Siknis in chapter 1. Another relevant area is indigenous curing methods (see Morley and Wallis, 1978; Reid, 1983).

Sociolinguistics and communication theory has been another primary source. From these fields, I learned about culture-specific modes of verbal and nonverbal communication manifested in therapy with families of various social groups (see Bonvillain, 1993; Corson, 1995; Ekman, 1978; Hall, 1990; Holdcroft, 1978).

The diagnostic and therapeutic applications of the concepts and observations borrowed from all these fields are discussed in detail and illustrated by case analyses in parts II, IV and V of this book.

All of these concepts and findings had to be synthesized and integrated into a coherent, rigorous and systematic theoretical model. Before I began thinking about the possibility of creating a family therapy theory incorporating culture, I had already developed a general integrative model of psychotherapy entitled *multisystemic therapy* (see Ariel, 1987, 1992, 1994, 1996; Ariel, Carel and Tyano, 1984). In Ariel (1987–1996), concepts, observations, findings and methods found in various schools of individual and family therapy had been explicated and systematized by being translated into a unified theoretical language. The vocabulary and syntax of this language had been collected from various disciplines, notably information-processing theory, cognitive science and cybernetics, linguistics, communication theory and general systems theory (see Bertalanffy, 1973; Bonvillain, 1993; Eckhardt, 1993; Gardner, 1985; Globus, 1995; Lieb, 1993). I soon learned that culture, as represented by the above-mentioned disciplines, could be assimilated into this framework naturally and easily.

This model does not constitute just a set of armchair speculations. It rests on a solid empirical basis. The main sources of empirical data have been cases studied in the framework of various training courses I conducted in Israel and abroad or treated by my colleagues and myself in various private and public settings.

CHIEF CONTENTS

The model includes three major components:

Concepts and terms for describing the family as a dynamic cultural system
Concepts for analyzing culturally determined family dysfunction
Principles and techniques for resolving such dysfunction

Concepts and Terms for Describing the Family as a Dynamic Cultural System

The practice of culturally competent family diagnosis and treatment requires of the therapist to be aware constantly of the cultural characteristics of the family as these manifest themselves in the family's behavior. This model includes concepts and terms that can help the therapist focus his or her attention and thoughts on such elements and their dynamic interactions. As noted above, these concepts and terms have been borrowed from a wide range of relevant fields of research.

One class of concepts and terms refers to the family's dealings with its human and nonhuman *ecological environment*. The family is said to have proximity and control goals with respect to the environment. The environment imposes constraints on reaching these goals (e.g., natural, demographic, political or social constraints). The family interprets these constraints according to its characteristic culturally prescribed modes of representing reality (realistic interpretations, magical interpretations, spiritual interpretations, etc.). In the introduction to this book concepts and terms belonging to this class are labeled *ecological programs*.

Another class specifies the family's modes of representing reality. It includes the family's basic epistemological and ontological premises, its beliefs, opinions, attitudes and values with respect to the human and nonhuman world in general and family life in particular. It also comprises the family's modes of structuring experience and relating to it emotionally, along with its self-image. This class comprises the categories called *existential programs* and *family identity programs* in the introduction.

Another class covers the family's structure, its everyday functioning and lifestyle and its characteristic modes of verbal and nonverbal communication. This class includes the categories entitled *family structural programs*, *family functioning programs* and *communication programs* in the introduction.

Finally, a class of concepts and terms describes the family's crisis management techniques and coping styles. In the introduction this class is labeled *coping and problem-solving programs*.

It is not claimed that all these concepts and terms are relevant to every particular case treated. However, when a therapist works with a specific family she has this general pool of concepts and terms at her disposal and can select the ones that are relevant to the case at hand.

The following cases illustrate clinical applications of concepts and terms of these four classes.

Case 1: A therapist worked with an ultra-Orthodox Jewish family that owned a grocery shop in Brooklyn, New York. The shop went bankrupt because a supermarket was opened in the neighborhood. [Ecological constraint on the family's control goal.] Following the loss of the shop, the father, a man in his forties, sank into depression. He locked himself up in his room and spent all day praying and studying the Talmud. [A culture-bound coping strategy.] The therapist, a secular Jew, attempted to help the family cope better with the crisis by encouraging the family to analyze the situation in realistic terms and adopt effective problem-solving strategies. However, the family failed to respond to this intervention.

What the therapist did not know was that the family had explained their misfortune by evoking a magical interpretation. They believed that their family business went bankrupt because the *mezuzah* (encased parchment inscribed with biblical verses) attached to the doorpost of their home had a blemish. [Beliefs with respect to the human and nonhuman world.]

The therapist could not possibly construct an effective therapeutic strategy for this family without being aware of this interpretation. His theoretical repertoire, however, did not include concepts and terms that could have helped him turn his attention and thoughts in this direction.

Case 2: A Taiwanese American youngster worked hard and got admitted to a prestigious university. His parents bought him a car. They said he had earned it. The car was stolen shortly afterward. The boy did not show any signs of disappointment, anger or sadness. He could not concentrate, however, on his studies and failed the term exams.

The therapist, whose leaning was symbolic-experiential, tried to help the boy by encouraging him to express his emotions with respect to the loss of the car in the presence of his parents. But neither the boy nor his parents cooperated.

What the therapist did not know was that both the boy and his parents would consider it a great shame if he expressed his emotions openly. In this family's culture, feelings of disappointment, sadness and anger were acceptable only if these emotions were not related to one's self-interests. Selfish emotions were not available to the individual even as private, inner subjective experiences. [Constraints on subjective emotional experience and its communication.] No therapeutic approach could succeed with this family unless these constraints were taken into account. The therapist's theoretical model, however, did not include concepts and terms that could help her become aware of these constraints.

Concepts for Analyzing Culturally Determined Family Dysfunction

Cultures derive explanations for individual or family dysfunction from their own world representation. For example, they attribute dysfunction to sins, to madness, to spirit possession, to the Gods, or the like.

According to the model presented in this book, different types of culture-bound dysfunction can take place in each of the following situations.

Situation A: The family does not come under the sphere of influence of a physical or social environment that is incongruent with its traditional way of life.

Situation B: The family does come under the sphere of influence of such an environment.

In Situation A, dysfunction is a traditional way of expressing deviation from normative cultural programs. (Such programs can involve any of the classes of concepts and terms listed above.) In other words, this sort of dysfunction is a temporary departure from homeostatic functioning of a social system. Culture, as stated in chapter 1, brings into being both order and disorder. Prototypical examples of this type of dysfunction are the culture-bound syndromes, that is, Grisli Siknis (see chapter 1).

In Situation B, dysfunction is the external manifestation of errors ("bugs") in the interpretation of the unfamiliar environment and failure to develop effective strategies for coping with the challenges imposed by it successfully.

Let us call the type of dysfunction that occurs in Situation A *intrasystemic dysfunction* and the other type *intersystemic dysfunction*.

Principles and Techniques for Resolving Dysfunction

Cultures have their own traditional, mostly effective ways of curing intrasystemic dysfunction. Characteristically, these indigenous forms of therapy use various techniques designed to correct the deviation and restore the homeostasis, while partly satisfying the psychological or interpersonal needs that produced the deviation.

Let us look again at Case 1. In this case, the father locked himself away in his room. He spent his time praying and studying the Talmud, the traditional book of Jewish law. To an external observer who is unfamiliar with Orthodox Jewish culture, these manifestations are likely to be viewed as symptoms of depression. A member of the Orthodox community, however, would possibly take these to be manifestations of repentance. To the external observer, this behavior would be considered the illness. To the internal one, this behavior would be regarded as the cure, because it redresses the sin committed. Case 1 represents one way in which a culture can solve intrasystemic dysfunction.

Modern professional family therapy is required mainly when the family manifests intersystemic dysfunction. The main objective of therapy is to help the family derive better coping strategies from its existing repertoire of traditional family programs. The therapist serves as a mediator between the family and its new environment. Case 3 represents intersystemic dysfunction.

Case 3: A family emigrated from a North African Muslim country to France. Due to the high costs of living, the husband's salary was insufficient to support his family just by his own income. So, his wife had to work outside of the home. In order not to be too conspicuous and subjected to harassment, she wore modern European clothes to work. Although her husband had encouraged her to go to work, he could tolerate neither the fact that she worked outside of the home nor the fact that she did not adhere to the traditional Muslim dress code. Once, when she came back from work, he called her "a whore" and beat her up. This was reported to the local social service agency. A social worker attempted to handle the case by talking with the couple about the cultural differences between the two societies.

The therapeutic alliance in culturally competent family therapy is governed by the following principles: Avoid ethnocentrism. Be aware of your own culture-centeredness. Acknowledge differences, and join the family's culture.

The therapeutic process can be assisted by a variety of techniques, which can be classified as follows:

1. Techniques developed in the framework of the various schools of family therapy, modified to suit the special requirements of culturally sensitive therapy
2. Traditional healing techniques, adapted to the needs of culturally competent family therapy

Both techniques involve the use of art, drama, play, metaphors, storytelling, imagination and ritual. On the other hand, many techniques are reality oriented. They involve direct attempts at identifying and solving the problems.

THE CONCEPTUAL-TERMINOLOGICAL FRAMEWORK

As mentioned above, all the concepts and terms discussed in this chapter, namely the cultural characteristics of families, the types of dysfunction and the principles and techniques for resolving dysfunction, have been explicated and systematized in the framework of a single theoretical model, formulated in a unified language. In this model the family is represented as an information-processing system. Each family member is viewed as a kind of living computer. He or she can take in external information (input), process it in characteristic manners, store the processed information in memory and retrieve it from there. Then he or she can produce output, which is related in all kinds of ways to the internally processed information.

Processing the information involves interpretation and various combinatory operations (e.g., disconnecting bits of information and reconnecting them to other bits). Processing is regulated by programs. The term *program* was borrowed from computer jargon. It refers to a series of instructions that organize the information processed in fixed, routinized, recurring patterns. As a rule, human information-processing does not proceed randomly or haphazardly. It is patterned, therefore structured by programs. This applies to every aspect of human life, including interpersonal relations. Activities such as face recognition, responding to friendly gestures or to threats, laughing at a joke or reacting with shock to bad news are all regulated by programs.

A subset of human information-processing programs is *family programs*.

This term is designed to be a formal explication of well-known family therapeutic concepts such as *family rules* and *family interaction patterns* (see Ariel, 1987; Ariel, Carel and Tyano, 1984). Family programs are series of instructions describing patterns of information-processing shared by at least some of the members of a family. Familiar patterns of family interaction (e.g., dominance-submission, pursuing-avoiding, detouring, double-bind) can be represented rigorously, in detail, by formulating family programs describing the series of information-processing operations involved in their production.

In the Chief Contents section above, categories and concepts are offered for describing the family as a dynamic cultural system and for analyzing dysfunction. All of these categories and concepts can be coded into family programs (see chapters 7 and 8 for details). Family programs into which such categories and concepts have been coded are termed *cultural family programs*. The set of cultural family programs possessed by a particular family may be said to represent the family's culture. This set represents relatively stable, routine patterns into which a family molds its experience. Some parts of the family's culture are common to the family and various communities to which it belongs. Other are unique to the family.

Cultural family programs may be classified into the following types:

Axioms—e.g., general ontological and epistemological premises

Categories—e.g., classifying people into "of us" and "alien"

Explanations—e.g., attributing demographic changes in the family's environment to the wrath of the gods

Rules—e.g., sexual behavior codes

Cases 1, 2 and 3 include cultural family programs of all these kinds, although these programs are not specified in detail in these examples.

The information-processing system of the Orthodox Jewish family mentioned in Case 1 includes the axiom that every event in the world is brought about by divine will. This axiom may be formulated as a program determining how this family processes all kinds of information, including the information that a supermarket has been opened in their neighborhood.

The information-processing system of the same family also includes categories, that is, programs that classify entities into kinds in particular ways. For instance, they classify sins of omission, like the presence of a flawed *mezuzah* in their home, together with sins of commission, within a single category. Both can bring calamity to the family. Case 1 also includes a program of the explanations type. This family explained its economic misfortune as caused by the fact that their *mezuzah* was flawed. Finally, this case exhibits a program of the rules kind. The information-processing system of this family includes the rule that to avoid further calamities the father is obliged to repent for a religious transgression by locking himself away, praying and studying.

The family in Case 2 has in its information-processing system a program of the categories type, which classified emotions and their outward manifestations as "egotistic" versus "altruistic." They have a program of the rules types that forbids the experience and expression of egotistic emotions. Another program of the rules type is that efforts to excel academically for the benefit of the family may be rewarded materially.

The information-processing system of the husband in Case 3 included a program categorizing women who work outside the home and wear modern European clothes as "whores." Another program, a rule, forbids married women to work outside the home and wear modern European clothes.

People treat their programs as scientists treat their theories. They implicitly assume that the set of programs at their disposal is the best—that is, the simplest, the most elegant and satisfactory representation of their world. Therefore, it is also the best guide to action with the world. In the language of this model, this assumption is termed *optimal simplicity*. An information-processing system may be said to be optimally simple when it is:

Complete—includes all the programs and instructions needed to process the information to which it is usually exposed

Parsimonious—has no redundant programs or instructions

Consistent—that is, includes no contradictory programs or instructions

When the world seems to change in ways not experienced before, the information-processing system loses its optimal simplicity. This often happens when people are exposed to a new ecological or cultural environment. In such situations, the information-processing system becomes incomplete, overly complicated or inconsistent. In other words, its simplicity can be lost in the following three ways:

1. Reduced completeness—the system lacks programs or instructions for processing the new, unfamiliar information. Example: Foreigners often have a hard time understanding the nonverbal language of people in the host country. They lack programs and instructions for deciphering the codes underlying some gestures or facial expressions.

2. Reduced parsimony—some of the system's existing programs or instructions have become redundant. Example: Immigrants from countries in which the only way to get anything from government officials is to bribe them have no use for this pattern of behavior in a host country in which public administration is not corrupt.

3. Reduced consistency—the new information contradicts some of the system's programs or instructions. Example: Laws protecting wildlife in the modern state contradict the programs of families whose traditional way of making a living has been hunting.

When an information-processing system loses its simplicity, it does not necessarily become dysfunctional. It goes through the necessary adaptative
change and restores its simplicity. One might say that a new theory, which
fits the new reality, is constructed.

The fundamental simplicity assumption and the mechanisms of restoring
simplicity may be viewed as *metaprograms*. These are higher-level programs
that control and regulate the system's set of programs. The metaprograms
may be compared to central ground control in an airport. They are constantly on the alert. If the system loses its simplicity, they are automatically
set into action to restore it. Some metaprograms are in charge of restoring
the system's completeness. They generate new programs or instructions that
are capable of processing the unfamiliar information. Other metaprograms
are in charge of restoring parsimony. They put programs or instructions
turned redundant out of use. Still other metaprograms are in charge of restoring consistency. They modify programs or instructions to make them
consistent with other programs or instructions.

There are, however, circumstances in which the metaprograms cannot do
their job. They become paralyzed or disordered. In such circumstances, the
system's simplicity cannot be restored at all or cannot be restored fully. The
family's cultural information-processing system becomes dysfunctional,
"bugged." Characteristically, this happens when the new reality is radically
different from the family's former, familiar reality. The information-
processing system is flooded with an overwhelming amount of unfamiliar,
often stressing, intolerable, information.

Let us look again at Case 3. The husband's information-processing system
included the categorization program "Decent, respectable, married women
do not work out of the home or wear modern European clothes. Only
whores do." The new social environment into which this family emigrated
contradicted this program. Although initially the husband endorsed his wife's
working out of the home, his information-processing system was unable to
restore its simplicity. The metaprograms restoring consistency stopped functioning. His information-processing system became bugged. The external
symptom was a violent outburst.

Apparently the husband's symptomatic behavior was not due to inherent
irrationality, stupidity or violent personality. It was due to his system's inability to settle a stress-inducing contradiction. Adapting to the new culture
was too confusing, too demanding, too painful for this man.

The goal of culturally competent family therapy is to weaken or get rid
of the information-processing bugs underlying the presenting complaints.
When the bugs are removed or weakened, the metaprograms become active
again and the system restores its simplicity. It goes through the necessary
adaptive changes. If this is achieved the symptoms simply disappear.

How can this be achieved? The therapist serves as a mediator between the family and its unfamiliar environment. He translates the unfamiliar information to a language—in the wide sense of this word—the family can understand. He simplifies the new information, organizes it and softens its impact. And, most important, he helps the family derive adaptive programs from its existing repertoire of programs. If operating properly, the meta-programs are activated and the system restores its simplicity. The bugs disappear together with the symptoms.

Let us go back to Case 3. In order to help the family overcome the crisis, the therapist would be advised to approach it in the way described above. The main thrust of the intervention would be helping the husband reduce the dissonance between his deeply ingrained traditional concepts concerning the place of women in the family and society and those of modern Western society. The husband's existing repertoire of cultural programs will be explored with the hope of finding programs there from which an accommodation between these two cultural systems can somehow be derived.

THE GENERAL STRUCTURE OF CULTURALLY COMPETENT FAMILY THERAPY

Culturally competent family therapy with a particular case proceeds along the same steps as most other forms of therapy: Intake, diagnostic assessment, designing a therapeutic strategy, carrying out and monitoring the process and outcomes. What distinguishes this form of therapy, however, is that the family's cultural programs are high priority for the therapist throughout the therapeutic process. The following lists the main therapeutic considerations at each stage.

Intake and Establishing Therapeutic Alliance

Apply principles such as know your own culture, avoid an ethnocentric attitude, get an insider status, use intermediaries, try to influence within the frame of reference of the family's own culture, and so forth (see chapter 11).

Diagnostic Assessment

Collect information through the presenting problems interview, history of the case interview and naturalistic observations. It is essential to: (1) analyze the information—perform microscopic and macroscopic analyses of information collected and formulate culturally relevant family programs; (2) identify and explain bugs, the sources of the family's inability to restore simplicity in unfamiliar or stressing cultural circumstances and (3) explain the presenting problems (see chapters 9, 10).

Strategy

Choose an overall line of intervention, a general approach to the problem of removing or weakening the bugs in the family cultural-information-processing programs. Help the family derive bug-free, adaptive programs and instructions from its existing repertoire of programs.

Therapy

Choose appropriate techniques of intervention for each stage of the therapy. Sources of techniques are current family and other therapeutic methods and traditional problem-solving and healing techniques. The therapist should modify original techniques to fit the family's cultural programs (see chapter 12) and carry out the therapy in a culturally sensitive manner, as well as trace the processes of change with an eye to operative family cultural factors.

SUMMARY

This chapter includes a brief outline of the model of culturally competent family therapy presented in this book. It lists the main sources of the model and its chief contents. It sketches the information-processing conceptual-terminological framework in which these contents are synthesized and systematized, and it delineates the general structure of the culturally competent family therapy process.

The main sources of the model's contents are the culturally competent family therapy literature, anthropology and sociology of the family, cross-cultural psychology and psychiatry and linguistics. The conceptual-terminological framework borrows on general systems theory, cognitive science, linguistics and communication theory. All these have been incorporated into the author's own model of integrative, multisystemic therapy.

The model contains concepts for describing the family as a dynamic cultural system, concepts and terms for analyzing and explaining culturally determined family dysfunction, as well as methods and techniques for repairing such dysfunction. All these are incorporated into an information-processing, cybernetic theoretical framework.

Culturally competent family therapy is required mainly to solve intersystemic dysfunction, that is, bugged cultural information-processing due to a family's encounter with unfamiliar, stress-inducing cultural information. In such encounters, the metaprograms in charge of restoring the simplicity of the family's cultural information-processing system cannot function properly. The family cannot process the new information in complete, parsimonious and consistent manners. Its bugged, that is, incomplete, inconsistent, redundant and confused processing of the information is dysfunctional. This is often manifested in various psychopathological symptoms. The role of culturally competent family therapy is to mediate between the family and its unfamiliar environment and help the family derive adaptive information-processing programs from its existing repertoire of programs.

Culturally competent family therapy utilizes a variety of culturally sensitive diagnostic instruments. The information collected by these instruments is analyzed with a view to exposing the culturally determined bugs in the family's information-processing programs. A variety of strategies and techniques is employed to weaken or remove these bugs.

PART II

FAMILY-CULTURAL CONCEPTS RELEVANT TO DIAGNOSIS AND TREATMENT

In the introduction and in chapter 2, it is claimed that family dysfunction stems from the inability of the family's cultural information processing system to adapt itself to unfamiliar information. Culturally competent family diagnosis and treatment demand that the therapist locate and define those parts of the family's cultural information-processing system that are afflicted with this weakness. The therapist must also identify, delineate and describe the relevant facets of the unfamiliar information to which the family is exposed. To be able to accomplish this, therapists must be equipped with the appropriate conceptual and terminological apparatus. This part of the book provides the necessary concepts and terms. Any formulation of culturally sensitive family programs and bugs in these programs will include some of these concepts and terms. When a therapist takes a family of any sociocultural background to therapy, she should ask herself which of these concepts and terms are relevant and should include them in her diagnostic evaluation and treatment.

The concepts and terms introduced in this part cover the following content areas: (1) the family's structuring of its own subjective experience—the basic premises and axioms by which it interprets its reality and reacts to it, its categorization of its external and psychological environment, the explanations it offers to life's problems and difficulties and the principles by which it regulates its problem-solving behavior and (2) the family's structure and interactional rules.

3

The Family's Conceptualization of Its Environment

BELIEFS AND VALUES WITH RESPECT TO ITS ENVIRONMENT

People's beliefs and values often reflect basic principles dictating to the members of the culture how to understand the ecological and existential constraints they encounter and how to respond to them. Different groups react differently, for instance, when subjected to political and social oppression. One group would be guided by the principle of resignation and passivity. Another group would act according to the principle of active revolt and struggle. Furthermore, the same group can adopt different guiding principles in different stages of its development. Confronting a biological fact such as life's finiteness, one culture would embrace the belief that "all is vanity" and guide its members to passive behavior. Another culture would hold the value, "We should prepare a better life for future generations," and guide its members to invest efforts in building the future.

In the following list, beliefs and values are classified primarily according to the types of ecological constraints on reaching the family's goals with respect to the environment. There are *constraints on reaching control goals* (ownership, deriving benefits from others, leadership), and *constraints on reaching proximity goals*. (These concepts are discussed in greater detail below.) The same beliefs and values can be classified secondarily, according to the family's ways of coping with the constraints. The main modes of coping are:

Purposeful or *efficient* coping (directed systematically and rationally toward actually reaching the goals) versus *purposeless* or *inefficient* coping.

Active coping (involving externalized actions toward reaching the goal) versus *passive* or *internalized* (abstaining from actually working toward reaching the goal).

Optimistic coping (based on beliefs that the goal can actually be reached) versus *pessimistic* coping.

Immediate coping (directed toward reaching the goal as soon as possible) versus *long term* (reaching the goal is postponed to some future time).

Constructive coping (approaching the goal in a way that does not cause damage) versus *destructive* coping.

Not all of these coping modes are relevant to the meaning of each concept. Some of the words labeling values and beliefs have more than one meaning. Therefore, these words are likely to appear in the list several times, classed under different categories or subcategories.

A general comment: The concepts included in the following list should be viewed as general variables to be filled with particular contents. To learn the exact, specific meaning of each concept for each family, one should carefully examine the particular contexts in which the family uses the concept at hand. One should also investigate how the family defines each concept in relation to other concepts. Take, for instance, the concept of *modesty*. As long as some specific uses of it have not been examined, it says something general, vague and ambiguous. To know what modesty means for a particular family that belongs to a particular culture, one should examine its distinctive uses and their verbal and nonverbal contexts. Thus, for instance, in an Orthodox Jewish family, this concept is more likely to occur in contexts such as, "A woman should be dressed modestly," or "People should lead a life of modesty, abstinence and purity." In a secular Jewish family, the same concept is more likely to be used in contexts such as, "They have a lot of money but they live in a modest apartment"; "Despite all his academic degrees, he is a modest man who never boasts about his achievements." For the Orthodox family, this concept would be related mainly to the semantic field (range of meanings), centering around religious commandments concerning sex and matrimony. For the secular family, the same concept would be associated mainly with the semantic field centering around economical and academic achievements.

Beliefs and Values Related to the Environment

Ownership of Property and Resources
Materialism versus spiritualism, comfort, capitalism versus socialism, welfare, communism, consumerism.

Thriftiness, stinginess, abstinence, modesty, self-control versus lavishness, hedonism, addiction.

Giving, generosity, charity.

Work, diligence, punctuality, perseverance, methodicalness, responsibility, honesty, practicality, dutifulness, orderliness, professionalism, laziness, idleness, impermanence, gambling, adventurism, survivalism.

Conservatism, continuity, vision, perpetuation.

Deriving Benefits from People

Selfishness, altruism, profiting, parasitism, exploitation, deprivation, stealing, robbery.

Leadership and Power over People

Education, responsibility, superiority, inferiority, conceit.

Honor, respect, disrespect, dependency, surrender, devotion, dedication, passivity.

Respect for old age, respect for youth.

Gratefulness, modesty, dutifulness.

Discrimination, racism, exploitation.

Rebellion, evasion, anarchism.

Legalism, lawfulness, justice, injustice, coercion, militarism, pacifism, defeatism.

Cruelty, violence, terrorism.

Tolerance, intolerance, being humane, benevolence, charity.

Freedom, independence, nationalism, chauvinism, identity, free love, free choice.

Proximity

Confidence, loyalty, suspiciousness, criticism, accusation, keeping promises, breaking promises.

Keeping up appearances, good name, secretiveness, privacy, hypocrisy, shame, piety.

Respect, appreciation, modesty, disrespect, insolence.

Violence, cruelty, revenge, racism, discrimination.

Accusation, forgiveness, pacifism, conciliation, appeasement.

Identification, merging, devotion, Westernization, absorption, assimilation, dependence.

Independence, free choice, freedom, separate identity, nationalism, isolationism, separatism, seclusion, alienation, estrangement, rejection, distancing, self-realization, individualism, selfishness, free love, permissiveness, promiscuity.

Purity, impurity.

Guilt, shame, curiosity.

Solidarity, fraternity, mutuality, consideration, equality, friendship, mutual obligation, loyalty, collectivism.

The following case illustrates the importance of taking the clients' values into account in therapy.

Case 4: A university student of a Navajo family was depressed and unable to concentrate on her studies. She was treated by a clinical-psychology trainee in the university's consultation services. Her therapist attempted to empower her by encouraging her to "find her own distinctive voice"; explore her own personal strengths and abilities. She also urged her to participate in recreational activities on the campus and date boys. This approach did not work because it was based on the therapist's own mainstream American values and ignored the girl's own cultural values. The latter's symptoms were related to the fact that she was isolated from her extended family and community. She could not feel a whole person when she was on her own. She also felt guilty for having left her family behind. Dating boys was considered, by her, immoral.

In this case, the girl's symptoms were, in the terms of our model, the outward manifestations of bugs in her information-processing system. The latter could not accommodate some of the values of the social group she had joined, for example, individualism, self-realization and permissiveness. These contradicted her own internalized values of collectivism and abstinence. The theoretical and methodological apparatus at the therapist's disposal did not include concepts and terms for analyzing the girl's problem in this manner. Therefore, she misdiagnosed the problem, devised an unsuitable therapeutic strategy and failed to establish a fruitful therapeutic alliance.

BELIEFS AND VALUES WITH RESPECT TO EXISTENTIAL PROBLEMS

Culture creates beliefs and values to deal not just with constraints imposed by the external environment. It also devises beliefs and values that serve the family in its attempts to struggle with general existential problems. These problems arouse anxiety because they do not lend themselves to simple answers. This applies to questions such as life's finiteness and the certainty of death, the transience of time and of everything in the world, the apparent unpredictability and chaotic nature of events in nature and human life, the question of the purpose and meaning of the world and of human existence, man's insignificance in relation to the universe and so forth. The family faces such questions mainly in periods of transition or crisis, such as death, illness or other serious trouble.

Below is a small sample of beliefs and values of this sort. They are classified according to the modes of coping adopted by the family as a representative of its culture.

Beliefs and Values Related to Existential Problems

Attribution of Value to Life and Existence
Value of life, superiority of man, ethics and morality, nihilism (nothing has any value),

stoicism (giving up all wishes and desires and accepting fate without resistance), existentialism (human life has no general purpose or meaning; every person is responsible for his or her own life and its value), skepticism.

Bringing Order into Chaos

Harmony, divine justice, aesthetics.

Immortalization, Eternalization

Immortality, everlasting God, continuity of time, continuity of the soul, reincarnation.

Attribution of Spirituality to Matter

Materialism, spiritualism, profanity, divinity, impurity, purity, body, soul, holiness, sacredness, naturism, belief in deity.

Documentation and Interpretation of Reality

Art, literature, history, myth, science, humor.

The following case illustrates a therapeutic use of existential cultural values.

Case 5: A Japanese American family came to consultation because the school performance of their ten-year-old son deteriorated considerably following the death of his grandfather. The therapist, also a Japanese American, attempted to help the boy and his family by talking with them about their belief in continuity of the soul after death and reincarnation.

Unlike the therapist in Case 4, the therapist in this case did devise a successful strategy based on the family's own cultural values and beliefs. This was not necessarily related to the therapist's specific theoretical or methodological background, but to his being a member of the same cultural community as the family.

PROXIMITY AND CONTROL GOALS

Families and individuals orient themselves toward particular *goals* with respect to their human and nonhuman environment. These goals belong to two broad categories: *proximity goals* and *control goals*.

Proximity goals: belonging (to a specific group) versus autonomy; separatism; intimacy; fusion with other people versus differentiation; collectivism versus individualism.

Control goals: ownership or rights of use (of territory, property, resources, means of production or means of purchase).

Deriving benefits (work, services, help, etc.) from other people or groups.

Leading, governing.

The choice to concentrate just on these two types of goals is not arbitrary, but is based on numerous studies in fields such as ethology (see Cranch and Ploog, 1979; Eibl-Eibesfeldt, 1989), small group behavior (see Brown, 1988) and family therapy. The family's proximity and control goals are intimately interrelated with its values and beliefs (see above).

Constraints on Reaching the Goals

The family's human and nonhuman environment imposes constraints on reaching its goals. Some types of constraints are:

1. Natural constraints (climatic conditions, volcanic eruption, air pollution)
2. Demographic constraints (changes in population parameters such as the rates of birth and death, migrations, age of marriage and patterns of residence)
3. Technological constraints (industrialization, introduction of advanced technology)
4. Economic constraints (recessions and slumps)
5. Political constraints
6. Constraints caused by war, revolution or persecution
7. Social constraints (social barriers to upward mobility, discrimination)

Types of Interpretations Assigned by the Family to Ecological Constraints

The family's modes of coping with the environmental constraints on reaching its proximity and control goals are decisively influenced by how it interprets these constraints. The extent to which the constraints constitute stressors, causing problems and difficulties, is partly determined by their subjective meaning for the family. The interpretations given to the constraints by the family are, in turn, derived from its basic premises (see chapter 4) and its beliefs and values (see above). Here are some types of interpretation:

"Scientific" Interpretations

These are interpretations based on empirical, factual data and on logical inference. They are often derived from a popular version of the findings of science. To be classified as "scientific" in this context, the interpretations need not necessarily be correct or valid.

Spiritual and Mystical Interpretations

The family attributes the constraints to abstract supernatural forces such as "fate," "luck," "karma" or other spiritual powers not anchored in any concrete entity.

Magical Interpretations

The family attributes the constraints to the magical influence of people or quasi-human agents (animals, devils, gods, etc.)

Mythical Interpretations

The family interprets the constraints by referring to myths shared by the social group.

Philosophical (Evolutionist, Historiosophic, Ethical, etc.) Interpretations

Evolutionistic and historiosophic interpretations attribute the historical development of human society to general principles, such as the principle of progress (humanity progresses) or the principle of self-destruction (humanity moves toward destroying itself). Ethical interpretations account for major events of nature and human life by evoking ethical principles such as justice or equality. For example, the principle of reward and punishment is a central explanatory construct in Jewish tradition. Mythical or historical events such as the Flood, the destruction of the Temple and the Exile are explained in the Bible and later Jewish Scriptures as punishment for the people's wickedness, sins and immortality.

Psychosocial Interpretations

The family attributes the constraints to psychological and social forces such as hatred, racial prejudice or snobbism.

Some of the concepts introduced in this chapter are illustrated through the following case.

Case 6: The family described in this case consists of Israelis of Iraqi Jewish origin. Following the 1948 Israeli war of independence, they, like many other Jewish families, had become victims of persecution by the Arabs. In Iraq, they had been well off, but all their property was confiscated by the Iraqi authorities, and they could not manage to smuggle anything out. When they arrived in Israel, they were housed in a transit camp. The father of the family, forty-five-year-old Shalom, was offered a temporary job as an agricultural laborer. He refused. In Iraq, he used to be a respectable merchant. He saw it as a degradation that he should do dirty manual labor in the field, like a *falah* (Arabic for "peasant"). He also saw himself as too old to work. Back in Iraq, at his age, he would retire and rely on his grown sons to support the family. He also wanted his sons to finish high school and go to the university and bring honor to the family. Yet, he was unable to finance their studies. Israel could not yet afford state-subsidized, free secondary education then. Following a family consultation, it was decided that his wife, Miriam, and his oldest daughter, Tikva, would work as housemaids. The sons should be free to study and finish high school. However, things did not go as planned. The sons dropped out of school and strayed from the straight-and-narrow, joining a gang of delinquents. The father, Shalom, fell into depression and stopped functioning. The mother, Miriam, contracted diabetes and could not continue working. The whole family deteriorated. They spoke bitterly about Israel and its government. They saw the State of Israel as wholly responsible for all their troubles. They looked around and saw that their next-door neighbors in the transit camp, immigrants from Rumania, managed quite well. They opened a shop in Tel Aviv and could afford to leave the camp. Shalom and his family were convinced that they were discriminated against because of their Iraqi origin.

Let me analyze this case using the terminology introduced in this chapter. In Iraq, the main *proximity goal* of this family was to remain a part of the Iraqi Jewish middle class and the main *control goal* to continue owning their property and capital. These goals could not be attained because of political persecution. The family became moneyless refugees. In Israel, their goal was to regain their previous socioeconomic status and become a part of the educated middle class. They did not seem to have the goal of becoming a part of the mainstream Zionistic Israeli society of the time. They could not reach this goal due to demographic and economic constraints (unemployment and poor housing conditions in a country that had to deal with war, with a great wave of moneyless immigrants and with a shortage of economic resources). The dominant beliefs and values held by Israeli society of 1948 were socialism, respect for manual labor, equality between men and women, collectivism and putting the community's interests first before the individual and the family. These contrasted sharply with this family's beliefs and values: Materialism and capitalism, viewing manual labor as inferior, unequal gender roles, family honor and respect, and early retirement for the male head of the family. This contrast prevented the family from adapting to its new environment and overcoming the new ecological constraints. In order to succeed, Shalom had to come to terms with the necessity to do whatever jobs were available at the time. Both males and females of the family had to do their share of work. The girls and the boys should have had equal schooling opportunities. The parents should have served as strong, reliable role models for the children. All of these could not materialize because of the family's traditional values and beliefs. Furthermore, the family could not face their own responsibility for their failure. They erroneously blamed it on deliberate political and social discrimination.

As explained in the introduction and in chapter 2, bugs in the family's information-processing system are generated by the system's inability to adapt itself to unfamiliar information. This inability is often sited in the family's conceptualization of its environment. In terms of our model, the information-processing system of the family described in Case 6 became bugged because their original conceptualization of their environment had been incompatible with many aspects of the new reality they encountered in Israel. To diagnose such a family and construct an effective therapeutic strategy and achieve adequate therapeutic alliance, the therapist needs concepts and terms for detecting and describing such incompatibility. Equipped with such concepts and terms, he can ask questions that would lead him to the right track.

To be able to formulate even an oversimplified, relatively superficial analysis of Case 6 (such as the analysis offered on p. 42), a therapist would need to have most of the concepts and terms introduced in this chapter in his toolshed.

SUMMARY

This chapter is devoted to the question of how the family as a cultural system interprets its human and nonhuman ecological environment and reacts to it. The first part of the chapter examines the family's beliefs and values with respect to its environment and with regard to general existential questions. These beliefs and values are said to constitute the concepts and principles by which the family interprets its environment and decides how to respond to it.

A list of ecologically relevant beliefs and values is proposed. The classification is based on the roles of the beliefs or values in question with respect to the family's proximity or control goals. Another list is offered, including beliefs and values related to general existential problems.

The next topic is the family's proximity and control goals in relation to its human and nonhuman ecological environment and various types of environmental constraints on the possibility of reaching these goals. The family's modes of coping with these constraints are partly determined by how the family interprets them. Various characteristic types of interpretation are listed. The relevance of the concepts introduced in this chapter to family diagnosis and therapy is discussed as illustrated by Case 6.

4

The Family's Cultural Identity

FAMILY STRUCTURE

The structure of a family may be defined as the set of rules or programs regulating relations of proximity and leadership among the family members. Families of different cultures vary considerably in their structural organization.

Culturally determined aspects of family structure include:

1. The membership of the family (who belongs to the family and who does not).
2. The degree of cultural homogeneity of the family.
3. Subsystems of the family. Who belongs to each subsystem? The relations of proximity and control among family members and subsystems. How do family members attempt to reach these goals, and how successful are they in reaching them?
4. The level of organization of the family. To what extent is the family structure rigid and stable? To what extent is it flexible and capable of changing with varying circumstances?

Membership

The concept "membership of the family" refers to the following three questions:

1. Who belongs to the nuclear and extended family and who is considered an outsider? Is a distant relative who lives in a different country considered a member of the extended family? Does the family include, according to its own conceptions, members who we, from our own cultural standpoint, would be reluctant to count as family members (e.g., fictitious family members, nonblood relatives who are labeled blood relatives, animals, plants or

inanimate objects, deities, or ancient ancestors)? In some cultures, inclusion of such members is normative. Are there blood relatives who are not considered members of the family; for example, relatives who have been ostracized, relatives who are feeble-minded or mentally ill, relatives whose existence is denied?

2. What are the residence arrangements of the family? Who lives at home and who out of the home? How distant are those who live in a separate house? What is the distribution of territories inside the home?

3. What are the rules of descent in the extended family? Rules of descent determine a particular group of relatives with whom an individual is to be affiliated and with whom he or she is to enter into reciprocal obligations. There are four types of rules of descent: *patrilineal*—the child is affiliated by mutual rights and obligations mainly with the relatives of his or her father; *matrilineal*—the child's main affiliation is with his or her mother's kin group; *bilineal*—the child is affiliated with a special group consisting of some of the members of his or her father's kin group; and some of the members of his or her mother's (usually the closest genealogical kinsmen). This is the most common pattern in our society.

Other societies have *double descent*—the society possesses both patrilineal and matrilineal kin groups, and a person is simultaneously affiliated with the patrilineal group of his father and the matrilineal group of his mother.

Some societies exhibit various combinations of these rules of descent, for example, patrilineal descent for males and matrilineal for females.

In the Chinese community of Taiwan, patrilineal cousins are the people to whom a man turns when he needs a peacemaker, emergency funds, a job for his son, an introduction or letter of credit, or sympathetic advice in the quarrels between his brothers and himself. (Wolf, 1981, p. 136)

The Degree of Cultural Homogeneity

This concept is determined by the following questions:

1. Is the marriage *endogamous* (spouses belong to the same cultural community) or *exogamous* (an intermarriage between spouses belonging to two different ethnic, religious, etc., communities).
2. To what extent does the family exhibit cross-generational cultural continuity?

Proximity/Control Relations inside or among Subsystems

The term *subsystem* refers both to formal subsystems, such as the parental one or the sibling one, and to informal subsystems, such as a strong coalition between a mother and her son or a dominance-submission relationship between a father and his married son. It will be noted, however, that the question of which subsystems are considered formal or normative and which informal or deviant is a matter of cultural relativity. In some cultures, subsystems that we consider informal and deviant, for example, a coalition between a mother and her son against the son's wife, would be viewed as both formal and normative.

The proximity and control goals of family members with respect to each other and the constraints on reaching them (and, consequently, the structure of subsystems in the nuclear and extended family) are dictated in many cases by sociocultural norms characteristic of specific groups.

Subsystems and proximity-control relations among them are often reflected in the structure, design and internal organization of the family's dwelling place.

Moskos (1981) describes control relations among siblings in a Greek American family: "Evangelos, my father's oldest brother, assumed the mantle of family head in the traditional style. At times my father would chafe under Evangelos' heavy patriarchal hand. There was a time when Evangelos forbade the purchase of a suit." (P. 389)

The Level of Organization of the Family

In some cultures, the structure of subsystems and the proximity and control relations inside and among them change flexibly, according to the situational context. In other cultures, such interrelations are more rigid. In the rigid type of cultures these interrelations are determined by fixed traditional rules. In such cultures, some aspects of the interrelations of proximity and control in the family are barely open to negotiations or manipulations. Roles, rights and duties are determined by age, gender or one's status as a parent or as an older sibling. If anybody disobeys the rules, he or she is punished severely. The level of organization of the family is related to the question of to what extent they are flexible, negotiable and determined by changing circumstances.

The following case is cited to demonstrate the importance of taking into account the family-structural concepts and terms defined above in a culturally competent family diagnosis and treatment.

Case 7: A multiproblem family of African descent lived in an extremely overcrowded small run-down apartment in a deteriorated area of London, England. The family consisted of twenty people belonging to four generations. Their difficulties included chronic disease, psychiatric disturbances, delinquency and substance abuse. The social worker in charge of the case attributed the family's problems to poverty and overcrowding. She recommended to rehabilitate the family by taking the following measures:

1. Dividing the family into unigenerational units, each consisting of a single nuclear family.

2. Housing each family unit in a small modern apartment, in a subsidized housing project allocated to low-income families.

3. Moving some very old and infirm members of the family to a public nursing home.

4. Moving some of the children to special education boarding schools.

5. Providing medical and psychiatric care to the needy family members.

6. Doing family therapy with each small family unit.

This strategy failed. At first, the whole family refused to leave their home and move to the designated places. They were forced to move after they had been informed that all the houses in their neighborhood were to be destroyed for redevelopment. The old and the young members of the family, who had been removed from their home, left the nursing homes and the boarding schools in which they had been placed, never to go back there. Most members of the family rarely used their own apartments. They practically lived in one of the new apartments. This was the apartment in which the oldest woman of the family, a widow, lived with two of her unmarried daughters. The family pretended to cooperate with the family therapists assigned to help them, but never really let them achieve real joining. The family became its old self again, including all the original problems.

In her written diagnostic evaluation, the social worker in charge of this case used many concepts taken from Minuchin's Structural Family Therapy (Minuchin, 1974). The social worker wrote that this family was enmeshed and chaotic, lacking clear generational boundaries. She recommended to help the family organize itself and develop internal boundaries.

These were not, however, the structural concepts and terms needed to diagnose this family, develop an effective therapeutic strategy or achieve meaningful therapeutic alliance. A therapist applying the concepts and terms introduced above is likely to arrive at something like the following description:

Membership—the basic family unit is the extended family rather than the nuclear family. Breaking this family into small nuclear families amounts to destroying it.

Rule of descent—matrilineal.

Residence arrangements—martilocal, that is, the whole extended family lives in the same location, centering around the oldest female figure.

Degree of cultural homogeneity—Endogamous, cross-generational continuity.

Proximity/control relations—whatever the structure of subsystems in this family, it does not coincide with the structure of its constituent nuclear families.

Any therapeutic strategy for this family must be based on such an analysis.

FUNDAMENTAL SPIRITUAL IDENTITY

Every family, as a representative of a particular culture, holds some basic premises about the world as it knows it. These premises may be viewed as fundamental, unshakable axioms. Although axioms and premises of the kinds discussed below are very general and abstract, they often have a decisive influence over families' outward behavior and problems. They are also reflected in families' response to therapy. Their clinical relevance is unquestionable.

Ontological and Epistemological Axioms

The terms *ontology* and *epistemology* may be borrowed from Western philosophy to describe the nature of some of these premises. Ontology is that branch of metaphysics that investigates the properties of existence, the essence of things. Epistemology is another branch of philosophy that deals with the question of the nature and origins of knowledge.

Below is a list of ontological premises held by families of various cultures. Some of the premises are illustrated by examples and case material.

1. Only tangible, concrete things are real. This premise is an offshoot of the materialistic and pragmatist world-view professed by some modern ideologies, for example, Marxism and behaviorism.

2. This world is not the real world. The real world is "the other world." This premise is held by families who adhere to certain Orthodox Jewish traditions. It is also a part of some Buddhist traditions.

Case 8: A recently widowed diabetic woman from an ultra-Orthodox Jewish community in the Williamsburg community of Brooklyn, New York, refused to take her medicines. When she was warned by her doctor that this could cost her her life, she said: "I want to join my husband in The Other World and leave this illusive world."

3. The material world is just one outward manifestation of a divine, spiritual world. This premise is also held by families who adhere to certain Buddhist, Hindu or Orthodox Jewish traditions.

4. The material and the spiritual worlds co-exist.

5. There is no such thing as a permanent existence. This premise is included in some Chinese traditions.

According to the ancient Chinese text, the I Ching or Oracle of Change, everything in the universe is in a state of flux. Every end is also a beginning. The process of change can be seen everywhere; in the flow of the tides, the phases of the moon, the cycle of seasons and the fortunes of mankind. (Tseng, 1976, p. 169)

6. Knowledge is acquired by divine inspiration.

Basic Causal Premises

Families of different cultures differ in their general premises about the causes of the phenomena and events of nature and human life. Below are some examples of different types of causal premises.

7. Phenomena and events are caused by supernatural powers.

8. Phenomena and events are caused by magical acts performed by human beings. In many cultures all over the world, people believe that natural phenomena such as rain, drought and floods are caused or influenced by rituals and magic.

Premises about the Reasons for Phenomena and Events

Families, as representatives of different cultures, attribute different reasons (to be distinguished from causes) to the phenomena and events of nature and human life. Such a premise follows.

9. Major events in nature and human life happen as a reward or punishment for people's compliance or noncompliance with some prescribed standards of conduct. This is one of the central premises of the Jewish religious tradition. Major events in the history of the Jewish people, for example, the destruction of the Temple, the Exile and the Holocaust are explained as punishment for transgressions and sins.

Case 9: The oldest daughter of a religious family living in a small settlement in the West Bank left the settlement and led a permissive life in Tel Aviv. One day, Palestinian terrorists penetrated the family's home, murdered the father and wounded the youngest daughter. The family explained this disaster as a punishment for the daughter's transgression and the family's failure to prevent it.

Premises about the Meanings and Purposes of Phenomena and Events

Causes and reasons should be distinguished from meanings and purposes.

10. The purpose of human life is to conquer the self and become godlike. This is the basic premise underlying many Hindu traditions.

"A man of realization is the one who has conquered his ego. . . . The idea is to remind the dissipating mind constantly of the purpose of its existence in the world, which is to unfold the self, to realize his godhood." (Parthasarathy, 1989, p. 25)

11. Events in human life and nature are signs or omens through which people can decipher God's will or His "state of mind."

Basic Guiding Principles

Families' values, attitudes and rules of behavior are guided by different culturally prescribed basic principles. Below are some examples of such principles.

12. The family's honor should be protected by all means. This is a basic guiding principle in many Muslim societies.

13. People of the same community should always strive to be and remain together.

14. Physical and moral purity should be always preserved and pollution avoided. The principle of purity is one of the central guiding principles of the Jewish religion. Jewish family life is regulated by many laws and rituals designed to achieve purity and avoid pollution. One law forbids sexual intercourse during the wife's period.

Case 10: A religious Jewish man in Miami, Florida, had a compulsion to act in a self-defeating manner, which caused him to fail in his business and social life. In therapy, he confessed that he used to have intercourse with his wife during her period. The self-defeating behavior was interpreted as self-punishment for this transgression.

The following case illustrates the unavoidability of taking the family's basic premises and guiding principles into account in culturally competent diagnosis and treatment.

Case 11: A family of devout Hindus from Calcutta spent two years in London, England. The male head of the family, a professor of Hindu law, had a temporary post as a lecturer at London University. His seventeen-year old son, Ravi, created and produced a record, presenting an interesting blend of traditional Indian and Western pop music. Fortunately or unfortunately, the record became a hit, a bestseller. Overnight, Ravi and the whole family became rich and famous. One evening, Ravi was assaulted and badly hurt by a group of skinheads, who were waiting for him outside a TV studio in which he had been interviewed. Following this attack, Ravi stopped attending his grammar school. His father decided to resign his job, leave everything behind and go back to India with the whole family. All attempts by the president of the college in which he lectured to persuade him to stay were turned down politely. He also refused offers to provide the family with police protection.

Ravi was invited with his parents to meet the counselor of the grammar school. The counselor expressed her deep regret for what had happened. She reassured Ravi and his parents that the offenders represented just a negligible minority. The great majority of the people of Britain were not racists or xenophobic. She suggested some measures to guarantee the family's security. She tried to persuade Ravi to come back to school. However, Ravi's father did not change his mind, and the family left for India.

The president of the college and the school counselor thought that this family's withdrawal had been motivated by fear and disappointment. They believed that the family had been traumatized by the assault and felt threatened and unwelcome. These were not, however, the main reasons why the family decided to disengage themselves from their commitments and go back home. This decision was motivated primarily by the following basic premise and guiding principle: *The purpose of human life is to conquer the self and become godlike* (premise 10 above) and *One's fate must not be resisted*. The family anticipated that Ravi's success in the world of pop music would lead the whole family to self-indulgence and divert it from its spiritual course. This would be incompatible with the above basic premises. They saw the assault as a signal that they had deviated from the right track, as a blow of fate that must not be resisted but submitted to.

No therapy or consultation with this family would have any chance of succeeding unless these hidden culture-bound motives for their responses were taken into account.

THE FAMILY'S REPRESENTATION OF ITSELF

Self-Concept

Families, like individuals, have a self-concept. The family as a culture includes its self-concept. Defining the family's self-concept involves the following questions:

1. Which groups does the family consider itself a member of? The affiliation groups can be a nation, a religious group, a local community, a socioeconomic class, a profession, a group defined by areas of interest, values and world-view, or the like. For example, a Native American family can identify itself as "American," "Navajo," "Christian" and "farmers."

2. What are the distinctive, peculiar characteristics the family attributes to itself, which distinguish it from its affiliation groups? A family that defines itself as Anglo-American can also see itself as something special and deviant in American society; for instance, as members of some esoteric cult.

3. How stable is the family's self-concept? Cultures vary with respect to the stability of their members' self-concept and sense of identity. A striking example of an unstable cultural self-concept is that of the Vezo of Madagascar.

"Malagasy people share a concept of the person which . . . can be glossed as "cumulative personhood,'" that is, as "something achieved gradually and progressively throughout life, and even after death, rather than ascribed and fixed definitely at birth" (p. 467). The Vezo, a Malagasy tribe, "are not a kind of people," that is, not "inherently Vezo . . . were not born to be Vezo. We see a person who, instead of being, is becoming, and instead of knowing is learning. The Vezo person has no history," for the past is constantly shed when one moves from one context to another, from one moment to the next. (Astuti, 1995, pp. 467–468)

4. Does the family's self-concept include stereotypes and prejudices attributed to it by outsiders?

5. How positive or negative is the family's self-concept?

6. To what extent is the cultural self-concept contrasted with the image of cultural others? Many societies all over the world build their own self-image by looking at other groups as nonhuman or as lower genres of humanity.

Symbols, Images, Myths and Rituals

Symbols, images and myths are usually taken from the written and oral cultural tradition the family is affiliated with. A *symbol* is a verbal idiom or a nonlinguistic entity, such as the features of a person, an animal or creature, a picture, a geometrical shape, a structure, an object or the like, which has acquired important meanings in the cultural tradition. These meanings constitute an associative field of contents drawn from history, religion or social life.

An *image* is a symbol that expresses the idea it stands for indirectly, in a way that reminds one of the idea or alludes to it, relying on partial similarity between the symbol and the idea. For example: The dove, representing peace, is an image, as are the words "doves" and "hawks" standing for political left and right wings.

Littlewood and Dein (1995) define the concept *myth* as "some narrative about ultimate reality to which we have particular recourse when everyday cause-and-effect explanations are inadequate, and which to the observer exemplifies our society's fundamental values." Many myths take the form of a story purporting to describe historical events. Its purpose, however, is not to give an exact, objective description of the events, but to transmit an important message through the description. The meaning of the message can be religious, political, ethical, social or the like.

The family's self-concept and its subjective identity include the symbols, images and myths the family adopts as a part of its world. Here, again, one can distinguish among those symbols, images and myths that the family shares with its identification groups and those that serve to stress its unique, separate identity.

Ferreira (1966, p. 86) defines *family myth* as "a number of well-systematized beliefs, shared by all family members, about their mutual roles in the family and the nature of their relationships." Following marriage the couple constructs not only their present reality but reconstructs past reality as well, fabricating a common memory that integrates the recollections of the two individual pasts (see also Bennet, Wolin and McAvity, 1988, and Handel, 1967).

Case 12: My parents were born in Kishinev, Besarabia (now in Moldavia), on the border of Russia and Rumania. It was a time of pogroms against the Jewish community and the Jews of Kishinev endured the greatest share of suffering. My parents grew up in homes that may be labeled Zionist and Enlightened (these two expressions are, themselves, verbal symbols). They imigrated (made *aliyah*, in Hebrew "ascended"; itself a verbal symbol) to Palestine in 1925. For the marriage ceremony, my father insisted on wearing khaki shorts. This item of clothing was then a symbol of the anti-bourgeois, young Jewish pioneering laborers. Other central symbols I grew up with were Hebrew writers and Hebrew books, which were central representatives of Enlightened socialistic Zionists. My parents strove, in word and deed, to emphasize their being book-loving people, affiliated with Hebrew writers and books. However, they had no lesser love of Russian literature. A central family myth I grew up with was fighting anti-Semitism with an attitude of Zionistic Jewish pride. My parents used to tell and retell scenes in which they encountered anti-Semites and pogromists and stood up against them with pride and courage.

Bennett, Wolin and McAvity (1988) argue that rituals and myths both enact, represent and perpetuate family identity over time. *Family rituals* are condensed versions of family life as a whole. Their performance clarifies roles, delineates boundaries and defines rules. With repetition, they serve to stabilize the family and affirm its shared belief system. Rituals are celebrations, traditions or patterned routines. Examples of celebrations are weddings, funerals, baptisms, bar mitzvahs and Christmas. Traditions are visits from extended family members, anniversary and birthday customs, parties and special meals. Patterned routines are regular family dinner time and bedtime.

Subjective History

The subject of family myths is related to that of family history. Family history, however, includes more than family myths, since telling the family history does not serve just the purpose of transmitting educational or other messages. The story includes pieces of reality that can help us understand the family and its current problems. For example, when Vietnamese refugees in America tell their children and their grandchildren the history of the war, it is more than just a myth.

In 1984, a mass exodus of the Jews of Ethiopia began, mainly from villages in the areas of Gonder, Vogera, and Semyen. Thousands of families made their arduous way by foot toward the Sudan, to settle temporarily in transitional refugee camps that had been set up there.

The Jews stayed in the refugee camps in the Sudan for many months, trying to hide their ethnic identity. They suffered from hunger and disease.

Those whose Jewishness was exposed were killed or tortured by the Sudanese. They died in multitudes in the camps or on the way there, without being able to bury their dead in accordance with their traditional customs.

In November 1984, and March 1985, the Jews were delivered from these camps by air by the Israeli government in two missions called Operation Moses and Operation Queen of Sheba. In Israel they were housed in various temporary dwellings: houses, hotels and mobile homes spread all over the country. Over 90 percent of the children and youth were placed in religious boarding schools, away from their families (Bodovski et al., 1994).

This series of historical events is directly reflected in the following excerpts of a family history. This history was taken and related by Shosh, a social worker who participated in one of my courses on culturally competent family therapy. Parts of it are reproduced below verbatim. It should be pointed out, however, that this is not a clear-cut case of the subjective history of the family as told by itself, but a mixture of the family's voice and the voice of Shosh herself:

Case 13: Boaz is a homeless person, the only homeless Ethiopian immigrant I have ever heard of. Boaz is now twenty-seven. He was born in an all-Jewish small village in northern Ethiopia, close to nature. In such a home, the father chooses one boy, who looks to him spicy and perhaps also a softy, one who cannot tend to the sheep and chase the wolves away, and sends him to school, a three-mile walk every day. After school, hard work out in the field. A happy childhood. Warmth from the mother; father admired.

The next page: Sent by his family to Israel through the Sudan. People made eight weeks on foot in 1984. The Jews did not run away from the civil war or from the famine. They just used the opportunity that many Christians and Muslims escaped. Pure love of Zion. Boaz was seventeen. "You come, kiss mommy and granny." Daddy gives a blessing. Have never seen most of the rest since. Daddy said: "Bring your father's word to the Wailing Wall." Biblical people. "You'll be my messenger. Pave the way for the whole family by praying in Jerusalem. We'll meet soon. I am coming after you." He had nothing. They put the nothing in two little bags. In the Sudan he faced reality. Sudanese beat and raped the women. Death. Terrible diseases. Hate the Jews. Boaz, however, got along surprisingly well. Had contacts, learned the language, was the connection man between the camp and the Sudanese. Worked. Found a first love, no matchmaking. His time came to be taken to Israel. He refused to go on the plane. Said: I'm not going without my family. Then some white men came and told him: If you don't go on this plane you'll be thrown away, back to Ethiopia.

In Israel, he was sent to a residence home. He was forcibly separated from his girlfriend. They said she was too young. Afterwards he was ashamed to see her again. Never saw her since. They sent her to a religious girls' boarding school. They told them: After both of you grow up, when your parents arrive, if they agree, you'll be allowed to get married. Later she was married off to another boy by her uncles.

The rest of the family tried to come to Israel. Five out of nine died on the way, buried in the desert. His father and mother are here. He is the oldest brother now. Boaz has disengaged himself from his family completely. He cannot face their sorrow.

The funeral ceremony is as important to Ethiopian Jews at least as death itself. Boaz told me: I was the only one who did not attend the funerals. Died, died, all right, but I did not see their graves and never will. My brothers are lucky. They buried the dead. They can face my parents. Once I cried all my tears out, and then I had a mission, to stop my mother's tears. Mommy, if you cry for another year, will this bring the children back? Daddy gets into the room. Two men against one woman. I imagined I succeeded; no, daddy is crying too. Who can I go to calm him down with? Can Mommy interfere with father's crying? Then I stopped coming and I do not meet with them. I live out in the street; can't make a home of my own.

Emotionally Loaded Family Themes

The concept "emotive" will refer, below, to an emotionally central theme the family is preoccupied with always or in a given period. The family's emotives can be associated with any of the kinds of factors discussed in this part of the book (e.g., constraints on proximity and control goals with respect to the ecological environment, world-view, values and attitudes, symbols, images and myths).

Examples of emotives are:

Fear of losing the family's social status because of political and social changes; this is related to constraints on reaching control goals

Guilt feelings because of family members who violated the laws of purity and impurity; related to beliefs and values

Anger about family members who deviate from the family consensus; related to the family's conception of family life

Modes of Emotional Experience

Some anthropologists, social psychologists and cross-cultural psychiatrists have argued that different cultures experience emotions in different ways. They also contend that some emotional experiences, for example, depression, are culture specific. Some cultures simply lack this kind of experience (see Kleinman and Good, 1985).

Schieffelin (1985) stresses the cultural relativity of emotions, in general, and depression, in particular, and illustrates his arguments by examples from New Guinea and Chinese cultures:

Culture determines the evaluation of stimuli as stressors. The affects engendered by these stimuli, such as anger, anxiety, depression or guilt are known to the person only via cognitive processes: Perception, labeling, classifying, explaining, valuating, ... (P. 103)

Affects are social in that they are experienced and given meaning in the presence of others, respond to cultural rules of expression and legitimacy, communicate cultural implications and messages, and are necessary and appropriate concomitants to any social situation. It is because they are situated in the cultural system that they have the significance they do for the personality. . . . A highlander from New Guinea who is jumping up and down and yelling with rage may merely be expressing anger in a conventional manner, while an upper class Englishman engaging in the same behavior would, in the light of British expressive norms, be considered to be regressively acting out. . . . Particular feelings are socially expressed, or even required as part of appropriate participation in the situation. . . . There is a culturally normative way of how a person must feel. . . . (Pp. 105–106)

Kleinman (1980) asserts:

The somatic idiom for cognizing and expressing depressed feelings among the Chinese constitutes that affect as a vegetative experience profoundly different from its intensely personal, existential quality among middle-class Americans. Chinese reduce the intensity of anxiety, depressive feelings, fears and the like by keeping them undifferentiated, which help both to distance them, and to focus concern elsewhere. Other related coping strategies are minimization, denial, dissociation and somatization. (P. 148)

Lutz (1985) claims that "the distinction between the what and how of depressive experience and the dichotomy of 'emotion' and 'cognition' make sense only in the context of Euro-American cultural system." (P. 245)

The family's typical modes of emotional experience are a part of its sense of self. Families may be characterized, from their own subjective viewpoint, as "raging," "happy-go-lucky," "unsatisfied," "grumpy" and so forth. The ways families interpret their experiences and respond to them emotionally are integral parts of the family's culture.

The family's symbols, images, myths and rituals, its subjective history, the emotionally loaded themes it is preoccupied with and its modes of emotional experience must not be ignored in culturally competent diagnosis and treatment. Bugs in the family's information-processing system are often produced by the family's inability to adapt these subareas to new kinds of information it is exposed to. A culturally competent family therapist should be able to pinpoint and describe these difficulties.

Case 14 illustrates this requirement. The Cossacks are a group of ethnic communities living on the south and east frontiers of Russia. In czarist Russia, mounted soldiers used to be drafted from these communities to serve in the Imperial Guard. The mounted Cossacks were known for their loyalty to the czar, extreme nationalism, courage and ruthlessness. Recently, following the disintegration of the Soviet Union, there has been a revival of the Cossack tradition. Male Cossacks wear their traditional uniforms, hold horse races and engage in military training. They hold extremely nationalistic and militaristic views.

Case 14: A family of Cossacks from Ukraine emigrated to the Netherlands. Kolya, the father, found a job as a laborer in a factory, but he soon dropped out, neglected his family duties and took to heavy drinking. His oldest, 12-year old son Vanya soon followed suit. He became rowdy and rebellious at school and then dropped out.

The family was referred to a social worker, but was uncooperative. Kolya's wife Mareena and his other children did not seem too bothered by Kolya's and Vanya's behavior.

The conceptual and terminological repertoire available to the social worker in charge of this case lacked the concepts and terms that could direct her attention to the following crucial elements of the problems she was called to solve: The Cossack traditions this family had brought with it to the Netherlands were radically different from cultural traditions of the host society. Cossack men were not supposed to work. They were warriors. They were loyal to their king and country, otherwise free. Their central cultural symbols and images were the horse, a symbol of power and freedom, their distinctive uniform and their shotgun. Their rituals included mounted shooting matches they used to demonstrate their virtuosity and social gatherings they used to drink and boast their bravados. The main subject of their myths and subjective family histories were glorious battles of the past. Their main emotives were related to pride, loss of face and nationalism. Their emotional experiences centered around overcoming fears of injury or death. The sharp contrast between these elements of the family's identity and its new milieu was the source of the bugs in the family system.

VALUES AND BELIEFS CONCERNING MARRIAGE AND FAMILY LIFE

Marriage and Family as Values

Families differ considerably in their attitudes toward marriage. These attitudes range between a complete devaluation of marriage at one extreme and regarding marriage as a sacred, eternal bond that should never be dissolved, at the other extreme.

In many cultures, the value of marriage is related to conservation and continuity. Marriage is not considered a private affair of the spouses, and they do not enjoy the freedom to choose one another. The choice is determined by the extended family. The bond of marriage is a link between families or clans. In most modern urban societies, on the other hand, marriage is considered an agreement between individuals. The value of marriage is based on romantic love, attraction and mutual interests. This is related to the individualism, social mobility and achievement motivation of Western society.

What is noted above, about the value of marriage, also applies to the value of the family. In this respect, too, there are different attitudes, ranging from viewing the family as sacred to attaching no special importance or value to it. The value of the family is partly derived from the family's proximity and control goals and its other beliefs and values. For example, in the early days of the Israeli kibbutz, the value of collectivism and work brought about the devaluation of the family. Some kibbutzim actually attempted to abolish the family and replace it with free love and collective child care. In the present-day kibbutz, however, the goals and values have changed toward individualism, high-tech industry and detachment of the community from other communities. The value of the family has become central again, as it used to be in traditional Jewish society.

The Honor of the Family

In many cultures the value of the family also includes the concept of "family honor." This concept has different meanings in different cultures and in different contexts. Generally speaking, it has to do with obligations binding every family member to behave according to certain codes. Violating the codes stains the family's reputation and self-respect. Members of the family are also obliged to defend the family's honor against offense coming from people outside the family.

In some sections of Muslim society, the penalty for violating the family's honor is death. For example, if an unmarried woman gets pregnant, some family members (her father or older brother) are obliged to kill her in order to reinstate the honor of the family.

Case 15: A news report in the Israeli newspaper *Ha'Aretz* of February 19, 1996: "The body of 20-year old Haleema Bishari was found in an olive grove near the Arab village Yarka, near Acre in the Galilee. Nearby, the body of her 30-year old brother Hameed was found hanging from a tree. The police suspect the brother strangled his sister to death and committed suicide.

Yesterday, it was reported that Haleema's two older brothers had been applying heavy pressures on her during recent months to withdraw the charge she had filed with the police against their father, Nageeb. According to the charge, the father used to beat Haleema and her two sisters, 12 and 13 years old. Haleema had also consulted the International Association of Children's Rights in Haifa."

Hameed murdered his sister and committed suicide to protect the honor of his father and of the whole family. Haleema's acts of exposing her father's deeds and enlisting the aid of external authorities had been most serious violations of the traditional codes of family honor respected by many Muslim societies.

In a study of African American youth in the south of Chicago, Kochman

(1981) describes a verbal ritual called "sounding" in which a group of young-sters competes for wit and verbal skill by jokingly abusing each other:

"Most of their witticisms include insults directed at the opponent's family, mainly his mother. By being placed in the frame of a game, these verbal exchanges serve to confirm rather than devaluate the central importance of the honor of the family in these youngsters' culture.... However, if sounding is produced in a different context, without the presence of the peer group, or when the jocular intent is not self-evident, it will frequently lead to a fight involving, in some cases, killing.... In the classroom from about the fourth grade on fights among black boys invariably are caused by someone 'sounding' on the other person's mother." (P. 67–68)

Sexual Fidelity

There are cultures in which sexual fidelity is a supreme value. Other cul-tures, however, exhibit a high degree of tolerance toward extramarital affairs. Some societies prescribe a death penalty on a wife who betrays her husband. An extramarital affair on the part of the husband is not considered such a serious crime. At the other extreme, in modern urban society there are "open marriages" in which the two spouses have open extramarital affairs that they tell each other about.

Shared Responsibility

The concept of family honor is tied to the concept of mutual responsibility among the family members. There are families in which each person sees himself/herself as responsible for his or her own well-being. In other fami-lies, all the members feel obliged to do whatever necessary to help the person in need.

Families also differ with respect to the areas and contexts in which there is mutual versus individual responsibility. Relevant contexts are, among oth-ers, health, financial problems, interpersonal difficulties and major decisions.

Another differentiation among families is where and when mutual re-sponsibility begins and where and when it ends. Does it apply only to the nuclear family or also to the extended family? Does it hold with respect to adult married children? In wide sections of the Israeli population, it is cus-tomary for parents to assist their children financially through higher edu-cation, marriage or purchasing a home. Children, for their part, take responsibility for helping aging parents if they need medical or nursing care. In other societies, such mutual responsibility is not the norm.

Traditionally, Native American societies have placed a high premium on shared responsibility. Deyhle and Margonis (1995) state: "Navajos share re-sources, including cash, food, tools, or labor. Having something another individual needs creates an obligation to provide for the person in need.

Navajo people assume a cooperative social context in which each individual is obligated to help others." (P. 152).

The Family as a Collective or as an Aggregate of Individuals

A factor directly related to mutual responsibility is the unity of the family. Some families regard themselves as a single organism whose parts are strongly tied to each other. Other families see themselves as a group of separate but interrelated individuals. These different conceptions are expressed in modes of thinking, speaking and behaving.

Personal Autonomy vs. Mutual Merging

The conception of the family as a collective or an aggregate of individuals is related to the degree of separateness of each individual in the family. The issue here is to what extent each individual in the family conceives of himself or herself as a separate person, with his or her own distinct identity, as opposed to being a part in a collective being. How subjectively real are the boundaries around the self and the body of each family member?

Minuchin's terms *enmeshed family vs. disengaged family* and Bowen's term *undifferentiated ego mass* refer to the degree of personal differentiation versus fusion in the family. These, however, are structuralistic terms describing the degree of interpersonal distance in the family. This section does not deal, however, with the family's structure but with how the family and each of its members conceive of himself or herself in relation to the others.

The issue of the family as a collective is also related to the question of to what extent the family tolerates individual peculiarity and deviance and whether it sees individuation processes as legitimate.

Nomura, Noguchi, Saito and Tezuka (1995) attempted to investigate Japanese families by Moos and Moos' Family Environment Scale. The results were surprising. They showed how vulnerable the research instrument itself had been to cultural specificities. The authors conclude: "*Independence* as a construct may be less universal and more culture-specific than we generally assume. It may be more germane to the Western framework of self and individual, but difficult to convey in Japanese culture" (P. 80).

In his study of the Massim of Melanesia, Macintyre (1995) came to realize that "loss is not conceived of as the loss of a person, but as the 'dismemberment' of a specifically constituted social entity that has to be disintegrated" (P. 32).

In families where personhood is derived from mutual merging with others, loss of family connections and roles is likely to result in a sense of loss of self. Let us go back to the case of Boaz, the young Israeli immigrant from Ethiopia (Case 13). Boaz's choice to become a homeless person, a street-dweller, may be explained as an outward expression of his inner experience of loss of self and meaningful personal identity due to the losses of family members, family connections and family roles that he had experienced.

The Degree of Interpersonal Openness

The attitude toward individual autonomy is reflected also in the extent of openness among the family members. There are families in which members expose themselves, share their thoughts and feelings and disclose information about their personal affairs. Other families keep secrets and hide their thoughts, feelings and actions from other family members.

Boyd-Franklin (1989b) refers to the issue of secrets kept from other family members in the African American community. She lists informal adoption, extramarital pregnancy, white ancestors and mentally ill family members as the most common types of avoided issues.

The Right or Duty to Leave Home

There are implications for the subjects discussed above with respect to the extent to which the family tolerates distancing, manifested in a family member leaving home or being removed from home. Situations in which such distancing can take place are divorce or separation, placing children in foster or residential care, or children who reach maturity, moving to their own residence.

In a study of the Navajo, Deyhle and Margonis (1995) mention the case of a husband who wanted to go to the city for a job. His family decided: " 'It is his job to stay here with his family, not to go to the city for some kind of job.' " . . . The older son wanted to move with his girlfriend from another part of the reservation. His older sister said: 'We told him not to go. We need him, and we don't want to lose him to the family' " (p. 141). This family had low tolerance of distancing.

Attitudes toward Expressions of Emotions, Love, Warmth and Intimacy

Families differ in the importance they attach to intimate love and its verbal and nonverbal manifestations. Some cultures encourage and some discourage such expressions. Cultures also vary in in their attitudes toward open expressions of emotions such as grief, dismay, embarrassment, fear and compassion.

Equality vs. Inequality in Rights and Duties

Equality or inequality apply to differences of age, gender or generation. The relevant rights are related to many different areas such as food, clothing, money and personal belongings, education, medical care, freedom of speech and expression, leisure and recreation, sexual gratification, a person's right regarding his own body, violence and physical protection and even the right to live. The relevant duties apply to work, house chores, child care, sustenance and earning a living, medical care and various services. Families of different cultural groups vary considerably in the extent to which younger and older, male and female members of the family enjoy equal rights in any of these areas.

The following examples represent two extremes on the scale of egalitarianism:

The egalitarian relations between Navajo men and women was recognized in early accounts of the Navajos by Anglos. These accounts included the cultural patterns that positioned women at the core of Navajo religion and on an equal footing with men in agriculture pursuits, child rearing, religion and political activities." (Deyhle and Margonis, 1995, p. 137)

Confucius (551–479 BC) taught a cosmic order in which dyadic relationships were preordained in superior-inferior ranking. Of the five cardinal relationships: Sovereign-subject, father-son, elder-younger brother, husband-wife, and friend-friend only the fourth made reference to woman, assigning her the inferior position. Her relegation to a subordinate role was not a simple status arrangement, but an all-encompassing subjugation modeled on the primary relationship—sovereign and subject. Her husband was not to be questioned and even carried the power of life and death over her. (Bennet and Meredith, 1995, p. 1)

Honor and Respect

Inequality often goes together with the duty to respect and honor the dominant subsystems (e.g., males, elders). Families of different societies differ in the importance they attach to the honor of men, parents and older people. In most traditional Muslim societies, for instance, younger siblings must pay respect to older siblings. This is not the rule in most present-day WASP families.

Tolerance toward Aggression, Violence, Sexual Promiscuity and Deviant Behavior

This category applies to such manifestations both inside the family and between the family and people outside the family. There are families that not only tolerate such behavior, but even encourage it. Other families suppress it forcibly.

Attitudes toward Illness and Death in the Family

Some families conceive of illness and death as normal, expected life events. Other families regard them as terrible catastrophes. Families also differ with respect to whether it is possible or desirable to try and prevent such events.

Families attribute different meanings and causes to illness and death. These are influenced by the family's basic premises, beliefs and values. Many concepts introduced above are relevant here, for example, culture-determined interpretations assigned to the ecological constraints (rational, spiritual, mystical, magical, philosophical, etc.), beliefs and values concerning existential problems (e.g., value of life, nihilism or immortality), the family's ontology and epistemology, and so forth.

Families of different cultures vary with respect to whether death is a final, terminal state. Lock (1995) states:

Whereas in most parts of Euro-America a scientific approach to death is apparently widely accepted today, in Japan this seems not to be the case. In many Japanese households family members talk with recently deceased ancestors whose photographs are placed in the family altar. The biologically deceased are anthropomorphisized and eventually attain social immortality. (P. 15)

Conceptions of Periods of Transition and Change in the Family

Families of different cultures mark different particular periods as significant transitional stages. For example, in Israeli society, birthdays, bar mitzvahs and enlisting in the regular armed forces are recognized as important life stages, but many societies attach no particular significance to these stages and do not celebrate them with any family rituals.

Families vary with respect to the age considered by the culture as life's turning point. Different cultures assign stages such as adolescence, maturity or old age to different chronological ages. Accordingly, these transitional ages are institutionalized by formal acts such as starting or finishing school, joining organizations such as youth movements or fraternities, leaving home or retirement.

Different societies treat different life stages as important. Some cultures, for instance, view the transition from childhood to adolescence as extremely important. Other cultures regard the passage to adulthood as more important.

Families of different cultures attribute different religious, economic, psychological and social meanings and functions to particular life stages. For example, in Orthodox Jewish communities, the bar mitzvah ritual, applying to thirteen-year-old boys, marks the stage at which the boy begins to be bound by the religious commandments. This is the central meaning of this stage and of the ritual marking it. Although the same ritual also is celebrated by nonreligious Jewish communities it has, for the latter, different meanings and functions. For nonreligious Israelis, for instance, it marks the passage from childhood to adolescence and the transition from elementary to high school.

The family's values and beliefs concerning marriage and family life must be taken into account in culturally competent diagnosis and treatment. Bugs in the family's cultural information-processing system are often produced by the incompatibility of the family's values and beliefs concerning marriage and family life with unfamiliar information the family is exposed to. Consider, for instance, Case 15. The tragic death of Haleema Bishari and her brother Hameed was the ultimate result of the incompatibility of their traditional family values and those of modern Israeli society. In their family, honor of the family and of its male head was a primary value. These values are not shared by mainstream Israeli culture. In Haleema's family, inequality between men and women was a norm. Violence perpetrated by male members of the family toward female members was not considered a major offense. Outsiders were not supposed to know about or interfere with such acts of violence. In mainstream Israeli culture, men and women are considered equal. Violence within the family is illegal and is condemned by public opinion. Haleema, who had been influenced by Israeli culture, defied her own family's values and paid with her life. The murder and suicide in this case cannot be explained without evoking this incompatibility of cultural values.

Therapists are advised to be especially attentive to the parameters of the family as a collective or as an aggregate of individuals, personal autonomy versus mutual merging and attitudes toward expressions of emotions. These parameters stand for fundamental cross-cultural differences in the ways people experience their own selves and other people. It is not at all easy to set oneself free of one's own modes of experiencing in these domains and empathize with other people's radically different modes.

SUMMARY

This chapter is devoted to the family's identity as a representative of culture. The family's identity consists of its distinctive, culture-bound structural properties, its basic tenets, its self-representation and its values and beliefs concerning what marriage and family are all about. Families vary considerably on these parameters. A family's cultural identity, as defined in this chapter, must be taken into account in culturally competent diagnosis and treatment. The family's problems, the possible solutions and the response to therapy will be decisively influenced by the distinctive features of the family's cultural identity.

Family structure is defined as the set of programs regulating relations of proximity and leadership among family members. The aspects of family structure discussed are: *membership* (which kinds of people or nonpeople are qualified as family members, rules of residence and rules of descent); *degree of cultural homogeneity* of the family; subsystems and relationships of *proximity and control* inside and among them and the *level of organization* of the family.

The family's basic tenets constitute, together, its spiritual identity. They include fundamental premises and axioms guiding the ways the family perceives the world and responds to it.

The family's subjective representation of itself consists of its self-concept and of symbols and images through which it conceives of itself. Other aspects of the family's self-representation are myths and stories through which it describes its own origins and past. Another constituent of the family's sense of self includes the central emotional concerns the family is preoccupied with and the characteristic color of its emotional experience.

The family's values and beliefs concerning marriage and family life include the following four sets. The first set consists of values and beliefs that are related to the importance of the institutions of marriage and family for the culture. The second set may be classed under "cultural differences in family cohesion." Categories discussed are the family as a collective or as an aggregate of individuals, tolerance of deviance, personal autonomy versus merging, shared responsibility, privacy, interpersonal openness, the right or duty to leave home, attitudes toward expressions of love and intimacy, sexual fidelity and attitudes toward illness and death. The third set has to do with family hierarchy. Relevant categories are equality versus inequality, honor and respect, division of labor and roles. The fourth set has to do with family development. The main category is transitional life stages.

5

The Family's Functioning and Lifestyle

The previous chapters deal with the subjective conceptions of the family with respect to the world in which it lives and to itself. In this chapter, we shall move on to external manifestations of these conceptions in the family's functioning and behavior. Families' modes of daily functioning and lifestyles vary considerably across cultures.

CONTENDING WITH ECOLOGICAL CONSTRAINTS

In chapter 3, various types of ecological constraints on the possibility of reaching the family's proximity and control goals with respect to the environment are listed and discussed.

An active solution for ecological constraints requires investment of resources: time, money, work, study. The questions arising at this juncture are: Who is responsible for allocating resources? How are the decisions concerning these resources carried out? Who consumes the resources?

According to Moskos' description of the history of his own Greek American family (1981), the authority to decide how ecological constraints on the family's goals should be overcome was in the hands of the author's uncle Evangelos, his father's older brother. However, the author's father and his wife had to execute these decisions. Responsibility for overcoming ecological constraints in the African American community often falls on women (Lawson and Thompson, 1995).

DIVISION OF LABOR AND ROLES

Different families have different conceptions concerning allocation of roles and duties. This applies both to formal roles such as financial management, earning a living, child care or preparing meals, and informal roles such as who listens and provides emotional support and who is a trouble-maker. There are cultures in which even such informal roles are partly in-stitutionalized; for example, in most families of a particular community, the grandmother on the mother's side settles disputes, the middle son is the scapegoat and the older daughter is the bad girl.

Families also differ in the extent to which the division of labor and roles is flexible or rigid. Thus, for instance, there are families in which the mother cares for the baby, but if she is busy, the father takes over. And there are families in which the father will never take such a task upon himself because it is considered shameful for a man to take on baby care.

THE FAMILY'S BUDGET

The subject of family budget is partly derived from the solutions to the ecological constraints and partly from other categories of data discussed above, for example, the family's values concerning material possessions, equality versus inequality and division of labor and roles. Relevant questions are: Who determines the family's budget? How are the decisions carried out? Who wins which slices of the family's cake? What is the money spent on?

DAILY LIFE

This category includes daily agendas and timetables. Who does what, at what times and where? What is done together and what alone? Daily life agendas cover areas such as child care, household chores, leisure time and activities and eating habits.

PRIVACY

Families differ considerably in their attitudes and habits with respect to privacy in the sense of time, territories and property owned exclusively by specific individuals. In most of the families in our society, clothes, shoes and articles such as a toothbrush and a comb belong to specific individuals, but there are many families in which such items change hands, and no one has exclusive rights over them. There are households in which each person has his or her own private room, which can be locked. In other households, no individual person has exclusive rights to any territory.

NUDITY AND TOUCH

Different families behave differently with respect to body exposure and tolerance of physical touch of an intimate or even erotic nature. Mondykowski (1982) claims that Polish American families are very tolerant with respect to overt expressions of sexuality in the family:

It would not be unusual for a man to come home from work and, in front of the children, to squeeze his wife's breasts or slap her behind playfully. . . . Within the family, expressions of sexuality have a joyous and overt quality that the Polish Americans consider lusty and that non-Poles have often considered vulgar. (P. 399)

FORMAL AND INFORMAL DAILY RITUALS

Family rituals are discussed in chapter 4 as an aspect of the family's subjective identity. Here they are mentioned as manifestations of the family's daily life. Family rituals can be described by the following parameters: degree of regularity, time and place, participants and scenario.

RAISING THE CHILDREN

Child-rearing practices are culture specific too. Families differ considerably with respect to the following parameters: Father and mother's parental roles and responsibilities; amount and manners of disciplining and limit setting; tolerance of children's autonomy and respect for their rights; manners of socializing; expressions of affection; the extent to which children are nurtured or exploited.

Case 16: Nicos, a thirty-five-year-old American of Greek origin, was married to Jane, an American of mixed North-European origin. One of the family therapy sessions dealt with three subjects:

1. Jane complained that Nicos did not give her enough money for the household expenses. He had promised her to put money in their joint bank account, but had not done so for over a year. One day she called him at work and told him that she needed money for shopping. He said that he had some cash under his shirts in the wardrobe. She took $400. Nicos was a construction contractor. The next day he looked for the money under his shirts to pay his Greek laborers and found out that most of the money was gone. He erupted in a stream of dirty words and threatened her with his fists. She called him "primitive" and since then they have not been on speaking terms.

2. Jane had a pottery workshop in the basement of their house. Later she opened a shop in which she sold her products. Nicos objected to the shop. He argued that it was not profitable and that since Jane had started the shop she had been neglecting the children. Jane called him a male chauvinist pig. She contended that he had to take an equal share in the burden of household chores and care for the children. She explained that she needed the shop to sense her own worth and to be free of her husband's financial favors. Nicos ridiculed these arguments.

3. The children, sixteen-year-old Bob, ten-year-old Mary, and four-year-old Anthony used to fight and yell continuously. Jane could not control them. All three children lived in one room. Bob and Mary demanded a separate room. Nicos ob-

jected. He said: "Everybody for each other and all together for everybody." Jane said that he did not understand their needs. She argued that the family could afford a larger apartment, but Nicos's refusal to let the children have a separate room was sheer obstinacy.

This case illustrates a number of concepts discussed in this chapter, as well as chapter 4. Nicos and Jane differed in their values and attitudes concerning shared responsibility, the family as a collective or as an aggregate of individuals, personal autonomy, privacy, equality in rights and duties, division of labor and roles, the family's budget and raising the children.

VERBAL AND NONVERBAL COMMUNICATION

All the areas discussed above are externally manifested in patterns of verbal and nonverbal communication. Families differ in the modes and styles of communication. One should distinguish between communication among the family members and communication between the family and external bodies. There can be considerable differences in styles of communication between these two contexts. Here are some of the relevant parameters.

Amount of Communication

Cultures differ in the average amount of verbal and nonverbal exchanges among family members. In some cultures silence is considered a sign of respect (see Bachran, Lee and Yoo, 1995).

Expressions of Feelings and Emotions

Here below are some relevant parameters:

1. To what extent do family members externalize feelings and emotions?
2. What kinds of feelings are expressed more and what kinds less?
3. How are emotions expressed (dramatically, reservedly or the like)?
4. What is the amount of verbalness or verbosity?
5. Is there directness versus indirectness in expression (weeping, shouting, nonverbal gestures versus controlled expressions or talking about feelings)?

Culturally competent family therapists must not confuse the nature of emotions with their outward expression. Families that overdramatize their emotions are not necessarily in greater stress than families who keep their feelings inside or use understatements.

The following citation from Reena, a student in a culturally competent family therapy training course for social workers, is relevant here.

My experience with the Ethiopian community is, "If I'm emotionally overwhelmed I say little, although, for me, it is saying much." The more powerful the emotions and the greater the emotional difficulties, the less they are verbalized and the greater the expectation that the other will understand without explanation. If the others do not understand, let them go on not understanding. I am not going to overburden anybody with my emotions.

Directness vs. Indirectness of Talk about Sensitive Matters

There are considerable cultural differences with respect to the readiness of families to talk freely about sensitive subjects such as sex, health or financial problems. Some families pretend that everything is all right and keep up appearances. Other families use euphemisms or indirect modes of communication (e.g., insinuations, double talk, humor and sarcasm).

Case 17: The Connoly's, an Irish American family, were referred to therapy because their fifteen-year-old daughter Nikki developed bulimia. Her mother Janice had been suffering from severe diabetes. Her father Sean had lost his job as a mechanic and was unemployed for several months. Her seventeen-year-old brother Brian was caught by a neighbor while trying to steal his car radio. When the therapist tried to discuss any of these problems with the family, he met with various evasive tactics such as changing the subject, turning the question into a joke, saying something vague or highly ambiguous, making wisecracks or speaking for another person. For example, when the therapist asked Brian about the incident with the neighbor, his father Sean said with a smirk: "He needed the radio to listen to the sermon on Sunday." When the therapist addressed Janice about her diabetes Brian said: "She's Nikki's sugar mama."

Body Language: Kinesics and Proxemics

Kinesics is the science of body language. Proxemics is the science of the use of space in communication. Families differ considerably in their kinesic and proxemic rules. Relevant questions are: How much and how are the body and various parts of it involved in communication? How expressive are the faces? Is there eye contact? How physically close do people get to each other when they communicate? Do they touch each other as part of their communication? Hall (1990) gives many examples of misunderstandings in interpersonal communication that are due to cross-cultural differences in the variables listed above (see also Richmond, 1991).

Main Kinds of Communicative Intents and Presuppositions Employed

Communicative intents are the purposes of verbal or nonverbal communicative acts. The relevant question is: What does the performer of the act want to achieve by having produced the act? A presupposition is what the producer of a communicative act holds to be true of the receivers of the act or the situational context. For example, a man boasts about his achievements. His intent is to impress his listeners. He presupposes that they are not aware of his achievements or do not appreciate them.

The main relevant diagnostic question is: How prevalent are specific types of communicative intents or presuppositions in the family's interactions? For example, in some families, many communicative acts are based on the presupposition, "The other people in the family do not respect me." The most frequent intent is to force the other family members to respect the producer of the communicative act. In other families, many communicative acts are based on the presupposition, "The other family members are very concerned about my emotional well-being." In such families many communicative acts will have the intent of making one's feelings known to the other family members.

McGill (1987), discusses major communicative intents in Japanese culture: "The Japanese customarily speak in terms of the other's feelings (*aite chusin*)" (p. 284). "Many of their expressions obey 'the principle of indecision, evasion and indirection' (*hi dantei*). . . . The principle of 'apology' . . . permeates Japanese discourse" (p. 286).

Kochman (1981) describes various kinds of conventionalized speech games used at that period by inner-city African American Chicago youth. Each of these games makes ritualized uses of different kinds of intents and presuppositions.

"rapping," "shucking," "jiving," "running it down," "gripping," "copping a plea," "signifying" and "sounding" . . . describe different kinds of talking. Each has its own distinguishing features of form, style and function. (p. 55)

Rapping is a performance to project personality, physical appearance and style on the performer. Personality and style might be projected through non-verbal means: stance, clothing, walking, looking. One can speak of a "silent rap." *Shucking and jiving* (S-ing and J-ing) is a form of speech used with The Man (the white man, the establishment, authority figures). Its purpose is to disguise one's real intents, in order to be protected from being mishandled or victimized.

Running it down is a style of speech used for giving information, explanation, advice. *Gripping* and *copping the plea* are expressions of partial or total submission to a powerful, dangerous opponent. *Signifying* is goading, begging or boasting by indirect verbal or gestural means. *Sounding* is a verbal ritual in which friends insult each other to relieve tension.

Efficiency of Communication

Therapists should be aware of cultural differences in clarity, consistency, contextual relevance, rationality, caution and responsibility and truth value of families' communications. Cultural difference with respect to the notion "truth" can be confusing. The cultural relativity of the notion "telling the truth" comes out clearly in the following excerpt from a course of culturally competent family therapy for social workers.

Shlomo: I can tell you a funny story. When I conducted field work in a Bedouin encampment in the Sinai desert some years ago, a young man named Hamed fell in love with Smadar, my assistant, a young Arabic speaking student with exotic good looks. He courted her with ardor and proposed to marry her at least ten times. Smadar complained, in Hamed's presence, about an old man, Bakr, who was pestering her with intolerable obscene expressions. When Hamed heard that, he became very upset. He cursed Bakr and his whole family, and promised to kill him if he dared to insult Smadar again. Smadar and I planned to leave the next day. Hamed implored us to stay till Friday. He said: It would be worth your while to stay. There's going to be a big Bedouin wedding, a big feast, with a camel race and all. We decided to stay, and guess whose wedding it was? Hamed's of course. And another surprise: Old Bakr was Hamed's father.

Reena: Amazing! This reminds me of a story I read in the paper last week. All the orange trees in a *moshav* [a Jewish communal village] in the Galilee were stripped of their oranges overnight. A *fallah* [an Arab peasant] from a neighboring village was caught at dawn by the night watch with ten donkeys carrying 20 bags full of oranges. When handed over to the police, the thief insisted that he took only one bag of oranges. He stubbornly stuck to this claim and refused to admit the obvious truth.

Galila: I don't think people like Hamed or that *fallah*, from their own point of view, tell a lie. They sort of create a reality by saying words. I think this is typical of peoples whose reality is that of being oppressed.

Shlomo: Maybe. I think we can only speculate about the motives and reasons for other people's modes of behavior that look strange and alien to us. Saleema, as an Arab, do you have any explanation for Hamed's and the *fallah's* responses?

Saleema: I am not sure. I guess it has to do with conflicting codes of behavior about honor and self-respect. Hamed's self-respect requires of him to protect the honor of a woman he loves against a man who has insulted her. However, his self-respect requires of him also to protect the honor of his own father. He "solves" this problem by cursing the man who insulted Smadar, but at the same time failing to mention that the man in question is his own father. His self-respect requires of him to honor a woman he courts by proposing marriage to her, but at the same time honoring her by not mentioning the fact that he is engaged to be married. A man's self-respect requires of him not to admit that he is a thief. If he confesses to the theft of only one bag of oranges, the injury to his honor is not so great, because the theft of one bag only can be considered as a forgivable necessity of feeding only one's hungry family. If people find out the truth by themselves the injury to one's self-respect and the loss of face are smaller than when one openly admits a dishonorable fact.

Ethnotheories about Communication

All the characteristics of the family's communication discussed above are decisively influenced by the culture's general premises about communication and its functions. Ethnotheories about communication are developed to answer some of the following sorts of questions: What is the function of words? Are they to be interpreted as acts of expressive or internal events, as vehicles for exercise of power, as disguises for actual intentions or meanings? Can intentions differ significantly from either acts or words (see Lutz 1985; Mageo, 1995)?

The following examples paraphrased from Corson (1995, p. 190) illustrates cross-cultural misunderstanding that can arise in situations in which the communicants hold different ethnotheories about communication.

The following speech acts are characteristic of Koori (Australia) child-discourse in conventional classrooms: Empty bidding in response to teacher questions, followed by silence, deferred replying to a question, after a longer than normal pause, shadowed replying, etc. Teachers often interpret these responses as reflective of intellectual inferiority, rather than as norms of language use dictated by the cultures ethnotheory about communication.

All the parameters specifying the family's functioning and its lifestyle discussed above must be taken into account in culturally competent diagnosis and treatment. Therapists are advised to be especially alert to the parameters division of labor and roles, raising the children, privacy, nudity and touch and verbal and nonverbal communication. People are emotionally invested in their own culture-bound modes of thinking and behaving in these domains and often find it difficult to overcome ethnocentric preconceived ideas and prejudices when these domains are concerned. For obvious reasons, the parameter verbal and nonverbal communication requires therapists' special attention. Adequate therapeutic alliance will never be reached if the therapist has not assimilated at least partly the family's own modes of verbal and nonverbal communication.

SUMMARY

This chapter is devoted to the manifestations of the family's structure, self-concept, values and beliefs in its daily functioning and lifestyle. These manifestations vary considerably among families of different cultural backgrounds. The chapter covers the following areas: the family's modes of contending with ecological constraints on its proximity and control goals, the way it handles its budget, its daily life habits and rituals, its approaches to tasks such as educating the young and its style of verbal and nonverbal communication. Important concepts for analyzing communication introduced are intents, presuppositions and ethnotheories about communication.

6

The Family's Coping with Problems and Difficulties

THE CULTURAL RELATIVITY OF DISTRESS

Culturally competent family therapists must realize that families of different cultural backgrounds do not conceive of their problems and difficulties and do not attempt to solve them in the same ways. Families differ in what they identify as symptoms or problems, in how they define and explain the difficulties and in their modes of coping and help-seeking. Psychopathological phenomena, personal and interpersonal crises and other difficulties are culturally relative both in their root causes and in their outward manifestations. People of different cultures do not suffer from the same things. Different combinations of factors cause distress in different social groups.

Lebra (1982) discusses sources of psychological pain and well-being in Japanese culture.

The Japanese in general are socialized to reflect upon themselves (*hansei*) instead of accusing someone else suspected to be the source of frustration . . . one's suffering is to be understood as a consequence of the sufferer's negligence of her duty as a daughter, wife, mother, descendant or believer. (P. 272)

Bilu and Witztum (1993) in a study of psychopathology in an ultra-Orthodox Jewish community in Jerusalem cite culture-bound psychological risk factors peculiar to growing up in a strictly religious ambiance. They note overindulgence in the spiritual while neglecting pressing real-life issues. They also discuss factors that counterbalance these real-life issues, that is, the structural, benign environment of the Yeshiva. The authors also describe culture-specific external manifestations of psychopathology in this community, such as torturing guilt about religious negligence or psychotic delusions based on religious contents.

THE CULTURAL RELATIVITY OF SYMPTOMS

Manifestations that most clinicians would definitely regard as psychopathological symptoms such as hallucinations, paranoid productions, encompresis or postpartum depression will not necessarily be viewed as serious problems by the culture to which the family belongs. In some cultures such symptoms may even be seen as normative behavior. Even if the family and the therapist identify a particular set of behavioral manifestations as symptomatic, they still can identify very different features as the constituents of the symptom. This is illustrated in the following case.

Case 18: A white American family initiated therapy. The identified patient was the thirteen-year-old son Winston. His parents were worried about his being shy and socially withdrawn. Winston's father was a teacher of philosophy and his mother was an artist. In their youth, they spent some time in a hippies' commune. During the intake interview they told the therapist that Winston had sexually assaulted his ten-year-old brother. When the therapist expressed her concern about this incident, both parents played down its importance. They considered it a natural by-product of adolescence.

Therapist and family can also differ in what they consider situations of stress or crisis. For example, a father's heart attack may not be viewed by the family as a major crisis, but the son's decision to marry outside the family's ethnic group would be considered as such. Likewise, violence against children can be viewed as a family problem by the therapist and as normative behavior by the family. Conflicts between a teenage girl and her parents, however, can be seen as normal by the therapist and as a serious family problem by the family.

Case 19: An African American single-parent family in south Chicago, a mother and four children, was referred by the school to the local welfare agency. The social worker who had interviewed the family filed a report, saying that the mother neglected her children. The children spent most of their time with relatives and neighbors living in the vicinity of their home. It was the children who decided where to stay and when, not the mother. For the mother and her relatives, however, this did not mean that the children were neglected. For them, the mother's functioning with her children was normative and in no way harmful.

ATTRIBUTION OF CAUSES, MEANINGS AND FUNCTIONS TO PSYCHOPATHOLOGY

Families often explain symptomatic behavior differently than the therapist. For example, what the therapist would call hysterical symptoms would be viewed by the family as behavior controlled by a devil that penetrated the sufferer's body. The penetration of the devil would be interpreted as a sign that the symptomatic girl should break her ties with a young man her parents do not find acceptable. Following are some examples of explanations for psychopathological phenomena, offered by different cultures.

According to Littlewood and Dein (1995), among members of a Jewish Hassidic [Chabad] sect:

Physiological and psychological dysfunction is attributed to failure to perform ritual correctly, to disharmony and conflict within the family, and to the historical exile of the Jews, as well as to separation from the divine. To recover one's health is to restore our alienated world. "The universe itself is in need of healing." Since the shattering of the vessels God himself is in exile.

Traditional Chinese medicine is based on the concepts of two opposing elements in cosmic forces, *yin* and *yang*, which must remain in harmony to produce health. Mental and physical troubles are explained as manifestations of disharmony between these two forces. (Kinzie, Teoh and Tan, 1976, p. 103)

In the Chinese view "feelings" are private and embarrassing events that are best not explored. The goal of therapy cannot be the analysis of feelings. They are not implicated as the perceived root of distress, nor do they represent a moral concept. What Kleinman describes as "limited psychological insight" on the part of his Chinese patients represents a limit in terms of the goals of therapy within a psychodynamic framework. Within the Chinese framework, limited social insight would appear to be the more serious problem, as this might lead one to cause shame to one's family by allowing a stigmatized nonphysical diagnosis for one's symptoms. The American's "psychological insight" is the Chinese person's "self-absorption." The heavy value loading evident in each of the latter two phrases indicates the extent to which the theories underlying both therapies and definitions of depression are simultaneously descriptive and evaluative. (Lutz, 1985, p. 70)

Bourguignon (1976) lists traditional explanations offered for psychopathological phenomena in different parts of the world. The list includes, among other explanations, spirit possession, soul loss and possession by insects or animals.

Situations of stress and crisis can also be interpreted very differently by therapist and family. So, for instance, a religious family may interpret the decision of a family member to marry a nonreligious girl as punishment from heaven for having failed to provide a stricter religious education and as a message that they have to reinforce their observance of religious commandments. A secular therapist, on the other hand, can see this fact as a manifestation of the family's secularization, which is a part of the natural process of acculturation of religious and ethnic minorities.

INDIGENOUS HELPERS

Most social groups single out institutions and individuals whose function is to treat symptoms and intervene in crises. There are groups in which this function is assigned to certain people in the extended family, such as the husband's father or the grandmother. In other groups, these are the roles of functionaries in the community, such as religious leaders, shamans, doctors or fortune-tellers.

It is important for family therapists to know which people and social bodies the family is accustomed to consult with. In some cases, it is advisable to cooperate with them or seek their assistance. It often happens that the family turns to professional therapists who represent the dominant culture's establishment and at the same time, "to be on the safe side," goes to traditional helpers. Various types of indigenous helpers are described in chapter 12.

COPING STRATEGIES

Families of different cultures employ different strategies for coping with life's difficulties, in general, and situations of emergency or crisis, in particular. The strategies are partly determined by the other characteristics of the culture. Following is a small sample of coping strategies found in various cultural communities.

Hill et al. (1995) list the following coping strategies inner-city African American women have adopted for coping with environmental violence: Resourcefulness, flexibility of roles, positive self-concept, reliance on kinship ties, mutual respect and social support among other African American women, spirituality and political activism.

Gideon Levi, an Israeli journalist who works with Palestinian refugees in the Gaza Strip, was interviewed by me for the newsletter of the Israeli Association of Family Therapy. In the interview, he described the extremely trying living conditions in the refugee camps: Poverty, hunger, unemployment, intolerable overcrowding, extremely poor housing. Before the Israeli armed forces evacuated the Gaza Strip in 1995, the refugees in the camp suffered, on top of all these, long periods of total curfew by the Israeli army, surprise night raids into homes by units searching for terrorists or hiding places for weapons and explosives, killing of family members who participated in terrorist attacks or in violent demonstrations. According to Levi, the refugee families have adopted the following coping strategies for dealing with these hardships: Adherence to fundamentalist Islamic ideas and to conservative beliefs, values and attitudes concerning the traditional social order and the family, passive resignation and endurance, skepticism and cynicism with respect to any political authority, including their own political leadership, and an almost-messianic belief in the eventual return to the places in Israel from which they ran away or were driven away in the 1948 war.

HOW ARE PROBLEMS TREATED AND SOLVED WITHIN THE COMMUNITY?

Every cultural community has its own institutions and procedures for curing mental distress, deviant behavior and personal and interpersonal problems. Native therapeutic methods are organic to the culture. That is, they are systematically interrelated to other aspects of the culture, as listed and discussed above.

A culturally competent family therapist must understand the cultural relativity of mechanisms of therapeutic change. Since curing is culture bound, interventions that have proven effective with members of one culture can be found ineffective with members of another culture.

To understand how the family is aided by indigenous helpers, one should know their method of functioning. How is the connection between family and helpers established? Where and how is the help provided and by what means? What is the therapeutic procedure? Which mechanisms of change are effected by the procedure? When and how is the intervention terminated?

HOW IS SUCCESS OR FAILURE OF INDIGENOUS INTERVENTION EXPLAINED?

To understand the culture's own subjective understanding of cure, the following questions should be answered: What is considered a success by the family? Disappearance of the symptoms? Removal of the sufferer from the community? Coming to terms with the symptom? How does the family explain success or failure? For example, does it attribute success to the therapist having successfully enticed a devil to leave the sufferer's body? In the following case the client attributed the success of the therapy to her guardian angel:

Case 20: A young religious Jewish woman and her boyfriend came to me for couple therapy. They loved each other but had some differences to bridge. The girl held the traditional Jewish belief that the matching of each specific couple is predestined, "written in heaven." Before she met her boyfriend she had a dream in which she saw him very clearly and a voice said: "Here is your future husband." Following some sessions, the couple solved their difficulties and marriage was soon to follow. The girl told me that she believed I had been subtly guided by the angel in charge of matchmaking, who told me what to say and what to do so that the therapy could reach its happy end.

ATTITUDE TOWARD MODERN PROFESSIONAL HELP

Recruiting motivation for therapy and achieving good results depends, to a large extent, on the family's attitude. Different families can have radically different attitudes, ranging between deep suspicion and hostility at one extreme to blind, unjustified faith and admiration at the other. Families hold a great variety of views and prejudices with respect to professional help. These are partly derived from the family's own internalized cultural programs. Furthermore, people of disadvantaged sections of the population often mistrust mainstream professional helpers and the organizations they represent. Unfortunately, the distrust is often justified. Phenomena such as institutional racism and preferential treatment for certain segments of the population are well documented. See for instance McGoldrick (1998).

The ambivalent relationships between many African American families and professional helpers is thoroughly discussed by Boyd-Franklin (1989b). Bilu and Witztum (1993) discuss the problematics of offering modern psychiatric services to the ultra-Orthodox Jewish community of Jerusalem. They point out incompatibilities between the religious and the medical psychological models of reality. They claim, furthermore, that therapists are viewed as representatives of the impure secular world, which must be avoided. Despite these difficulties they have attempted to reach this community by adopting a therapeutic language suited to their world-view and values.

All the parameters referring to families' coping with problems and difficulties discussed in this chapter must be taken into account in any culturally competent family diagnosis and treatment. An essential ingredient of the art of culturally sensitive therapy is adapting the therapeutic strategies, the choice of techniques and the style of therapeutic communication to the family's own culture-bound conceptions of distress, coping and help.

SUMMARY

This chapter is devoted to cultural differences in the ways people identify, define and explain symptoms, problems, crises and stresses and in their help-seeking attitudes and behavior. These differences co-vary with the family's world-view, ecological goals, values and beliefs.

In designing a therapeutic intervention, the therapist should take into account the family's representation of its problems, its traditional help-seeking attitudes and habits, its sources of help within its own community, and its attitudes with respect to modern professional help. Communication between therapist and family has to be sensitive to anxieties, suspicion and prejudices on both sides.

PART III

THE INFORMATION-PROCESSING FRAMEWORK

This part of the book introduces a general model and a theoretical language for integrating, organizing, formalizing and systematizing all the knowledge relevant for providing a comprehensive culturally competent diagnosis and treatment for any particular family of any social and cultural background. The knowledge included can belong to any of the types discussed and illustrated in part II of this book.

The model and language include:

Description of the family as an information-processing system, an intercommunicating system of "living computers"

Formalizing cultural information-processing programs

Explicating culturally determined family dysfunction as information-processing "bugs" in family programs

Explaining bugs as unsuccessful attempts to restore the system's overall simplicity

Often simplicity cannot be restored in intercultural encounters that cause misunderstandings and stress. Also discussed are principles and methods for removing or weakening such bugs. Therapeutic "bug-busters" are derived from the family's own existing repertoire of programs.

7

The Family as an Information-Processing System

In part II of this book, the family-cultural concepts relevant to diagnosis and treatment are defined and illustrated in informal, ordinary English. In this chapter, a theoretical language is introduced, which enables therapists to apply the same concepts in their work in a more explicit, exact, detailed and systematic manner.

Admittedly, a culturally competent diagnostic evaluation, a therapeutic strategy or a treatment description can and usually will be formulated in informal, everyday language. Why a specialized technical language then? There are a number of reasons why such a language is needed.

A stage is reached in the development of every science, in which the insights, findings and techniques that have been accumulated since its inception are explicated, synthesized and systematized in the framework of a formal theoretical language. Such a language facilitates the construction of a unified, coherent body out of the existing heterogeneous pieces. Fuzzy concepts and propositions can be explicated and defined in rigorous, exact terms in such a language. The logical interconnections among them and their corollaries can be explored and defined. Only then can their empirical validity be tested.

Therefore, a diagnostic evaluation and a treatment description formulated in such a language is likely to be more exact, more detailed, more profound and more testable than an evaluation or description expressed in informal, everyday language. Although ordinary language formulations seem on the face of it more communicable, they are in fact less so, because they are characteristically vague and ambiguous. Furthermore, formalized concepts and propositions are more susceptible to empirical research.

Once a therapist has mastered the theoretical language, understood the logic behind it and practiced it in her work, her ability to formulate systematic, detailed and exact diagnostic evaluations or treatment descriptions will be enhanced, even if she uses everyday, informal discourse.

A complete description of the theoretical language of information-processing includes a highly technical, quasi-mathematical notational system whose acquisition requires specialized training. What is presented below is just a nontechnical summary of its main features, with a few simple examples.

THE FAMILY—A NETWORK OF "LIVING COMPUTERS"

The family is analogous to a network of living computers, a metaphor that cognitive scientists and family therapists have employed for a number of years. In this analogy, each family member is visualized as a separate information-processing machine. The sense organs (eyes, ears, skin, etc.) are the instruments by which the family member receives information (*input*) from the outside. The motor nerves and muscles are used to produce and send *output* to other family members or to outsiders. Data can be stored in and retrieved from *memory*. Input or retrieved information is processed in fixed, routine manners by *programs*.

The output each family member produces becomes input, which is received and processed by other family members. Input can also be received from sources external to the family. Likewise, output can be sent outside the family. Some data are common to some or all family members. This shared information is stored in the memory of at least some family members. The family also shares some commonalities in the way each member processes data. This subset of programs is called *family programs*. The family programs that constitute the *family's culture* (see the introduction and chapter 2) and termed *cultural family programs*.

Formulating Cultural Family Programs

Cultural family programs include two kinds of *instructions: data manipulation* and *data interpretation*, which an individual uses to process information.

The data manipulation instructions are: *switch* the information-processing system *on* or *off*, *store* information in memory, *retrieve* information from memory, *select* data, *apply* instructions to selected arrays of data, *compare* arrays of data, *transform* arrays of data, *order* data and *substitute* arrays of data with other arrays of data.

The data interpretation instructions are: *name an* array of data *as, distinguish* between arrays of data, *make* new *distinctions, symbolize* arrays of data as, *attribute a property or a process to* arrays of data, *attribute* arrays of data *to a property or a process, place* arrays of data *in a logical, spaciotemporal* or *sets relation*.

The *logical relations* are *negate, imply* and *state equivalence*. The *spaciotemporal relations* are *cause, predict, coordinate, precede* and *follow*. The *sets relations* are *creation of a new set, introducing items or subsets into an existing set, mutual exclusiveness of sets* and *overlapping of sets*.

The instructions are linked together by *operators*, namely AND, NOT, OR, IF . . . THEN, ALL/EVERY/ANY/SOME/PROPER (that is, applying to one specific case) and ITERATE.

The format for constructing family programs begins with identifying the family member and programming in that individual's proximity and control goals (discussed in chapters 3 and 4). Next, the therapist formats the family member's relevant stored information with sequential instructions for processing input and producing output, that are tied together with appropriate operators.

It will be noted, that although some of the terms introduced above refer to conscious actions in ordinary language, their use in formulating family programs does not imply a conscious awareness of information-processing by family members. The terminology introduced here is just a way of explicating predominantly implicit processes.

REFORMULATING CONCEPTS AS CULTURAL FAMILY PROGRAMS

Each of the concepts and terms introduced in part II of this book can be redefined in the technical vocabulary and grammar introduced above. As stated in the introduction and in chapter 2, these concepts and terms may be classified into the types *axioms, categories, explanations* and *rules*. Each of these types may be viewed as a mode of information processing. Every specific axiom, category, explanation or rule can therefore be formally explicated as an information-processing program. Below are some examples.

Programs Representing Axioms

The following ontological premise (axiom) was discussed in chapter 4: "The material world is just one outward manifestation of a divine, spiritual world." This premise may be viewed as a shorthand representation of an information-processing program. It summarizes a fixed pattern by which information is processed. The input is the material world. It is out there, to be grasped and perceived by people. This input, as well as its traces in the memory of people, become associated in the minds of certain people with an abstract idea stored in their memory: "the divine, spiritual world." The exact nature of this association will be specified in the actual formulation of the program by data manipulation and data interpretation instructions. Let us try to construct the program step by step.

The first line in the general format for organizing and ordering all the instructions and operators in a program is *ID of family member*. Since this program is not restricted to a specific family, we may write something like *any member of the culture*.

The second line is *proximity/control goals*. This line is irrelevant in this juncture, because this premise has nothing to do with ecology or with family structure.

The third line is *relevant information stored in memory*. The relevant information in this case is that there is such an entity as "the divine, spiritual world" and that this entity has various properties, which are not the same across cultures. A full formulation of the program will specify these properties. Another kind of relevant information stored in memory are traces of the material world.

The last line is *instructions for processing input and producing output, ordered in a sequence and tied together with operators*.

Let us look at the list of *data-manipulation instructions* above and pick the instructions that should be included in the program. Naturally, the information-processing system should be *switched on*. Input data must be *selected*. Information should be *retrieved* from memory.

Now let us pick the relevant *data-interpretation instructions* from the above list. It seems that the instruction *symbolize* is the best approximation to what we need (the material world and its traces in memory, being conceived as outward manifestation of a divine, spiritual world, may be said to be a *symbol* for this world).

The instructions should now be ordered in a sequence and tied together with operators. The right sequence is obvious: First the system must be *switched on*. Then input data should be *selected*, taken in from outside the system or *retrieved* from memory. Since the premise explicated refers to every aspect of both the real and the divine worlds, the instruction *symbolize* should apply to all arrays of input or retrieved data and to every property of these data. Therefore, the operators ALL and EVERY should be used.

Here is the resulting program:

ID: The following applies to EVERY member of the cultural community.

Relevant information stored in memory:

I. A *set* of concepts, images and *properties* constituting together "the divine, spiritual world."

II. ALL memory traces of the material world.

Instructions for processing input and producing output, ordered in a sequence and tied together with operators:

    1. *Switch* the information-processing system *on*.

    2. *Select* ALL input data belonging to the material world AND *retrieve* the *set* "the divine, spiritual world" from memory.

3. *Symbolize* the *set* "the divine, spiritual world" by ALL the input data *selected* AND by ALL the memory traces of the material world.

Programs Representing Categories

Categories can also be expressed as cultural family information-processing programs because they spell out how people of various cultures classify information.

The following proposition was mentioned in chapter 4: "Physical and moral purity should be always preserved and pollution avoided." This proposition, a central guiding principle of the Jewish religion, presupposes a distinction between the categories "pure versus foul or defiled." These are interesting cultural categories. Each of them subsumes heterogeneous entities, of which the common denominator is not self-evident. The category "foul or defiled," for instance, includes, among other things, devils and evil spirits, menstruating women, beasts whose flesh is forbidden from being eaten, pagan idols and Jews who have committed certain transgressions and sinful thoughts.

In chapter 10, a technique called *componential semantic analysis* is proposed, whose purpose is to root up the common meaning underlying such heterogeneous subcategories. The main procedure by which this is accomplished is comparing the contexts in which each subcategory is used. This technique has been applied to these subcategories. The outcome was that the common semantic denominator of all the subcategories of "foul or defiled" was "everything that is prone to cause the mixing of the profane with the holy." The categories "profane versus holy" are also culture-bound categories that need to be defined, but this will not be done here.

To express this categorial distinction as a program, one should ask oneself how *input* data or data *retrieved from memory* are classified by people who conceive of the world in these terms. Such people have two *complementary sets stored* in their memory. The set "entities prone to cause the mixing of the profane with the holy" and the set "entities not prone to cause the mixing of the profane with the holy." The former set is labeled "foul or defiled" and the latter "pure." Each of these sets includes a finite number of specific *subsets*. The former includes, for instance, the subsets "devils," "pagan idols" and "menstruating women" and the latter the subsets "angels," "the Torah scroll," "nonmenstruating women," among others. When a person whose memory includes these complementary sets *takes in* a new datum (*input*), or *retrieves* a datum from memory, she asks herself, "Is this datum prone to cause the mixing of the profane with the holy?" IF the answer is "Yes," she *introduces* the new datum *into the set* labeled "foul or defiled." IF the answer is "No," she introduces this datum into the complementary set, labeled "pure."

The fully formalized program is too complex to be spelled out here. Its structure, however, is outlined in the informal analysis above, which also specifies the main instructions and operators included in it.

Programs Representing Explanations

The elders of a Nigerian family attributed the departure of the young members of the family to the city to sorcery committed by a rival family. This culture-bound attribution can be formulated as a cultural information-processing program of the type *explanations*, as follows:

ID: the elders of a Nigerian family

Their proximity/control goals: To keep the young members of the family in the village, in order to prevent the family's socioeconomic deterioration

Relevant information stored in memory:

I. The general axiom (which can be expressed as a subprogram) "Misfortunes are caused by magic and sorcery practiced by one's enemies and rivals."

II. The knowledge that a particular neighboring family in the village is our rival. It is set to undermine our socioeconomic position in the village.

III. The knowledge that the family's socioeconomic position in the village is deteriorating, contrary to the family's goals.

Instructions for processing input and producing output, ordered in a sequence and tied together with operators:

1. *Select input*—The departure of young members of our family to the city, contrary to the family's goals.

2. *Retrieve* the knowledge that the family's socioeconomic position in the village is deteriorating AND *attribute* the *selected input* (departure of young) to this retrieved knowledge as a *cause*.

3. *Retrieve* the general axiom (I) AND *imply* with respect to PROPER [that is, consider this axiom applicable to the specific case in hand]

4. *Store* "The departure of the young AND the resulting socioeconomic deterioration of the family are *caused by* sorcery practiced by the neighboring family"

Programs Representing Rules

Case 16, chapter 5, describes the culture-bound disagreements between Nicos and his wife Jane. Nicos justified his objection to letting each of the children have his or her own room, by citing the rule "Everybody for each other and all together for everybody." This rule can be written as a cultural information-processing program, as follows:

ID: Nicos

Proximity/control goals with respect to the rest of the family:

To control them; to keep them close together and make them show mutual solidarity, in accordance with the following principles.

Relevant information stored in memory:

I. The proximity/control goals mentioned above

II. The principles of mutual and collective responsibility and self-sacrifice within the family

Instructions for processing input and producing output, ordered in a sequence and tied together with operators:

1. Select ANY *input* array Ai referring to the behavior of ALL or SOME family members with respect to each other

2. *Retrieve* the information stored in memory (I and II above)

3. IF Ai is an NOT an *attributed* PROPER [that is, not considered by Nicos as a particular instance] of the *retrieved* principles, THEN Ai *negates* the *retrieved* proximity/control goals.

4. *Select output*—Words and actions designed to make the producers of Ai stop producing Ai AND *produce output* which does not *negate the retrieved* goals and principles.

Admittedly, the above programs are much more complex and stylistically more artificial than the original concepts or descriptions. Yet, the above programs have the following advantages:

The formulation-as-programs portrays the original concepts and principles as dynamic processes rather than as static entities. It elaborates the cognitive processes involved in applying these concepts in real time. It distinguishes between central and peripheral cognitive processes—information taken in from outside, actions, information retrieved from memory and various mental operations. At the same time it displays the dynamic interrelations among all these processing stages. This makes the formulation-as-programs more useful to clinicians than the original formulations. A therapist looking for the best intervention technique for a particular purpose must take into account the target stage of processing. Different techniques would be used for modifying input information, output information, actions or internal mental operations. In choosing a technique, furthermore, a therapist has to be able to predict how intervening in one processing stage is likely to influence the other processing stages. By specifying the processing stages and exposing their dynamic interconnections, then, the formulation-as-programs facilitates the choice of techniques.

Once the original concepts have been reformulated as programs, the interrelations among them become more explicit. For example, the program referring to the departure of young members of the family in a Nigerian village above ties together ecological concepts with concepts referring to popular beliefs. Nicos' program, presented above, connects family-structural concepts with concepts referring to values concerning family life.

This property of programs, too, is useful to therapists. It widens the therapist's vista and enables her to predict side effects of therapeutic techniques employed. Another advantage of formulation-as-programs is the clarity and precision accrued by the use of a standardized formal, rigorous language.

PROGRAMS ADD UP TO AN IDIOGRAPHIC THEORY

Learning and describing the family's culture is a part of the culturally competent diagnostic evaluation of this family. Being acquainted with the family's culture is also the very essence of culturally competent family therapy. When a therapist formulates the set of information-processing programs purporting to represent the family's culture, he constructs an *idiographic theory*, that is, a set of interconnected hypotheses about a particular case. This theory is necessarily tentative. It is continuously being revised as the therapy proceeds.

In constructing such an idiographic theory, the therapist attempts to answer the following three questions:

1. Which of the cultural information-processing programs included in the general theory applies to this particular family? Ideally, all the concepts introduced in Part II of this book would be reformulated as programs. Each program would be identified by a code name (e.g., the code name *the world's divinity*, standing for the program that explicates the axiom "The material world is just one outward manifestation of a divine, spiritual world," or the code name *collectivism*, standing for the program that explicates the rule "Our family must adhere to the norms of mutual and collective responsibility and self-sacrifice"). Then the therapist would ask himself: Does the program whose code name is such and such apply to this particular family? If it does, then it should be included in the idiographic theory describing this family's culture. If it does not, then it should not be included in this idiographic theory.

2. Does the culture of this particular family include any *local programs*, that is, programs not found in the general theory? If the answer is "yes," then the therapist attempts to formulate these local programs.

3. What are the interrelations among the programs that have been included in the idiographic theory? Are certain programs logically implied by some other programs? Do some programs overlap?

HOW CAN THERAPISTS ARRIVE AT IDIOGRAPHIC THEORIES AND TEST THEIR VALIDITY?

Since a family's culture is not directly observable, and can only be described by a tentative, revisable idiographic theory, the question arises how it can be reached. When a therapist meets a family, she only witnesses a jumble of verbal and nonverbal behavioral manifestations. She does not see or hear the family's culture. On rare occasions, family members will be aware of some laws governing their behavior and will be able and willing to spell them out. Usually, however, this will not be the case. How can the therapist unearth and describe the family's culture, then? Part IV of this book contains various methods for collecting, eliciting and analyzing data relevant to culturally competent family diagnosis and treatment. These, however, are only heuristic procedures, technical aids. They are not *discovery procedures*, leading from data to theory. As argued by Chomsky (1965), there can be no such discovery procedures. A theory is not just some kind of summary of the observed data. It is a system of abstract laws, hypothesized to govern not only the observed data but of a theoretically infinite set of data, of which the observed data are just one particular sample. These laws can be approximated only by intuition and creativity.

Chomsky (1965) argued further that not only is a discovery procedure an impossibility, but also a *decision procedure*. That is, there can be no procedure by which it could be decided whether a theory about a certain range of data is the correct one or not. In other words, there is no such thing as a theory that is absolutely valid. The only feasible test of validity is an *evaluation procedure*, by which two or more theories already proposed for a given sample of data are compared and the best one is chosen. A theory is preferred by criteria such as *completeness, consistency* and *parsimony*. In other words, the theory that summarizes the given data in the simplest, most complete and most consistent manner is considered the best.

The implications of these methodological principles with respect to culturally competent family diagnosis and therapy are the following: A therapist who works with a family attempts to learn the family's culture and describe it by a tentative idiographic theory, a system of interconnected information-processing programs, some taken from the general theoretical pool and some tailored for the specific family. The therapist is aided by various heuristic procedures, but his main tools in constructing the tentative idiographic theory are his own intuition and creativity. The empirical validity of the idiographic theory arrived at can be tested by an evaluation procedure. The therapist can attempt to construct a number of alternative systems of programs and then choose the most consistent, complete and parsimonious one. He or she can also ask colleagues to attempt constructing alternative theories and then compare the results by the same criteria. As the therapy proceeds, the therapist is continuously revising the original theory, with a view to restoring its consistency, completeness and parsimony. The similarity between this evaluation procedure and the process of assimilating novel cultural data attributed to families (see the introduction and chapter 2) has perhaps not escaped the reader's notice.

A CASE ILLUSTRATION

The following case illustrates the uses of the instructions defined above to formulate a program according to the suggested outline. It also illustrates the associated methodological principles.

Case 21: David and Edna. David, a twenty-eight-year-old man, and his twenty-seven-year-old wife Edna came to therapy to sort out their marital difficulties. Edna had a long list of complaints. She did not like David's lack of ambition. He seemed to be satisfied with his current level of occupation and income. He worked as an odd-job man and had no ambition for furthering his education and career. When David came in from work late in the afternoon, Edna said, he used to be tired and used to go to sleep early. He rarely entered into more than trivial conversations with Edna. He did not seem to be interested in her feelings. Edna thought David limited in his ability to formulate thoughts and ideas. In the company of her friends, he used to be extremely inhibited. He was usually trying to avoid her friends and was overly critical of their character.

Edna did not like David mother's attitude toward her. She used to accuse Edna of mistreating her son. David failed to protect Edna from his mother's accusations. Edna held David's whole family of origin to be primitive, dull, uneducated, unambitious and aggressive.

Edna was not on good terms with her own mother, too. Whenever they visited her parents, Edna was becoming extremely distressed. David was critical of Edna's attitude and thought she should respect her mother and be more tolerant of her. When Edna became distressed, he would not support her, but would avoid her and become cold and indifferent.

Edna was often lecturing to David that he should change. She threatened to leave him if he did not change, but she never did. She often used to cry and act miserable.

David had his own list of complaints. He accused Edna of neglecting him and their home. Edna used to work part time as a TV reporter. She attended a sculpture workshop. In the evenings she liked going out with her friends, who were all media people or artists. She liked intellectual discussions and gossip. David said that her friends looked down on him and could not understand why she was staying with him. They did not seem, to him, good or moral people. They were, in his eyes, obsessed with power, were snobbish and exploitative.

Edna used to get up late in the morning and her income was limited. She expected him to provide for her. She liked spending money on leisure activities and did not seem to do much around their home. When they visited his family, Edna would behave in a conceited and disrespectful manner. He thought of Edna as an aggressive, unloving, domineering, conceited person.

Here is the history of Edna's family of origin, as told by Edna. Her parents, Max and Rosa, emigrated from Rumania to Israel in the early 1960s, as political refugees. Rosa had to stop her studies in an art school, and Max had to quit his studies in an institute of technology. Their house and bank accounts were confiscated by the Communist party. When they came to Israel they could not afford to settle in a "good" neighborhood and settled instead in Beit Shemesh, a town populated mainly by North African and Iraqi immigrants, in which housing was subsidized by the government and living was inexpensive. They never resumed their studies. Max opened a small electronics business, and Rosa stayed at home as a housewife until Edna, their only daughter, was sixteen. Occasionally, Rosa painted and sculpted at home, without attempting to present or sell what she created. She became depressed and hypochondriac. When Edna was sixteen the municipal council gave Rosa a grant to open an art gallery, as a part of a policy to promote cultural activities in the town. After a short period of activity, during which Rosa attempted to develop the gallery, she neglected it and let it deteriorate. She said people in the town were too ignorant to appreciate art. Max and Rosa blamed the Israeli government for their situation. They said the government did not care for people of talent. They glorified the Rumanian communist government, which promoted the arts and sciences.

After Edna completed her army service, at the age of twenty, she moved to Tel Aviv. She did not continue her studies, but looked for a job in the electronic media. She found a part-time job as a reporter in cable television.

And here is the history of David's family of origin, as told by David. David's grandfather was a goldsmith in the Casablanca (Morocco) Jewish section. In 1948, after the Israeli Declaration of Independence, the community was the victim of riots by their Muslim neighbors. After deciding to immigrate to Israel, the government confiscated the family's house and property. The family arrived in Israel when David's father was five years old and were housed in a temporary camp near what was later to become the town of Beit Shemesh. The transitional stay in the camp lasted ten years. It was ten years of privation and difficulties. Finally, the family moved to a subsidized house in Beit Shemesh. David's father had to leave school and go to work in a factory when he was sixteen, and he worked there all his life. David's father met his wife in the transitional camp. Her family emigrated from a small village in the Moroccan Atlas Mountains. They were illiterate. After she married David's father, she bore four children, of which David was the second. She worked as a factory cleaning person.

David's older brother was considered "the genius in the family" and the rest of the family mobilized to help him devote himself to his school work. David's younger sister was "the good-looking one," who was supposed to marry up. David had to devote himself to the family and enable his older brother and sister to achieve their destinies. He was not a bright pupil and quit school at fifteen to help his family. Until he was inducted into the army when he was eighteen, he worked as a day laborer in an open-air produce market. After he was discharged from the army, he made his living as an odd-job man.

Analysis

The therapist, having obtained all this information, had to use his intuition and creativity to construct a tentative idiographic theory, a set of interconnected programs purporting to describe those parts of this family's culture that would be relevant to therapy. The resulting theory includes the relevant programs found in the general theory, represented by code names, and local programs, that is, programs not included in the general theory but found in this particular family.

Programs Taken from the General Theory (Represented by Code Names)

Ecological programs: Edna's.

Proximity and control goals: Remain a part of her intellectual and "artistic" family friends

Her family's interpretation of ecological constraints: Failure to reach goals blamed on external hostile authorities

Her family's values related to the environment: Personal, intellectual and social achievement, individualism, interesting life

Ecological programs: David's.

Goal with respect to the social, extrafamilial environment: Remain a part of his nonacademic, working-class family of origin and circle of friends

His family's interpretation of ecological constraints: Failure to reach goals is blamed on the family's decision to emigrate and economical and political circumstances

Family's environmental values: Parsimony (making do with what one has), work, diligence, practical attitude, dutifulness, conservatism, altruism, modesty, justice, intolerance toward deviance, upward mobility, good name, honor, self-sacrifice, solidarity

Structural programs: Edna's.

Proximity and control goals: Draw David close to herself emotionally and have him assume a more nurturing and supportive role [proximity]

Family's structure: Only Edna's father and mother are in Israel. Other members of the family were left behind in Rumania and contacts with them are rather meager. The family is culturally homogenous. Family rules are flexible. Wife is dominant family member.

Structural programs: David's.

Proximity and control goals: Do not let Edna control him

Family's structure: The extended family considered part of the immediate family. Very close daily ties are kept with them, husband is dominant in the family. The children never argue with their parents and always accord them respect.

Programs referring to the family's representation of itself: Edna's.

Her family's self-concept: Ashkenazi-Jewish (European), middle class, academic-intellectual, "artistic"

Edna's family's modes of experiencing: Aesthetic, intellectual

Her family's emotives: Sense of nonfulfillment and missed opportunities and anger at authorities

Programs referring to the family's representation of itself: David's.

Family self-concept: Israeli, Sepharadi, Moroccan, nonintellectual

Family's emotives: Fear of poverty and hardship, grief and anger related to the memory of losses and suffering

Family's modes of experiencing: Direct, reality oriented, emotional

Program's referring to the family's values and beliefs concerning marriage and family life: Edna's.

Family honor and sexual fidelity not primary values

Family viewed as an aggregate of autonomous individuals

Individual deviance tolerated

Equality in roles and duties valued

Openness about emotional experiences encouraged, but intimacy and personal warmth not of primary importance

Programs referring to the family's values and beliefs concerning marriage and family life: David's.

Marriage and family valued and sanctified

Family honor and sexual fidelity important

The family viewed as a collective

Individual achievements viewed as serving the family's goal of upward mobility

Deviant behavior not tolerated

Parents should be honored and respected

Men have a higher status than women

Gender roles clearly delineated

Sensitive emotional issues are evaded

Programs referring to the family's functioning and lifestyle: Edna's.

Husband responsible for providing for family, wife is free to spend time and money as she wishes, leisure activities include reading, visiting the theater and art galleries, and intellectual conversations, personal space and time respected

Family's communication style: Verbal communication ample and nonverbal communication minimal. Feelings are discussed and analyzed, main positive communication intents are directed toward creating interest, main negative communication intents are aimed at accusing other people of one's misery

Programs referring to the family's functioning and lifestyle: David's.

All adults responsible for providing for family. Major decisions are made by the father, in consultation with sons. Minor decisions made by the mother and daughters.

Leisure-time activities include meeting and talking with relatives, eating and watching TV. Personal space and time are not always respected.

Family's communication style: Main conversation topics are everyday concerns. Expression of feelings primarily nonverbal. Women touch and hug each other, but men and women do not touch each other in front of other people. Children are hugged and kissed freely.

Programs referring to problems and coping: Edna's.

Feeling of failure with respect to professional and social goals.

Family's coping style characterized by inaction, complaining and blaming.

Programs referring to problems and coping: David's.

Main problems related to money, children's needs, health problems, marital discord.

Problems solved inside the extended family.

Financial problems solved by men.

Health, educational and relationship difficulties solved by women.

Interrelations among the Programs

Many of the programs listed above by code names are interrelated. This will not be demonstrated here in detail, but here are some examples.

Edna's family of origin's values related to the environment were represented above by the code names "personal, intellectual and social achievement, individualism, interesting life." These are clearly related to their above mentioned modes of experiencing—aesthetic and intellectual, as well as to their self-concept—Ashkenazi-Jewish (versus Sepharadi, "oriental"-Jewish), middle class (versus working class), academic-intellectual (versus uneducated) and "artistic." All these are linked with Edna's goals with respect to the social, extrafamilial environment—to remain a part of her intellectual and "artistic" family and circle of friends.

Edna's family of origin's communication style is described above as follows: "Verbal communication is ample and nonverbal minimal. Feelings are discussed and analyzed. Main positive communication intents are directed toward creating interest." This communication style is related to the following elements of Edna's family of origin's functioning and lifestyle, mentioned above: "Leisure-time activities include reading, visiting the theater and art galleries, and intellectual conversations. Personal space and time are respected."

David's family of origin's emotives are described above by the code names "Fear of poverty and hardship. Grief and anger are related to the memory of the losses they suffered and the difficulties they were forced to go through." These are clearly associated with his family's values related to the environment: parsimony (making do with what one has), work, diligence, practical attitude, dutifulness, conservatism, altruism, modesty, justice, intolerance toward deviance, upward mobility, good name, honor, self-sacrifice and solidarity.

Local Programs

The therapist formulated some local programs, that is, programs not found in the general theory but specific to this particular family. Here is the main local program.

IDs: David and Edna

Goals:

Edna's goals with respect to the social, extrafamilial environment—Remain a part of her intellectual and "artistic" family and circle of friends

David's goal with respect to the social, extrafamilial environment—Remain a part of his nonacademic, working-class family of origin and circle of friends

Edna's goals with respect to David—Draw David close to herself emotionally and have him assume a more nurturing and supportive role

David's goal with respect to Edna—Not letting her control him

Relevant information stored in memory:

I. All the programs listed above

II. Edna's and David's respective subjective family histories

Instructions for processing input and producing output: A full formulation of these instructions in the vocabulary introduced above will be complex and hard to follow. Here is a paraphrase in ordinary English: If David behaves in a way that does not fit the cultural characteristics of Edna's family of origin (her family's self-concept, modes of experiencing, values in relation to the environment, conceptualization of family and marriage, family lifestyle and modes of communication), then Edna attributes this behavior either to David's family culture, which she considers primitive, dull, uneducated, unambitious and aggressive, or to David's personality, which she considers limited, insecure and passive. Following this interpretation, Edna considers David's behavior as incompatible with her goal of remaining close to her intellectual and "artistic" family and friends or with her goal of drawing David toward herself. This evokes in Edna emotions characteristic of her family of origin's emotives: nonfulfillment; anger at external authorities. In order to serve these frustrated goals, Edna criticizes and accuses David and his family. She tells David that he should change. She threatens to leave if he does not.

However, if David's behavior reminds Edna of her own family's lack of self-fulfillment, her mother's depression and hypochondria, the habit of blaming failure on external agents and considering intimacy and personal warmth of secondary importance, then she attributes David's behavior to his family of origin's culture, which she considers problematic, aggressive and lacking insight, or to David's personality, which she considers as being a failure, nonunderstanding and unloving. This also hinders her from achieving her goals, which evokes in her emotions related to her family of origin's emotives. She reacts, with the same goals in mind, by crying and acting miserable. She accuses David and his family and threatens to leave.

If Edna behaves in a way that does not fit into David's family of origin's culture, then David classifies her behavior as belonging to the culture of her family and friends, which he considers intellectually and verbally superior, powerful, snobbish, immoral and exploitative, or to Edna's personality, which he takes to be aggressive, unloving, domineering, conceited and crazy. Then he views Edna's behavior as hindering the reaching of his goals of remaining a part of his nonacademic, working-class family and friends, and his goal of not letting Edna control him. He responds by avoiding Edna and her friends, by sleeping a lot and minimizing verbal and nonverbal communication with her and her friends. He criticizes her friends and her behavior with her mother. He does not support her when she needs emotional support.

SUMMARY

This chapter is devoted to the presentation of a model and a theoretical language that make it possible to explicate, synthesize, systematize and formalize all the knowledge acquired about any particular family as a cultural entity. In this model and language, the family is represented through an information-processing metaphor. It is viewed as a network of living computers programmed to receive, process and produce information according to culturally prescribed routines. The set of programs is the family's unique culture.

Family programs consist of data manipulation instructions, second data interpretation instructions (name as, distinguish, introduce into a set, make distinctions, symbolize as, attribute a property or a process to, attribute data to property or process, place in a relation [a list of kinds of relations is provided]).

Family programs are constructed according to the following scheme: ID of family members, their proximity and control goals with respect to each other and the external environment, relevant information stored in their memory and instructions for processing input and producing output. The instructions are tied together by operators. This formula for coding diagnostically relevant family-cultural information into such formalized representations of programs was illustrated by a case and examples.

This chapter also includes a brief discussion concerning the following methodological problems: How does the therapist arrive at an idiographic theory, consisting of interconnected information-processing programs hypothesized to represent the family's culture? How does the therapist test the validity of such a theory?

It is argued, with Chomsky, that there can be no discovery or decision procedures for constructing and validating such a theory. There can only be an evaluation procedure, applying criteria such as completeness, consistency and parsimony to decide which of a number of alternative theories proposed for the same set of data should be considered the best.

8

Culturally Determined Family Dysfunction

In this chapter, it will be explained how culture-bound disturbances ("bugs") in a family's functioning can be described explicitly and rigorously in the framework of the information-processing model presented in chapter 7. By formulating such explicit and rigorous descriptions of dysfunctions in the family, the therapist pinpoints and clearly marks the targets of culturally competent family therapeutic interventions. Principles for "debugging," that is, removing culture-bound bugs and restoring the system's capacity for good functional adaptation, are formulated and illustrated.

THE CONCEPT OF SIMPLICITY

A general, overriding, universal principle hypothesized to underlie human information-processing systems is *simplicity*. That is to say, the set of programs "prefers" to process information in the simplest possible manner, with a minimum of redundancies, inconsistencies and complications.

The principle of simplicity is not an arbitrary dogma. Various versions of it underlie, under different names, numerous scientific theories dealing with human or natural systems. A tiny sample includes *homeostasis* in biology (see Gottfried, 1993; Purves, 1995), and in general systems theory (see Bertalanffy, 1973), Festinger's *cognitive consistency* (1962), Piaget's *equilibrium* (1971), Chomsky's *simplicity* (1965) and Freud's *preservation and catexis of mental energy* (1949).

METAPROGRAMS MAINTAINING AND RESTORING SIMPLICITY

In the context of information processing, the principle of simplicity can be explicated through a set of *metaprograms*. These are higher-level programs that are built into any information-processing system. Their function is to regulate the activity of all information-processing programs such that simplicity is maintained or, if necessary, restored.

The underlying assumptions behind the operation of the metaprograms are:

Completeness: The set of information-processing programs includes all the programs needed to process the information to which the system is exposed, providing this information is needed for the system's survival and smooth functioning. Each program includes all the instructions needed to process such information.

Parsimony: The set of programs includes just the programs needed to process the relevant information. No program is redundant and no program includes any unnecessary instructions.

Consistency: The set of programs is self-consistent. Programs or instructions never contradict each other.

The metaprograms can be logically derived from the following assumptions.

Metaprogram 1: Deriving New Programs or Instructions

IF new, unfamiliar but critical input information is received by the system, *AND* the system lacks programs or instructions for processing this information, *THEN* the system generates new programs or new instructions capable of processing this new information. In this way, *completeness* is restored.

The same metaprogram can serve the purpose of restoring *consistency: IF* new, unfamiliar but critical input is received by the system *AND* the new information contradicts existing programs or instructions, *THEN* new programs or instructions, which settle the inconsistency, are generated. The new program or instructions restrict the application of the existing programs or instructions to specific conditions or contexts.

In most cases, the new programs or instructions are not generated out of nothing but are *derived* from the existing repertoire of programs and instructions. In the following case, metaprogram 1 operated to restore completeness.

Case 22: A Native American family started a business of agricultural tools, serving Native American farmers. They soon had to cope with bitter competition with other businesses in the same field. Competing and struggling for material success was incompatible with their cultural family programs prescribing collectivism, sharing, non-materialism and family and community service. For the business to survive, they expanded their cultural information-processing system by adding to it the rule that competition, use of power and cunning are allowed in business matters. At the same time, they preserved their traditional values with respect to family and community affairs.

This rule was derived from other parts of their information-processing system, designed to deal with pressures coming from the side of the dominant American establishment. In the following example, metaprogram 1 operated to restore consistency.

In the Jewish community in Ethiopia, when a woman complained that her husband was beating her, the husband and wife were brought to a council of elders of the community. They would usually demand of the wife to obey her husband and reprimand the husband for having beaten her. In Israel, Ethiopian women learned that, when they are physically abused by the husband, they can complain to the police or the local social services department, and the husband can be sued. The community solved this inconsistency by bringing the husband and wife to the traditional council and going through the traditional procedure, but afterward leaving the continuation of the treatment in the hands of a social worker.

Metaprogram 2: **Deleting Programs or Instructions Rendered Redundant**

IF a system stops being exposed regularly to some kind of information, or previously crucial information loses its importance, *THEN* the programs or instructions that have become redundant are deleted. In this way, *parsimony* is restored. The same metaprogram can be used to restore *consistency*. In the following case, metaprogram 2 operated to restore the *parsimony* of the family's information-processing system.

Case 23: A family immigrated to the United States from Russia. In Russia, they lived a life of privation. Salaries were pitifully small. Basic goods were lacking and everything was extremely expensive. Accordingly, they developed family programs directed toward thriftiness and saving. Spending too much money on anything was not allowed. The grandmother controlled the family's economy. A penny could not be spent on anything without her permission. In the United States, they found an affluent society. They soon dropped most of the programs directed toward thriftiness and developed characteristic Western spending habits. The grandmother was no longer consulted about money matters.

Metaprogram 3: **Changing Programs or Instructions without Adding New Ones or Deleting Existing Ones**

The main function of this metaprogram is to restore *consistency*. Changes can take place in any of the constituents of a program or an instruction, for example, in the sequential order of the instructions in a program or in the kinds of data to which an instruction applies.

Case 24: In a Muslim family, the father used to have absolute authority over his wife and children. The teenage daughters were not supposed to date. This family, however, lived in Jaffa, a part of Tel Aviv, where the dominant culture prescribes equality within the family and tolerates sexual permissiveness. A program was added to this Muslim family that permitted the teenage daughters to date. However, this created an inconsistency with the traditional authority of the father. To resolve the inconsistency, the family did not change the program prescribing the father's authority. Rather, the fact that the daughters were dating was concealed from the father. The mother collaborated with the daughters in telling the father false stories about the daughters' whereabouts and behavior. In fact, the father knew the truth but, to preserve his honor and the consistency of the family programs, he collaborated in this pretending game.

CONDITIONS IN WHICH SIMPLICITY CANNOT BE RESTORED

Dysfunction in family programs occurs in conditions under which meta-programs 1 through 3 cannot operate properly. This happens usually when the family's cultural information-processing system is flooded with unfamiliar, stressful information. When simplicity cannot be restored, family programs become "bugged," that is, infested with errors in information processing that lead to malfunctioning. Some programs become redundant, some wrong, some too complicated, some too simple.

PUZZLES FACED BY BAFFLED CULTURAL INFORMATION-PROCESSING SYSTEMS

Below are some characteristic puzzles faced by cultural information-processing systems overwhelmed by unfamiliar information.

Inability to Settle on One Coherent Interpretation of the Data

This problem is faced by a system when the unfamiliar information yields itself to conflicting interpretations. The information-processing system lacks programs or instructions for choosing among them or reconciling them.

The immigration of the Ethiopian Jewish community to Israel was achieved as a result of great efforts by various public Israeli bodies to overcome the enormous obstacles and dangers involved in these *aliyah* operations. The immigrants were welcomed with very warm public ceremonies. The immigrants received many forms of administrative attention and public aid. The immigrants, however, whose immigration was motivated by religious fervor and Messianic beliefs, had also been badly mistreated by various authorities. The religious establishment questioned their very Jewishness and refused to accord recognition to their religious leaders. They were dispersed, by administrative decisions, to various parts of the country. The bureaucracy intervened insensitively in various aspects of their traditional way of life. Many

Israelis rejected them as "black," "dirty" or "primitive." Consequently, many families and individuals could not decide whether the Israelis were friends or enemies, whether Israel was really the Holy Land they dreamed about or an unholy, profane, cruel and corrupt society. Because these two contradictory interpretations of their experience in Israel have been equally emotionally invested, many could not settle on one single interpretation. In order to restore simplicity, these immigrants first had to settle on a single interpretation of the new data. Are the Israelis good or bad? Can they or can they not be trusted to take care of the community? Are they Jewish or some kind of new people? If they are bad, unreliable and alien, the existing programs and instructions for dealing with hostile non-Jews should be applied to them. If they are good, reliable and Jewish, the existing set of programs with which they made *aliyah* should be preserved. The inability to settle on any of these two possibilities, however, makes it impossible to decide which *programs* to apply. (see Ben David and Good, 1998)

Restoring Simplicity Would Cause Intolerable Distress

Before Hitler, the German Jewish community seemed to have been relatively well assimilated and integrated into the fabric of German society. With the advent of Nazism, they became, almost overnight, a persecuted, rejected minority. Many German Jews were unable to come to terms with this new reality, draw conclusions and adjust themselves to it. Restoring simplicity by changing would have caused them intolerable distress.

The System Is Unable to Digest the Overwhelming Amount of Unfamiliar Information It Encounters

Biolsi (1995) tells the story of attempts made by various U.S. governmental agencies to "civilize the Indians" starting in the second half of the nineteenth century. Most of these attempts failed, not just because they were forced upon a reluctant community, but also because modern capitalistic society, with its emphasis on free enterprise, individualism, competition and industry was the opposite of Native American society in many respects. The latter was a society of hunters-gatherers and horticulturists. It was collectivistic and egalitarian. It attached great importance to tradition and ritual.

In our terms, the cultural information-processing system of the Native Americans was unable to digest the overwhelming amount of new cultural information forced upon them by U.S. authorities.

ABORTIVE ATTEMPTS TO RESTORE SIMPLICITY AND ENSUING BUGS

When a cultural information-processing system faces puzzles and problems of these kinds, it does attempt to restore simplicity, but its attempts are often unsuccessful or only partly successful. Its faulty or incomplete attempts to restore simplicity engender bugs.

The following are the main kinds of dysfunctional strategies often employed by cultural information-processing systems in their desperate attempts to restore simplicity in unfavorable circumstances. Characteristic bugs produced by these attempts are listed and illustrated by examples:

Forgoing Completeness

The information-processing system ignores a part of the input. It processes just the parts that have not been ignored.

Some Ethiopian Jews ignore the disappointing aspects of Israeli society and consider the Israelis "all good." Other Ethiopian immigrants disregard the positive aspect of Israeli society and view the Israelis as "all bad." In this way they evade their inability to settle on one coherent interpretation of the data.

Forgoing Consistency

The information-processing system attempts to restore simplicity by giving up any attempt to restore consistency.

Case 25: A family emigrated from the former Soviet Union to the United States. The passage from a centrally controlled economy to a free market economy confused this family and caused them to behave in a random, disorganized and inconsistent manner in financial and business matters. They were thrifty in spending cash money, but used credit cards in an uncontrolled manner. They took a large loan to open an export business, selling to Russia, but changed their minds in the middle of the preparations and lost a great deal of money.

In our terms, the information-processing system of this family gave up any attempt to restore consistency.

Forgoing Parsimony

The information-processing system does not ignore the confusing new information, but also does not respond to it. Instead, it continues using its previous programs, which have become superfluous.

Many Native Americans simply ignored the pressures applied on them to "become civilized" and continued to behave according to their traditional codes. For example, if they received money to open a small business, they handed the money out to their relatives or spent it on ritual dances.

Case 26: An Orthodox Jewish family emigrated from an ultra-Orthodox Jewish neighborhood in New York to Israel and settled in a secular neighborhood in Tel Aviv. They were soon exposed to the very strong influences of the materialistic, competitive, permissive and hedonistic environment. They began adopting some features of this style of life. The wife went further ahead than the husband in liberating herself from the limitations imposed by the Orthodox way of life. This caused tensions and conflicts between her and the rest of the family. The peak of the crisis occurred when she confessed to her husband that she had an extramarital affair. Soon afterward, the family moved to an ultra-Orthodox neighborhood and adopted a style of life that was even stricter than they had had back in the United States.

This case illustrates both forgoing consistency and, later, forgoing parsimony.

Misconstruing Target Programs

The unfamiliar cultural environment a family attempts to adapt to is itself a cultural information-processing system whose functioning is regulated by programs. We shall use the term *target programs* for the latter.

When a cultural information-processing system attempts to restore its simplicity, it tries to simulate the target programs. In other words, it tries to change its own programs so that they approximate the target programs as closely as possible. However, the results of these attempts are not always satisfactory. The adjusting information-processing system is, of necessity, in a state of partial ignorance. It does not know or understand all the target programs. Nor does it possess all the data needed to reconstruct the target programs. Therefore, even if the adjusting information-processing system attempts to restore completeness, consistency and parsimony, it often misconstrues the target programs. It misses important distinctions or draws distinctions which, from the viewpoint of the target programs, are irrelevant. This is the source of many intercultural misunderstandings. In some contexts, such misunderstandings can have fatal results, as almost happened in the following case.

Case 27: The following incident happened to me when I conducted fieldwork in a Bedouin encampment in the Sinai desert some years ago. A young man named Waleed, who could speak Hebrew because he worked for the Israeli army, told me confidentially that I should pack all my belongings and run for my life as fast as I can, because the *sheikh* of the encampment had issued an order to kill me. When I asked him why, he told me, blushing all over, that this was because I was watching married women.

The purpose of my fieldwork was to study children's play and socialization. Indeed, I did sit on the hillock and observed the children play and interact with their mothers.

The *sheikh* excused me after Waleed explained to him that I had acted out of ignorance. During my stay in the encampment, I did my utmost to behave according to the programs of my hosts. Still, I kept committing errors out of ignorance. In my own culture, a man is not supposed to touch a woman without her consent, but there is no rule prohibiting men from watching married or unmarried women in public places. In the Bedouin encampment, I behaved as if this distinction was built into the target programs, the programs espoused by my hosts, too. This error could have cost me my life.

LIST OF BUGS

Below is a list of types of bugs engendered by the faulty or incomplete attempts to restore simplicity discussed above.

Bug 1: Blinders

This bug is engendered by the strategy of foregoing completeness. The information-processing system restricts the range of data it processes, just as horse blinders restrict the horse's panoramic view. An example is the above-mentioned blindness of some Ethiopian Jews to the disappointing aspects of Israeli society.

Bug 2: Extreme Ambivalence or Fluctuation

This bug is the result of forgoing consistency. The information-processing system is torn inside between opposing, contradictory ways of processing the information or exhibits extreme instability. An example is the unstable spending behavior manifested by the family of Russian immigrants in Case 25.

Bug 3: Cultural Fixation or Regression

This bug is the product of forgoing parsimony. The information-processing system fixates itself on, or regresses to, its previous programs and gives up all attempts to adapt itself to the unfamiliar reality it faces. An example of fixation is the refusal by many Native Americans to "become civilized." An example of regression is the adoption of a strict ultra-Orthodox lifestyle by the family of immigrants in Case 26.

Bug 4: Cultural Naiveté

This bug is reflected in misconstruing target programs. The information-processing system attempts to restore simplicity but fails due to its ignorance or cultural naiveté. An example is Case 27.

Bugs and Symptoms

Symptoms and other problems in the individual are direct external manifestations of bugs or indirect consequences of bugs. Let us go back to Case 21, chapter 7.

Rosa, Edna's mother, became depressed and hypochondriac. This was a result of bugs in her family's programs. She and her husband could not have adapted themselves to the open, free-enterprise Israeli society. They remained *fixated* on a totalitarian attitude, in which responsibility for one's successes and failures is in the hands of an all-embracing bureaucracy. Her symptoms were related to the passivity, helplessness and frustration necessarily associated with this *fixation*.

David and Edna's external symptoms of the difficulties in their marriage were also direct and indirect manifestations of the bugs in their programs. Edna's behavior included criticizing David and his family, pressuring him to change, threatening to leave, crying and acting miserable. David's behavior included minimizing communication with Edna and her friends, oversleeping, criticizing her and withdrawing emotional support. These responses were motivated by the partners' erroneous presuppositions concerning the reasons for the other person's attitudes and behavior. These erroneous presuppositions were due to *cultural naiveté*.

PRINCIPLES FOR REDUCING DYSFUNCTION AND DEBUGGING

It follows from this analysis that reducing dysfunction via a culturally competent family therapy should involve "debugging," that is, removing or weakening the bugs in information processing. If this is achieved, the information-processing system regains its ability to activate metaprograms 1 through 3 and restores simplicity spontaneously in those contexts wherein simplicity has been lost.

Debugging requires helping the family find better, bug-free solutions to the puzzles it faces, so that simplicity is free to be restored. Debugging principles can be derived from analyzing the following puzzles mentioned on pages 106–107.

Inability to Settle on One Coherent Interpretation of the Data

Solving this puzzle without getting bugs as complications requires helping the system to approximate the relevant target programs as closely as possible, without forgoing completeness, consistency or parsimony. If this is achieved, the information-processing system will be able to interpret the data coherently in bug-free manners. To the greatest extent possible, the constructed target programs should be derived from the system's existing repertoire of programs.

These principles are illustrated in the following case:

Case 28: Nicole, a young French woman, was married to an Israeli man, Oved, whose parents immigrated to Israel from Egypt. Nicole was not able to make up her mind whether Oved was her friend or enemy, her powerful protector or a weak man who lets people abuse her. Both worked in a factory. If anybody in the factory insulted or treated her with the slightest disrespect, Oved would fight for her bravely, risking his job, until the offender apologized. His parents, however, would often order her around, lecture to her and insult her. Oved would sit aside, listening meekly without objecting and even smiling as if he enjoyed the insults. Nicole was confused. Sometimes she thought Oved was hypocritical or unstable. At other times she thought he was mama's little baby who pretended to be a powerful man just to impress his friends.

In our terms, Nicole was unable to settle on a single interpretation of the data. In fact, both of Oved's contradictory responses were culturally coded and programmed into his system. As a man, he was supposed to be the protector of his wife's and his family's honor. As a son, he was obliged to respect his parents and never question their judgment or their behavior. Both of his seemingly contradictory responses were, in fact, self-consistent from the internal, subjective viewpoint of his cultural tradition. Both of them were designed to protect the honor and integrity of his family. His parents' behavior with Nicole was also culturally coded. She married into their family and was supposed to behave according to clearly prescribed norms, very different from the ways in which she had been brought up with respect to household duties and behavior. It was their duty to reprimand her, using strong words that would put her in place.

At first the therapist tried to explain these observations to the couple. Her explanations were rejected, however, because neither of the partners was able or willing to realize the cultural relativity of his or her attitudes, values and codes.

Then the therapist asked herself how she could help Nicole derive consistent interpretations of Oved's and his parents' behavior out of her own internalized cultural codes. Nicole told the therapist her life history. The therapist learned that she was brought up in Bergerac in the south of France. Her family considered themselves "modern" and "liberal." Nevertheless, they went to church regularly and preserved some Catholic rituals. Both at home and at school, the values of obedience to benevolent authority, nationalism, loyalty and public service were emphasized. However, direct coercion and strong language were never used. Her grandfather fought in De Gaulle's Liberation army, and the family was proud of him.

From talking more with Nicole it became clear that her decision to marry Oved and settle in Israel was partly motivated by her wish to set herself free of what she had felt to be a "stifling bourgeois environment of false liberalism and hypocrisy."

The therapist decided to adopt the tactic of deriving analogies to Nicole's present family situation from her family history and the cultural environment of her childhood. She led Nicole, by directive questions, to draw analogies between Oved's and his parents' values of loyalty, family honor and parents' authority and the values by which she had been brought up. Oved's chivalrous protection of her honor at work was compared to her grandfather's fighting for the honor of France against all odds. His obedience to his parents and their unpleasant lectures were compared to the respect paid to the priest during service and confession. Both behaviors were analogized to protecting *La Patrie*, tradition and the community. The therapist, however, pointed out that the element of "hypocrisy," double talk and false liberalism that she did not like in the world of her youth was not present in her current situation. Oved and his parents expressed their values, attitudes and feelings directly, openly and honestly.

As a result of this intervention, Oved's behavior began to make sense to Nicole. She was able and willing to give a consistent interpretation to his attitude and behavior in different contexts. This does not mean that she accepted his parents' behavior toward her and his compliance, but she understood. She began to realize that her current Israeli family was not that much different from her own family of origin. She realized that she had managed to escape what she considered the "hypocrisy" of her former world, but not the absence of true personal freedom. This was not easy for her, but the new ability to interpret the input consistently made it possible for metaprograms 1 through 3 to resume their operation and restore the simplicity of her information-processing programs. She spontaneously adopted the program of listening to Oved's parents respectfully, confessing her sins, like one does with the priest in church, while continuing to debate her rights and duties with Oved directly.

Restoring Simplicity Would Cause Intolerable Distress

Debugging requires showing the system alternative ways of restoring simplicity, which would not cause such distress, or teaching it how to reduce the resulting distress.

Case 29: A family of Ethiopian Jews was referred to the social services department in the city of Arad after a suicide attempt by the oldest son. The boy cut his wrists after the Israeli rabbinical authorities questioned the Jewishness of the mother, and, by extension, of her sons. The social worker, himself an Ethiopian Jew who was raised in Israel, suggested mediation between the family and the rabbis, to explain the complexities of the questions involved. The family, however, responded with passive resistance and depression. Apparently, attempting to understand the Israeli religious scene and learning to play by the local rules was too distressing for them, spiritually and emotionally. The therapist, a supervisee of mine in a course in culturally competent family therapy, decided to adopt a different tactic. He mobilized a *keisy* (a traditional religious and spiritual leader of the Ethiopic Jewish community). The *keisy*, together with the family and the therapist, read and interpreted verses of the Old Testament in a way designed to help the family understand and adapt itself to the Israeli religious scene without becoming so distressed by this process. The line adopted by the *keisy* and the therapist was to highlight, with the aid of the appropriate verses, the following points:

The Ethiopian Jewish community is an authentic ancient Jewish tribe. The great biblical prophets used to protest against institutionalized religion. They used to criticize its empty rituals, involvement in politics, accumulation of wealth, intolerance and moral corruption. They pleaded for resumption of moral values, justice, equality, humility and true spiritualism. The prophets would have been on the side of the Ethiopic community, not on the side of the rabbinical authorities. The Ethiopian Jews have a very important role in Israeli society, that of representing and defending authentic, true, uncorrupted religion. In order to fulfill this role in the best possible way, they must understand the Israeli religious scene better and make their own voice heard in it.

As a result of this intervention, this family got over their depression and began taking a more active role in the community's religious life. They spontaneously applied metaprograms 1 through 3. (This case is discussed again in chapter 12.)

The System Is Unable to Digest the Overwhelming Amount of Unfamiliar Information It Encounters

Debugging requires reducing the amount of new information to which the system is exposed, reducing the impact of the information (e.g., showing that it is less "strange or bizarre" than perceived), or helping the system process the information in less overwhelming ways.

These principles are illustrated in the following case.

Case 30: Orly, a student in a culturally competent course for social workers, presented the following case. A family immigrated to Israel from a small town in northern Iraq. Both parents were medical doctors who enjoyed a very high socioeconomic and professional status in Iraq. The husband, Habib, was a Muslim Kurd, and the wife, Rachel, Jewish. They considered themselves "Western" and liberal. Rachel wanted to emigrate to Israel to join a part of her family that had emigrated and to fulfill her Zionistic aspirations. In Israel, they encountered a very complex reality, extremely different from what they expected. They could not find jobs because of the flood of doctors who emigrated from former Soviet Union. Furthermore, the standards of the medical profession in the north of Iraq were considered, rightly or wrongly, too low by Israeli Western norms. Habib was looked upon with suspicion and hostility because he was a Muslim. However, he was not an Arab but a Kurd, so he was rejected by the Israeli Arab community too. The language barrier was another impediment. The family was flooded with distressing information.

Soon they went into a crisis. Habib, in particular, reacted with regression and disorganization. His responses were extremely unstable. One day, for instance, he told his wife three times: "I am hereby sending you away," which is the traditional Muslim divorce formula. But an hour later, he behaved as if nothing of the kind had happened. On the same day, he declared that he was going to go back to Iraq and join the Kurdish freedom fighters. This would have meant death, because he would have been murdered by the Iraqi soldiers either for having emigrated to Israel or for being a Kurdish terrorist. But then he said that he was going to emigrate to Germany and immediately afterward he cried and hugged his wife and children and said that he would never leave them.

Orly planned a strategy designed to reduce the amount and impact of new information to which the family system, in general, and Habib, in particular, were exposed, and help the family be less overwhelmed by the new information. The strategy included the following elements:

1. Mediating between the family and the various public and administrative bodies that had been or could be involved in their absorption in Israel. The family did not know that they could enjoy free participation in the programs designed to help immigrants.

2. Enlisting the Israeli branch of Rachel's family to facilitate the transition to Israel, especially for Habib. These members of the family disapproved that Rachel had married a Muslim and avoided contact with Habib. To change this attitude, Orly had to derive new programs from their existing repertoire. She emphasized the similarity of fate between the Jewish people and the Kurdish people: Both are small, persecuted nations fighting bravely for their independence. Both are hated by the Arabs. The Kurds have had friendly relationships with Israel. She also praised Habib's courage and his great love and loyalty to his wife; explained that for him to have come to Israel was a great sacrifice. She explained to them how badly he needed their approval and support.

Indeed, Orly managed to achieve the desired change of attitude. Habib was fully accepted into the family and received a great deal of warmth, honor and support.

Following this intervention, the family, in general, and Habib, in particular, got out of their state of regression and confusion. Their information-processing system began to adjust to the new Israeli reality, appropriately.

Misconstruing Target Programs

Debugging involves making the system aware of the bugs introduced blindly, out of cultural naiveté, and help it approximate the target programs as closely as possible. Let us return to Nicole, the French woman, and her husband, Oved (Case 28).

In one of the fights between the two, Nicole threw a shoe at Oved. He left and went to his parents' home, very upset. In the evening, Nicole joined Oved for dinner in his parents' home. After dinner his father asked Oved and Nicole to his room. He told Nicole that her parents had not known how to bring her up; that they had turned her into an indecent, disrespectful young woman. He said the marriage might have been a mistake, and that they ought to divorce. Nicole responded with fury. She told Oved's father: "You have no right to talk about my parents. I have many things to tell you about the way you brought up your son. If anybody is going to decide if Oved and I are going to stay married or get divorced, it is Oved and I and not you. Now that you have said what you said, your esteem in my eyes has gone down from here (she raised her hand above her head) to here (she lowered her arm and hand)." Oved's father was totally shaken by this response. He refused to have any contact with Nicole.

In this situation, a number of bugs were introduced blindly, out of cultural naiveté. Nicole was not aware of the fact that throwing a shoe at her husband had, in Oved's cultural tradition, a symbolic meaning of wanting to humiliate a man, trampling upon his honor and driving him away. The same applied to her gesture of lowering her arm and hand. It was interpreted by Oved's father as a traditional humiliating gesture meaning "I am putting you under my shoe, trampling on your honor." According to Oved's family's etiquette, Nicole was not supposed to talk back at all, but listen respectfully, because the relationship between her and Oved's father was not symmetric. She should honor him and pay respect to him as a man, as an older person, as the head of the family and as her husband's father. What made her transgression even graver, through the culturally calibrated lenses of Oved and his father, was that she talked back in the way she did when she was a guest in Oved parents' home. She should have respected their rights in their own territory. According to Oved's culture, it was not just his father's right, but also his duty to reprimand Nicole, criticize the way she was brought up and suggest the idea of divorce.

Oved and his father did not understand that, for Nicole, throwing her shoe at Oved was just an act of anger and frustration and had no symbolic meaning. In the way she was brought up, at least on the declarative level, men and women, older and younger people, parents, parents-in-law and their adult children were equal. Speech was free. Everybody had the right to talk back and express his or her view everywhere. When a couple was married, they became a separate, independent unit, and nobody had a right to interfere in their relationships, least of all in-laws or parents, unless asked by the couple to do so. A husband's loyalty was first of all to his wife and not to his parents, and, if necessary, he had to protect her from his parents.

The therapist suggested that the situation described above, with the father, his son Oved and Nicole be simulated in a role-play with Nicole, playing herself, Oved his father and himself, and the therapist playing, alternately, as the double of each of the three. The participants were asked to replicate the original scene, but also to voice their unexpressed inner thoughts. The therapist, as a double, explicated their culturally determined premises. Afterward, the three summarized, together, the misunderstanding that were created by cultural naiveté in that situation.

SUMMARY

The main purpose of this chapter is to explicate the notion of culturally influenced family dysfunction and to suggest hypotheses as to how such dysfunction comes into being. Another purpose is to suggest principles for healing or reducing such dysfunction.

Dysfunction occurs when the information-processing system loses its simplicity and is unable to restore it. This can happen when the family's ecological environment changes considerably, as a result of immigration, war, invasion, industrialization or the like. The notion of *simplicity* is defined as the systems "preference" to process information in the simplest possible manner, without complications, incompleteness and inconsistencies. Simplicity can be explicated by the notions *consistency*, *completeness*, and *parsimony*. When the family has to process a great amount of unfamiliar information (e.g., when the natural or demographic environment changes considerably, when the family emigrates to a new country or when strangers invade the family's territory), information can no longer be processed in the simplest, most complete and most parsimonious manner. The system loses its simplicity. And then the system, as it were, attempts to adjust to the new conditions and restore its lost simplicity by changing. It changes in manners that allow it to process the new information in the simplest possible ways. In this model, the accommodating changes are said to be governed by *me-*

taprograms. The latter are hypothesized to *add* programs, *delete* programs or *change* programs of the previous repertoire until simplicity is restored.

There are circumstances, however, in which this process of accommodation fails. The system is unable to restore its simplicity and becomes infested with *"bugs,"* crippling errors of information processing that breed dysfunction. Conditions under which this occurs include overtension created by being exposed to confusing, stressing or overwhelming unfamiliar data. Under such conditions, the system is faced with the task of solving problems such as interpreting seemingly inconsistent data, digesting data that cause it great distress, processing a great amount of unfamiliar data and approximating target programs from a state of ignorance. Some families attempt to solve these problems in bug-producing manners—forgoing completeness (bug-*blinders*), forgoing consistency (bug-*extreme ambivalence or fluctuation*), forgoing parsimony (bug-*cultural fixation or regression*), and misconstruing target programs (bug-*cultural naiveté*).

All these bugs can be manifested in a variety of culture-styled symptomatic behaviors in individuals and whole families. Principles for weakening or reducing such bugs can be derived readily from examination of their natures. An overall principle is helping the family derive correct, bug-free programs and instructions from its own existing repertoire of programs. The therapist represents the new situation in ways that enable the family to restore its simplicity in attempting to cope with the changing situation.

PART IV

CULTURALLY COMPETENT FAMILY DIAGNOSIS

This part deals with applying the theoretical model presented in the previous parts in constructing a culturally competent diagnostic evaluation for any particular family entering therapy. In chapter 9, various methods are proposed for systematically eliciting relevant diagnostic data, mainly observations and interviews. Chapter 10 includes techniques and procedures for analyzing the data on various levels of abstraction and generalization. The products of this analysis are descriptions of the family's main dysfunctional culture-determined information-processing programs in the family's past and in its present. The metaprograms (see chapter 8) are used as the explanatory constructs for tracing the development of the case. The presenting complaints are explained as derivatives of this idiographic theory of the case.

9

Data-Collection Instruments and Procedures

OBSERVATIONS

One of the most effective ways of collecting culturally relevant family diagnostic data is by observation of the family's behavior in various natural settings and in the clinic. Such observations can yield rich information of any of the kinds listed in chapters 3 through 6. What's more, this information cannot be obtained by other methods such as interviews, tasks or tests.

Families of different cultural backgrounds will vary considerably in their willingness to tolerate the intrusion of an external observer. Some will readily agree to be observed and videotaped in the clinic. Others will forbid any observation that is not incidental, by way of conversing or otherwise interacting, and certainly will not allow any kind of photographic or written documentation. Therefore, the observation and recording techniques proposed below should be put into practice flexibly, always taking into consideration the family's sensitivities.

TRANSCRIBING THE OBSERVATION

The observed behavior can be transcribed in detail from a videotaped or written protocols. The transcription techniques proposed below are arduous and time consuming but very useful, if a detailed analysis of short sequences of verbal and nonverbal behavior are required.

The Initial-Stage Chart

For the reader of a transcription protocol to be able to get a more-or-less clear picture of what actually happened in the interaction, the transcription

Figure 9.1
Initial Stage Chart, Vertical View

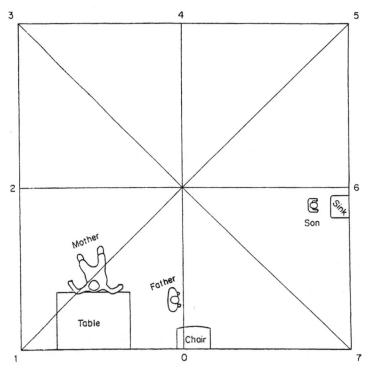

should refer to some initial state, which includes the relative positions of the participants and the relevant objects in the room at the onset of the observation or at some turning points in it.

The *initial stage* of an activity can be represented graphically by a chart, such as Figure 9.1, which is based on a single picture taken out of a videotaped or hand-recorded observation. In such a chart the initial stage is depicted schematically. It is represented as if viewed from above.

Crossing co-ordinate lines are drawn on the initial stage chart, as displayed in Figure 9.1. The points where these lines meet the perimeter line of the square are numbered clockwise, from zero upward, starting with the new central point on the bottom line. These co-ordinates and their ordinal numbers render it possible to specify the approximate direction of the objects and people in the activity area. For example, the front of the father's body in Figure 9.1 is turned to direction 6. The mother's elbows, which are placed on the table, are directed to 0. The sink is directed to 2, and so forth. If the direction of an object, a body or a part of a body is parallel to any of the coordinate lines, the + and − marks may be used. For example, the mother's left knee is turned toward 3+.

Figure 9.2
Initial Stage Chart, Horizontal View

If the location and direction of a body changes, the change can be described in relation to its location or direction in the initial state, as these have been specified in the initial-stage chart.

For example, with the initial-stage chart in Figure 9.1 as a description of the initial state in the room, one can write: "Son turns around through his left shoulder and walks three yards toward 4−, then he crawls toward 1 until his forehead touches his mother's knee." Looking at Figure 9.1, the reader of this statement can very easily visualize the movements of the boy crossing the room.

Figure 9.2 represents a horizontal view of the initial stage depicted in Figure 9.1.

The General Format of the Transcription Page

The videorecorded or written observation is transcribed on pages of standardized format, as displayed in Table 9.1. The vertical dimension is divided into columns, each of which is labeled by an ordinal numeral, from left to right. The numbers represent time units of a standard duration (e.g., 30 seconds, 60 seconds, etc.). The standard duration of the time units is determined by the transcriber according to his purposes and the technical devices available. The smaller the standard unit, the greater the refinement and accuracy of the transcription.

On the horizontal dimension, the verbal and nonverbal behavior of each of the participants in the play activity is transcribed. Four rows are allocated to each participant. One row is devoted to a general impressionistic descrip-

Table 9.1
Transcription of an Interaction Between a Father and His Three-Year-Old Son (each time unit represents ten seconds)

Time Units	1	2	3	4	5	6	7	8	9	10	11	12
Father												
General	Pretends to be a monkey. Picks son up and raises him above his head.											
Vocal-linguistic	Imitates the chuckle of a monkey, twice.											
Spatial-motional	Makes a funny "monkey" face bends toward son. Stretches his arms toward him.											
Touching							Takes hold of son, picks him up raises him above his head.					
Son												
General	Pretends to be a little monkey. Asks daddy to pick him up.											
Vocal-linguistic	Chuckles once. Says: "Daddy monkey, pick me up."											
Spatial-motional	Raises stretched arms toward his father.											
Touching									Lets his father pick him up.			

tion of the participant's behavior at each time unit, formulated in ordinary language. In the other three rows, the same behavior is described more accurately and rigorously. One row is devoted to the participant's vocal and linguistic behavior. Ideally, it is transcribed both in ordinary English and in a phonetic transcription. Another row (which is subdivided into a suitable number of lines) is devoted to the participant's spatial (proxemic) and motional (kinesic) behavior. Ideally, these aspects are transcribed by Eshkol and Wachman's movement notation (1958) and Ekman's Facial Action Coding System (1978). The fourth row (which is also subdivided into lines) is for transcribing the participants' touching (manipulative) behavior, that is, the contacts between his or her body (mainly his or her hands) and other human or nonhuman objects in the room. Ideally, this is transcribed by Touchnotation, a notational system developed by the author to transcribe behavior involving contacts (see Ariel, 1985).

Table 9.1 is an informal transcription of two minutes of interaction between a father and his three-year-old son. Such a score equips its readers with a clear, detailed picture of the verbal and nonverbal behavior of all the family members during a particular time span. Like the score of a musical ensemble, it tells what kind of music was played by each participant at any given moment, and which harmonious structures were created by the whole ensemble.

For a more detailed description of this transcription method see Ariel (1994, chapter 6).

INTERVIEWS

The Presenting-Problems Interview

Symptoms are culture bound. Family psychological problems have different outward manifestations in different cultures. To identify and understand the meaning of presenting symptoms, therapists should get the most exact and detailed behavioral descriptions of them possible. The presenting-problems interview is designed to get such descriptions. Coupled with direct observations, it can yield a fairly accurate picture of the presenting complaints.

When people complain about their difficulties, they usually use a subjective, emotional and rather vague language. One should bear in mind that even the style of such inaccurate presentations is often culturally coded. However, one should also aspire to adding a more objective description. Through the presenting problems interview, the therapist elicits a specification of the verbal, vocal, kinesic, proxemic and tactile elements of the symptom and an account of characteristic contexts of its occurrence: Time, place antecedents and consequences. Interviewees can be family members, doctors, teachers, neighbors, or anybody familiar with the people and problems. There can be no standardized format for conducting the interview. As in any cross-cultural contact, questioning should be conducted with sensitivity and care. If necessary, intermediaries who come from the family's culture, while also being familiar with the interviewer's culture, should be used.

Alfonso and Maria: A Presenting-Problems Interview

Interviewees are Alfonso and his wife Maria, both Mexican Americans living in Chicago.

Maria: We are worried about our eleven-year-old son, Carmelo. Yesterday he attacked Alfonso and threatened to kill himself.

Therapist: Can you describe exactly how this happened?

Alfonso: I collect old records. He picked one of my favorite records, Paco de Lucia, off the shelf and broke it into two.

Therapist: Were you in the room?

Alfonso: Yes; I followed him, because I knew he was up to something.

Therapist: What time was it?

Maria: 10 P.M..

Therapist: Is there anything special about this time?

Maria: Yes, after 10 he should stay home. His father does not allow him to go out and meet his friends.

Alfonso: (bitterly) Some kind of friends.

Therapist: Did you have an argument before he went for the records?

Maria: Yes, every evening, it's the same thing. His father threatens to beat him up if he goes out.

Therapist: And when he approached the records, did you say anything?

Alfonso: I warned him. I said: "If you dare touch my records I'll break your neck!" And then he did it. While he was doing it, he gave me this challenging look.

Therapist: How did you react?

Alfonso: I grabbed him from behind, and he hit my forehead with the back of his head.

Maria: I saw it! I saw him doing it!

Alfonso: Here, look! (Shows the therapist a black and blue bruise on his forehead.) He managed to free himself of my grasp and then ran toward the window, took hold of the curtain, tied it around his neck and yelled: "I'm gonna choke myself to death!"

Therapist: What did you do then?

Alfonso: I ignored him. I know my son. I know it's just empty threats. He's a coward. He'll never really do anything to himself. Just to us. But she (points at Maria) becomes hysterical. She cries and grabs him and begs him to stop.

This interview provides information about the time of the event (10 P.M.), the place (the family's apartment), the antecedents (Alfonso having forbidden Carmelo from going out and meeting his friends after 10 P.M.; threatening to beat him up if he did) and the consequences (Alfonso ignoring Carmelo; Maria grabbing Carmelo, crying, and asking him to stop). It also includes information about the symptomatic behavior itself:

Vocal-linguistic—yelling "I'm going to choke myself to death!"

Spatial-motional—e.g., facing Alfonso and looking at him in a challenging manner; running toward the window

Touching—e.g., breaking the record; winding the curtain around his neck

The Case-History Interview

The purpose of this interview is to collect data that will enable the therapist to trace the development of the case, in general and, in particular, its culture-relevant components, up to the time of referral. The interviewer aspires to learn as much as possible about the family's cultural information-processing programs at each stage of its history. He or she attempts to trace ecological circumstances that have forced the family to change these programs in order to restore the simplicity of its information-processing system, and to identify "bugs" that have invaded the system as a result of its efforts to change.

This interview, like the other instruments described in this chapter, is not molded in a rigid, standardized format. It should be administered flexibly, with caution not to alienate the interviewees by being insensitive to their cultural vulnerabilities. Interviewees, again, can be the family members themselves or any other person who is familiar with their history.

One useful way of conducting the interview is to begin by asking the interviewees to recount the history of the family and its problems, preferably as many generations back into the past as remembered. Then, during or after the telling, form hypotheses and ask leading questions that help to confirm or refute the hypotheses. The questions may refer to any of the categories of culturally relevant data discussed in chapters 3 through 6 of this book. The last stage of the case history refers to the current (present) situation, that is the state of the case at the time of the interview. Below are some excerpts of such an interview.

Nahum: A Case-History Interview

Nahum, the interviewee, is a thirty-four-year-old man who lives in Ashdod, an industrial town near Tel Aviv. The author is the interviewer.

Shlomo: Nahum, maybe you can tell me the history of your family: Where it comes from, who your ancestors were, major events, and so on.

Nahum: We made *aliyah*[emigrated] twenty years ago from Georgia [a former Soviet Union Republic bordering on Turkey and Iran, populated mainly by Muslims]. Our family lived in Tbilisi [the capital of Georgia]. My parents and grandparents were also born there. Our history is that, some hundreds of years ago, after the Land of Israel was invaded, they took certain Jews from the Land of Israel and they sold them as slaves in Georgia, and that's where they got stuck.

Shlomo: Who told you this story?

Nahum: When they give sermons in synagogues, they tell these things, and it also is transmitted from fathers to sons.

Shlomo: Are Jews treated well by gentiles in Georgia? [Univerbalized hypothesis: The history of Jews as slaves is a traditional myth intended to explain persecution of Jews by the Muslim majority.]

Nahum: Usually, they were not treated badly, but if somebody was murdered, it would be rumored that Jews murdered him, and then we had to be careful.

Shlomo: Can you tell me of relatives with whom you have close ties? [Purpose: To map the structure of Nahum's extended family.]

Nahum: I was close to an uncle of mine, my mother's brother. He was nice. He was helping us a lot. He also lives in Bat-Yam now.

Shlomo: Why does he live in Bat-Yam?

Nahum: His wife lives there, and her mother lives there.

Shlomo: It seems that you are closer to your relatives on your mother's side than to your relatives on your father's side. [Unverbalized hypothesis: Residence in Nahum's community seems to be matrilocal, and rules of descent are at least partly matrilineal.]

Nanum: Yes, they care more for each other, and they love me more than my father's relatives.

Shlomo: Can you tell me more about your childhood?

Nahum: I was breast-fed by my mother until I was five. I was very close to my mother.

Shlomo: Is this customary in your circles, for a child not to be weaned before he is five?

Nahum: Yes, it is. I was very close to her. I did everything she told me. I have three sisters. One seven years older than me, the second three years older than her. My mother used to dominate and control them very tightly. She married them off. All three lived with their husbands' mothers.

Shlomo: Is it customary for a woman who gets married to live with her husband's mothers and family? [Purpose: To reconfirm the hypothesis about matrilocal residence.]

Nahum: Yes, it is. One of my sisters was a third-year university student, and then my mother married her off to a man who was a nothing; a criminal. After she married him, there was a man she knew. The boy that was born to them, her husband said it was from that other man. When this boy was three, he died. Simply from all the beatings he took from his father. He used to beat my sister, too. He used to pour boiling water on her. But my mother refused to take my sister and her kids back. She used to take them but, in the end, because of the family honor, its good name, they would reconcile.

Shlomo: How were they reconciled? Your mother would conciliate between them?

Nahum: In most cases, she did. This sister won a gold medal in school. After she got married, she stopped her studies and her life was ruined.

Shlomo: A married woman cannot continue with her studies?

Nahum: No, she has to stay home and help her husband's mother.

Shlomo: Was it difficult for her to find a good husband? Maybe because she was too old?

Nahum: No, she could find a husband, but she did not want to get married. She wanted to study, but my mother forced her. The second sister also studied economics for two years, and then my mother married her off to a family that was no good at all. My mother and father knew that her husband was a drunkard, and when he came home he would pee in his pants a number of times. My sister said: "I can't live with him." My mother said: "Shut up! It is not nice to speak this way! It's a shame! People might hear you say that!" This sister of mine she is very nice. She won a silver medal, not a gold one. And after she got married, her life was ruined, too. Her mother-in-law was beating her. Her husband never worked. My parents knew that he was a drunkard before they married her off to him.

Shlomo: Was it your mother that married them off, or your father?

Nahum: My mother had the final say.

Shlomo: Was this so only in your family, or in other families too?

Nahum: In other families, too. The woman is the one who has the final say.

Shlomo: Why did your mother agree to the marriage if she knew he was a drunkard?

Nahum: She felt pity for his father, who was a little paralyzed, and she said, "He is ill so he will give her good pampering." Also they gave her two gold rings set with diamonds. But they really had nothing. Only outwardly they had something to give.

Shlomo: What was it like when you came to Israel?

Nahum: I was eleven years old. My mother became sick from sorrow, because my sisters did not follow us, and later, when they came, they went to Bat-Yam and not to Ashdod. Afterward I was a regular soldier. I did not have a girl. It was not considered right to have a girlfriend.

Shlomo: Why?

Nahum: I thought a girlfriend, excuse me for saying this, is a girl who is promiscuous, a whore. I got my satisfaction; it was all right, I was making it with girls, but for steady had to get married.

My mother showed me a number of girls. At last they showed me one who was also fourteen years old. I was twenty-three. I liked her. I agreed to get engaged to her. We took her to our home. At first, I used to force her to sleep with me. She rejected me. We had fights, and I would beat her up because she didn't want to have sex with me. She would hit back. A number of times, her mother came to us to intervene. The two of them would speak together in another room. I was afraid to go out to stroll with her, lest somebody will start with her and take her away from me. I was afraid that I would have to fight this man and kill him. Then I couldn't have intercourse with her. It's not that I wasn't a man. I just couldn't. My mother said that was because of the shoes her mother gave me. Her mother gave me shoes that her son didn't need, and my mother said her mother cast a spell on me through these shoes, to take my manhood away. But I was not sure about that, so I went to the doctor and he gave me something. Then she got pregnant and we had a boy. My mother brought him up. My wife was very, very impertinent. One day, my mother asked my wife for something clean to wipe the dishes. She brought her something so disgusting that I don't know. In our community, we have a custom that if a man and a woman have intercourse, then there is a special cloth with which she cleans herself. She brought that to wipe my mother's dishes. When I came home, she told me that my mother would keep her hungry. She was lying. She ate enough.

. . . I could not divorce her. I was ashamed. What would people say? They would say I'm no good. My mother also did not want me to divorce her.

And then she cheated on me. She would really cheat on me like a hen. Later, I found out that, even before she married me, she had men. There was someone who had sex with her and took her to men. She had a taxi driver and she had an old man, a neighbor. People saw him going downstairs from her. My mother told me to take a private eye. I took one, and he found that she worked in it. I did not tell anybody. They would make fun of me that I did not kill her; just divorced her.

In our community, we solve problems within the family. Here, I turned to other people. I went to a psychologist.

Shlomo: Why did you decide to do something unacceptable; turn to psychological help?

Nahum: My parents belittle me at home all the time. They call me Nahum Beduro, which means Nahum the No-Good. I could not rely on my family.

Shlomo: Why? You strike me as an intelligent man.

Nahum: Because I am the youngest, and I am a son and most of the family live in Bat-Yam. They want me to be their servant. Because they are old and sick. They don't want me to think: I am a big man, I am intelligent, I am strong, I'll marry an Israeli girl who is not a Georgian and I'll go away and leave my parents to die.

SUMMARY

This chapter presents methods and techniques for collecting or eliciting data for an overall culturally competent diagnostic evaluation of a family. These include naturalistic observations in various settings (home, street, the clinic, etc.) and interviews. A method for transcribing the details of the family's verbal and nonverbal observed behavior is proposed. Interviews are the presenting-problems interview, designed to obtain a detailed behavioral description of the presenting symptoms, and the case-history interview. The purpose of the latter is to trace the development of the case. This involves: (1) Learning about the family's culture-bound information-processing programs of any of the types discussed in this book, at each stage of the family's development; (2) detecting adaptational transformations in these programs, in response to ecological and developmental changes; (3) locating bugs in these programs, as a result of the failure to restore simplicity. Interviewees are family members or people in the community who know the family. During the interviews, the interviewer forms hypotheses and asks leading questions. The readers are warned to use all these techniques with caution and flexibility, always bearing in mind the family's cultural sensitivities.

10

Analysis of Diagnostic Data

In this chapter, methods and techniques are proposed for microanalyzing and macroanalyzing the data elicited by the techniques presented in chapter 9. The analysis leads to the construction of deduced functional and dysfunctional ("bugged") cultural family programs at various stages of the case development.

As explained in chapter 7, these methods and techniques cannot and do not constitute a "discovery procedure" leading from observed data to an idiographic theory representing the family's culture. The therapist can arrive at such a theory only by exercising her intuition and creativity. The methods and techniques proposed in this chapter are just heuristic procedures, helping the therapist order and organize the observed data in ways that would facilitate the construction of an idiographic diagnostic theory about the case in hand.

SEMIOTIC MICROANALYSIS OF BEHAVIOR

The technique proposed below can be applied to observation protocols, as well as to data elicited by the presenting-problems interview and the case-history interview. The transcribed behavior constitutes an initial microscopic description and interpretation of the behavior on the *raw material level*. On this level, the manifest, physical, partly observable behavior is described. However, raw material serves mainly as a medium for expressing meaning. Meaning is analyzed on two other levels: The *semantic* level, where the private thoughts and feelings expressed by raw material are analyzed and described, and the *pragmatic*, communicational level, at which *interpersonal thoughts* expressed by the same raw material are specified. For example, one of the symptoms of a thirteen-year-old boy reported in a presenting-problems interview was his habit of writing "TV series" in tiny, unreadable letters. He explained the fact that he wrote in this manner by saying that he wanted to save on paper. This was a part of the description of his behavior on the raw material level. On the semantic level, this was interpreted as a symbolic representation of his being worried about the family's financial situation. His father was a compulsive spender. On the pragmatic level, the same was interpreted as an interpersonal message: "You can't and shouldn't read my mind." Another example: In a free-play session, a six-year-old girl places two pointing fingers on either side of her head. This is a description on the raw material level. On the semantic level, this was interpreted as denoting "a devil." On the pragmatic level, this was interpreted as a message to her family: "You are scapegoating me, turning me into the family's devil."

Interpersonal thoughts are of two main kinds: *Communication intents* and *presuppositions* (see chapter 5). Thus, in the latter example, the girl *presupposed* that her family conceived of her as bad, and her *communication intent* was to show them that she was aware of this and disliked it.

The procedure of microscopic analysis consists of dividing stretches of observed behavior into raw material units and interpreting each unit or significant sequences of units on the semantic and pragmatic levels. An *activity unit* is a group of raw material features (vocal-linguistic, spatial, motional and tactual) that has a distinct semantic or communicational meaning. None of its subgroups is meaningful. Below is a microscopic analysis of a part of the presenting-problem interview with Alfonso and Maria (chapter 9).

Carmelo's activity units:

Unit 1

Raw material: Carmelo approaches the shelf containing his father's records.

Pragmatic—Presupposition—Alfonso has just used coercion by not allowing me to go out and meet my friends. He does not respect my freedom of choice or my friends who are dear to me.

Intent—threatening to punish Alfonso, get even with him by damaging a record that is dear to him.

Unit 2

Raw material: Carmelo breaks Alfonso's favorite record in two, giving father a challenging look.

Semantic—Damaging something that is dear to my father, like my friends to me.

Pragmatic—Presupposition—My father has just threatened me that he is going to break my neck if I touch his record.

Intent—To show daddy that I am not afraid of his threat. To punish him for his violent language by actually doing what I was just threatened to do.

And here is a microscopic analysis of an excerpt of the case-history interview with Nahum (chapter 9):

Nahum's wife's activity unit:

Raw material: Bringing Nahum's mother an after-intercourse cleaning-cloth.

Semantic—An object representing filth, impurity, associated with sex.

Pragmatic—Presupposition—Nahum, encouraged by his mother, forces me to have disgusting, filthy, impure sex. His mother deprives me of good food.

Intent—Retaliate by offering Nahum's mother a cloth that represents filthy, impure sex for "cleaning" the dishes that deprive me, but not the other family members, of good food.

MACROSCOPIC SEMANTIC ANALYSIS

The microscopic analysis yields a series of semantically and communicationally interpreted activity units. To complete the assessment, one has to expose and describe family programs, especially dysfunctional ones. The discrete units obtained by the microscopic analysis do not tell us much about such programs. The discrete units emerge from global interrelations among classes of such units. Such interrelations are exposed and described by semantic and pragmatic macroscopic analysis.

Techniques of semantic analysis designed to reveal the main dimensions of the meanings a culture attributes to its own subjective experience have been developed by anthropologists. Such techniques can assist anthropologists to describe the culture's world-view, its self-concept, its representation of the environment, its values and beliefs. Many of these techniques can be readily applied to a microscopic analysis of a family's behavior. This application can be a major step toward formulating cultural family programs. A good sample of techniques of this sort is included in the book *Cognitive Anthropology* (Tyler, 1969).

COMPONENTIAL SEMANTIC ANALYSIS

What is presented below is an adaptation of one of these techniques, namely *componential analysis*, to the description of the deep structure of the family's experience. This technique can be applied to an already microanalyzed observation or interview (referred to below as *the text*). The procedure of componential analysis proceeds through the following steps.

Step 1. List all the *semantic units* found in the text. A semantic unit is the meaning of an activity unit.

Step 2. List all the *semantic contexts* of each semantic unit. A semantic context of a semantic unit includes all the attributes of the units in question that are included in the text.

Step 3. Find *common semantic denominators* for all the semantic contexts of each semantic unit.

Step 4. Make pairwise comparisons among all the common semantic denominators of all the semantic units. In each comparison, attempt to identify *common meaning dimensions* and *meaning contrasts* or *differences* along these dimensions. The meaning contrasts or differences are the *values* of the dimensions.

Step 5. Attempt to identify *superdimensions*, that is common meaning factors across dimensions.

Step 6. Attempt to identify the emotions that are associated with the superdimensions.

Step 7. Attempt to organize the dimensions, their values, the superdimensions and the emotions associated with them in a configuration that displays the interrelations between all of them.

To illustrate, let us apply componential analysis to a small sample of semantic units found in the case-history interview with Nahum (chapter 9).

Step 1. List the semantic units. The analysis will be applied to the semantic units "mother," "father," "mother-in-law," "husband," "wife," "girlfriend," "man," "honor," "shame," "beating," "killing"

Step 2. List the semantic contexts of each unit. (Here are two examples, just for the purpose of illustration.)

Unit: "mother." A sample of contexts: My relatives on my *mother*'s side care more for each other and love me more than my father's relatives. I was very close to my *mother*. I did everything my *mother* told me. My *mother* used to control and dominate my sisters very tightly.

Unit: "shame." A sample of contexts: My sister said: "I can't live with him." My mother said: "Shut up! It is not nice to speak this way! It's a *shame!* People might hear you say that!" I couldn't divorce her. I was a*shame*d. What would people say? They would say I'm no good.

Step 3. Find common semantic denominators for all the semantic contexts of each semantic unit. Unit: "mother." Common denominators: center of matrilineage and of matrilocal residence; controls married daughters and unmarried sons; in charge of forming and protecting marriage of both sons and daughters; if daughters are mistreated by their husbands, protects the marriage rather than the daughters; blames wife and wife's mother for son's marriage difficulties.

Unit: "father." Common denominators: complies with mother insofar as her functions in the family, listed above, are concerned; punishes son for wife's (son's mother's) transgressions; pampers daughter-in-law; transmits cultural tradition to sons.

Unit: "mother-in-law." Common denominators: controls son's wife, who lives in her home and serves her; blames daughter-in-law for son's marriage difficulties.

Unit: "wife." Common denominators: married off by her mother; lives with her mother-in-law and serves her; fed and provided for by her mother-in-law; her husband is chosen by her mother and she has no right to refuse;

after marriage she has to discontinue personal occupations such as study or work and devote herself to mother-in-law, husband and children; has no right to leave her husband, even if mistreated; may be beaten, raped, abused or even murdered by her husband if refused to sleep with him or is suspected of having an extramarital affair; leaving husband and going back to mother considered a greater injury to family honor than being abused by husband and mother-in-law.

Unit: "girlfriend." Common denominators: considered a whore; dating and boyfriend-girlfriend relationships are unacceptable.

Unit: "man." Common denominators: a male person who possesses sexual potency; his "manhood" can be taken by away by sorcery performed by his mother-in-law.

Unit: "honor." Common denominators: the family's good name, its good reputation in the community; the family's honor is injured if a marriage breaks down; a man's bad character and behavior does not injure the family's honor.

Unit: "shame." Common denominators: injury to a family's honor.

Unit: "beating." Common denominators: a means of punishing one's wife or one's daughter-in-law for disobedience and refusal to perform her duties.

Unit: "killing." Common denominators: when one's wife has committed adultery, her husband is expected to kill her and the other man.

Step 4. Compare all possible pairs of semantic units with the common semantic denominators of their contexts and draw common meaning dimensions and differentiating values. (Here are two such comparisons, just for the purpose of illustration.)

Man/honor. Common dimensions: a property possessed by people; can be lost; can be redressed.

Differentiating values: a property of a male person versus a property of a family; independent of the person's character or behavior versus depending on the behavior of a family member; loss induced from outside (e.g., by sorcery) versus loss incurred by the behavior of a family member; redressing by fighting versus redressing by submission.

Man/girlfriend. Common dimension: sexuality.

Differentiating values: male versus female; allowed out of wedlock versus banned out of wedlock; morally right versus morally wrong.

As the procedure of pairwise comparisons continues, more common dimensions and differentiating values along these lines present themselves. Here is a partial list of the main dimensions and values found by a more or less exhaustive set of comparisons among all the units listed above.

Dimensions	Values	
source of rights and duties	blood bond	marital bond
authority	having authority (e.g., husband over wife)	not having authority (e.g., wife over husband)

Dimensions	Values		
tolerability of wife's transgressions	tolerable	barely tolerable	intolerable

Step 5. Identifying superdimensions (common meaning factors across the dimensions). All the dimensions and values found have to do with prerogatives and obligations derived from a person's marital and familial status. None of them is related to any other concerns, such as rights and duties not associated with family roles, achievement, intimacy or the like.

Step 6. Emotions associated with superdimensions. The main *emotive* (see chapter 4) manifested in the text is shame associated with failure to secure one's marital and familial rights or live up to one's marital and familial duties. It seems that such shame is experienced mainly by the privileged members of the family (husband, husband's mother, mother-in-law) and not by the underprivileged (wife, son, daughter).

Step 7. Configurational organization of the dimensions, values and emotions. All of the findings can be organized into the configuration displayed in Table 10.1.

A configuration such as Table 10.1 holds a great deal of information. First, it exposes some of the central ingredients of the family's cultural identity, namely its structural properties and its basic guiding principles. It also reveals some of its values and beliefs concerning marriage and family life. (All are discussed in chapter 4.) Furthermore, it X-rays the interrelations among all these entities. The same configuration also unmasks the main family-cultural emotional concerns (emotives). It conveys the idea that shame is a central emotion in the culture of this family. This emotion is experienced by both men and women, but not so much by wives. More generally, it is felt mainly by members of the family who have authority and privileges. It is more likely to be aroused in a mother's home than in a mother-in-law's home. It is associated with deniable entities such as honor and with protectable entities such as the marital bond. It is directed toward blamable people, whose transgressions are intolerable and severely punishable.

One can learn a great deal about a family's culture not just from what is included in such a configuration, but also from what is not included in it. The above configuration does not include, for instance, any concerns unrelated to familial prerogatives and obligations. The individual as a separate psychosocial entity—so it seems—does not exist in Nahum's family-cultural world. Nahum, as a young man who had gone through a rapid process of acculturation, had no way of asserting himself as an individual but breaking away from his family and its traditions.

A configuration such as Table 10.1 can serve as a standard family-cultural vocabulary for defining semantic units included in the text. Take for instance the semantic unit "cheat on," included in Nahum's case-history interview. It can be defined by the above dimensions and values as follows: female in

Table 10.1
Results of Componential Analysis of Nahum's Case History Interview

Emotions	shame	no shame
Superdimension— *Familial prerogatives* *and obligations*		
Dimensions and values		
gender	male and female	female (wife)
locality	mother's home	mother-in-law's home
source of rights and duties	marital bond	blood bond
authority	having authority (e.g., husband over wife)	not having authority (e.g., wife over husband)
entitlement (for services, protection, etc.)	entitled	not entitled
deniability	deniable (e.g., manhood, honor)	undeniable (e.g., maternal authority)
protectabiality	protectable (e.g., marriage)	unprotectable (e.g., wife against husband's abuse)
blamability	blamable	unblamable
tolerability of wife's transgressions	intolerable; barely tolerable	tolerable
severity of punishability	very severe (killing) severe (beating)	moderate

mother-in-law's home; source of rights and duties—marital bond; no authority over husband; subjected to husband's and mother-in-law's authority; deniable rights; not entitled to protection; blamable by husband and his mother; transgression intolerable; punishable very severely.

MACROSCOPIC PRAGMATIC ANALYSIS

Another step toward the exposition of family programs is macroscopic pragmatic analysis. The steps of this analysis are.

Step 1. List the *presuppositions* and *intents* of each sequence of semantic units of each family member.

Step 2. Attempt to find *superpresuppositions* and *superintents*, that is intents and presuppositions shared by sequences of presuppositions and intents yielded by step 1.

Step 3. Look at *turning points* in the stream of intents, that is, points at which previous intents are replaced by new ones.

Step 4. Attempt to find *super-super intents*, that is, intents that are shared by all the superintents. The super-superintents are the *goals* toward which a program is directed. The structure of the program can be traced by looking at the turning points.

The following case illustrates macroscopic pragmatic analysis.

Case 31: Beatrice and Her Family. Participants are Karen, who is twenty-eight, her mother Beatrice, her twenty-six-year-old brother James and his wife Gloria. The following scene takes place in Beatrice's apartment in northwest Chicago. It is Beatrice's forty-ninth birthday. The family is African American. Beatrice is a college graduate. In the 1960s she was involved in nonmilitant civil rights political movements. Her daughter Karen is a university graduate. She is active in a local black-white integration activity group. James and Gloria live with their father, who divorced Beatrice when James was four years old, in a low-income area in the south of Chicago. Their father is uneducated and unemployed. When he left Beatrice, he took James with him. James dropped out of school when he was eleven and was marginally involved in local gang activities. He does not have a regular job. Until James was ten Beatrice lived with Karen in the same neighborhood as his father, and he used to visit them regularly. But, then, Beatrice was offered a job in the northwest part of Chicago and moved there with Karen. Since then, James' visits became increasingly rare. His father refused to pay for the bus or train rides. When James visited them, he became more and more hostile and aggressive toward Beatrice and Karen. When Karen was sixteen he assaulted her and Beatrice asked him to stop coming. He did not show up at Beatrice's place until he married Gloria. Beatrice met him a few times on her own initiative, in public places. After James married Gloria, he resumed his visits to his mother's place, but only on special occasions, such as birthdays or holidays.

Below is the scene, as described by Karen to her therapist. Hypothesized presuppositions and purposes, with explanations, are attached to each expression:

Karen brings dishes with food and refreshments from the kitchen and places them on the table. She says: You will excuse me. I got a terrible headache. I'm going to rest a little bit.

[Karen's *presuppositions*: My family does not appreciate my efforts to help my mother, e.g., the fact that I did the hard work preparing this party. They will intimidate me, and my mother will not protect me. Karen's *intents*: Draw away from her family, to avoid being insulted. Demonstrate her vulnerability and resentment.]

She is going to her room and leaves the door ajar.

[*Presupposition*: They will talk about me. *Intents*: Being able to hear what they say; demonstrate her wish to remain in some kind of contact with the family.]

Beatrice is standing motionless by the table. She looks helpless.

[Beatrice's *presuppositions*: There's a rift between Karen, on one side, and James and Gloria on another side. The latter are also very bitter and resentful about me. Whatever I try to do can stir trouble and contribute to the tension. Beatrice's *intents*: Keep herself out of the conflict between the two parts of her family. Prevent aggravation of the conflict.]

James sits on an armchair, half-lying, his limbs stretched, smirking and saying nothing.

[James *presuppositions*: As usual, Karen is snubbing us, and mom does nothing about it. If I say or do anything this will end in an eruption and a renewed split. James' *intents*: To express his resentment and dissatisfaction but avoid an aggravation of the conflict.]

Gloria nears Karen's door, trying to take a look into the room with quick glances.

[Gloria's *presuppositions*: Karen does not have a headache. She is malingering. She is just snubbing us. She looks down upon us and does not want us near her mother. Gloria's *intent*: To call Karen's lie.]

Then Karen goes toward James and says: Typical!

[Gloria's *presuppositions*: James is not fully aware of Karen's offensive attitude. He is too passive and evasive, not protecting himself and me against Karen. *Intent*: Stir James to take a more active stand against his sister.]

James, without moving, is whistling "Happy Birthday to You." Then he shouts: "Hey, Sis, Its your mother's birthday!"

[James' *presuppositions*: Gloria wants me to be more active with respect to Karen. I am not sure whether Gloria does not overdo her reactions. It is not absolutely clear whether she is the aggressor or the victim. *Intents*: Partly complying with Gloria's expectations, while keeping a light, friendly atmosphere and avoiding increasing the tension.]

Karen (from her room): I'll be back with you in a few minutes. I got a terrible headache. I must rest a while.

[Karen's *presupposition*: They think I am not interested in their company. *Intent*: To reassure them that I am.]

James (smiling): Have you all noticed? I *talked* to her! (James and Karen were not on speaking terms for some time.)

[James' *presupposition*: My mother believes the rift within the family is my fault. *Intents*: To show his good will. To prove to her that he is the one taking an active step toward uniting the family and not Karen. At the same time, to show Gloria that he is not passive.]

Gloria: OK, as far as I'm concerned we can start the party.

[Gloria's *presupposition*: My point has been driven home to Karen and James. *Intent*: Show her readiness for a cease-fire.]

Gloria sits at the table opposite Beatrice. Beatrice does not move.

[Beatrice's *presupposition*: It is not clear yet whether the open conflict and tension between the parties have really receded. *Intent*: Avoid taking any clear stand that could stir up trouble again.]

James gets up, grabs Beatrice's elbow and says: Mom, sit down.

[James *presuppositions*: My mother is still displeased with my wife's and my own behavior. She hesitates whether she should start the party as if everything is OK. *Intents*: To help his mother overcome her hesitation and show his interest in bridging the gulf between himself and his wife and her.]

Beatrice obeys and sits. James sits on the only chair that's next to her.

[James's *presupposition*: Karen is going to take hold of this privileged position. *Intent*: take the position and prevent Karen from taking it].

Then he gets up, opens Karen's door and says: Party starting. He goes back to his seat. Karen emerges from her room holding her forehead. She walks slowly toward the table.

[Karen's *presupposition*: They still don't believe that I have a real headache. *Intent*: Showing her willingness to cooperate and stressing the fact that she is not malingering.]

She says faintly to James: That's my seat, but never mind. She takes a chair from the corner of the room and places it by the table, on her mother's other side.

[Karen's *presupposition*: James wants to take my place with my mother and depose me. *Intents*: Make the point that she is displeased with what James has done. Keep her position by her mother without entering into an open conflict with James.]

Gloria: I saw on TV a pissful demonstration yesterday.

[Gloria's *presuppositions*: Karen looks down on us. She thinks she does us a favor by having joined us at the table. *Intent*: Bring Karen low by insulting her and deriding her political opinions.]

Karen (hissing quietly): The word is *peaceful*.

[Karen's *presupposition*: Gloria is trying to insult me. *Intent*: Mark her objection without getting into an open conflict].

Gloria (loudly): These dudes say we don't even own ourselves! I get tired of that "one nation under God boogy-joogi" stuff. We are ourselves! We are our own nation or country or whatever you want to call it. We are not no one-tenth of some white something!

[Gloria's *presuppositions*: Karen identifies with whites and sets herself above us. She hardly tolerates us in the family and regards us as an inferior part in it. *Intents*: Challenging Karen's integrationist position and at the same time her supposed negative view of the part of the family represented by Gloria and James.]

Karen (hissing, as if to herself): What does she know about them? Talk talk talk.

[Karen's *presuppositions*: Gloria is ignorant of my political views and misinterprets my intentions. *Intent*: To express her resentment of Gloria's attitude.]

James (threateningly, to Karen): I heard you. If it wasn't mom's birthday. . . . He half rises. Looks violent.

[James' *presuppositions*: Karen hates me and my wife and looks down upon us. She insults my wife in the presence of my mother at her birthday party. *Intent*: Threaten Karen with violence, without actually committing an act of violence.]

Beatrice looks scared. She gets up, smiles and serves a dish to Karen, saying: Here are some goodies to my dudie.

[Beatrice's *presuppositions*: Karen has been attacked and insulted unjustly. The tension between them is threatening to erupt into open hostilities and violence. *Intents*: To appease Karen and at the same time reduce the tension.]

The four steps of macroscopic pragmatic analysis listed above had been applied to this scene. Here are the results (Step 4):

Results of Macroscopic Pragmatic Analysis

Step 4. Goals (super-superintents) and program structure (turning points).
Karen's

Goal: Remain close to her mother and be protected by her.

Program structure: She demonstrates good will, agreeing to cooperate with her mother's goal of preventing the aggravation of the conflict. She tries to avoid an open conflict, but IF attacked, she shows her vulnerability and resentment and attempts to enlist her mother's protection. If her position next to her mother is taken over by James, she does everything to protect it.

Beatrice's

Goal: Prevent aggravation of the conflict within the family.

Program structure: She avoids taking a stand. IF Karen is attacked, she does not take sides with her, but tries to appease her.

James'

Goal: Get close to his mother without losing Gloria's favor.

Program structure: Tries to get close to his mother and prove his good will to her, but IF Gloria incites him to confront Karen, he complies, partially.

Gloria's

Goal: Be protected against Karen's perceived hostility.

Program structure: She attacks Karen directly and indirectly, but IF James joins, she feels protected and is ready for a cease-fire.

FORMULATING FAMILY PROGRAMS

The information collected by observations and interviews, both those parts of it that have been semantically and pragmatically analyzed and those that have not, provide the building blocks for formulating the family programs. The proximity and control goals of each family member with respect to other family members can be found by the pragmatic-analysis method proposed above. Relevant information stored in memory can be found in the materials collected by any of the data-collection instruments described in chapter 9. This applies to data already analyzed semantically or pragmatically, as well as to unanalyzed data. Some instructions for processing the input and producing output can be inferred from the pragmatic analysis. Other are selected by the formulator of the programs, who uses his intuition and analytic powers.

To illustrate, below is a partial formulation of Beatrice's family program, including just Karen's and Beatrice's information-processing instructions.

Program of Beatrice's Family

ID of family members and their proximity and control goals with respect to each other: as above.

Relevant information stored in memory: The family's history and the general sociopolitical context.

Instructions for processing input and producing output:

Karen's:

> *Input* a behavior produced by James or Gloria
>
> *Retrieve* a memory trace
>
> *Compare* the input and the retrieved memory trace
>
> IF the memory trace has to do with James' having been hostile and assaultive toward me
>
> AND the input is hostile, threatening behavior
>
> THEN *Select output*—show vulnerability and resentment
>
> AND IF the memory has to do with James having been close to mother and the input is an attempt by James to get close to mother
>
> THEN *Select output*—protect position next to mother
>
> OTHERWISE *Select output*—demonstrate good will and avoid open conflict

Beatrice's:

> *Input* a behavior produced by James
>
> *Retrieve* a memory trace
>
> *Compare* the input and the retrieved memory trace
>
> IF the memory trace has to do with delinquent, aggressive and violent behavior and the input includes such elements
>
> THEN *Retrieve* from memory my conflicts with James' father, the bad years in the south of Chicago, the problems with James and Karen, etc. *Predict* that the input can lead to these problems being repeated. *Predict* that this can prevent me from reaching my proximity and control goals with respect to the ecological environment and to Karen.

AND IF I take sides with Karen

THEN these predictions are likely to materialize

Select output—avoid taking a stand

AND IF the input is the memory of James' having actually assaulted Karen when she was sixteen

THEN *Select output*—appease Karen

IDENTIFYING AND DESCRIBING BUGS

The procedure for identifying bugs includes:

- Identifying the new, unfamiliar information encountered by the information-processing system
- Singling out the puzzles faced by the system in attempting to adapt itself to the new environment (difficulty of interpreting the information coherently, restoring simplicity would cause distress, flooding, incomprehensible target programs)
- Identifying and describing the system's dysfunctional attempts to solve these puzzles and restore simplicity (forgoing completeness, consistency or parsimony; misconstruing target programs)
- Naming the resulting bugs (blinders, extreme ambivalence or fluctuation, cultural fixation or regression, cultural naiveté)

TRACING AND EXPLAINING THE HISTORY OF THE CASE

In this context, tracing and explaining the history of the case can be explicated as follows:

- Identifying and describing the major family programs in various points of the family's past
- Looking at periods of transition and change, during which the family had to face new, unfamiliar information and restore the simplicity of its set of programs
- Identifying and describing the bugs that emerged at each of these transition stages
- Describing the problems and symptoms arising from these bugs

How did this output affect the family's external and internal environment? The influences of the environment create new information that has to be dealt with to restore simplicity.

EXPLAINING THE PRESENTING PROBLEMS

As stated in chapter 8, symptoms and other presenting problems are direct or indirect manifestations and consequences of bugs in the family's information-processing system. Explaining the symptoms requires tracing the underlying bugs and exposing their connections with the symptoms. This is facilitated by the semantic and pragmatic analysis of the presenting-problems interview.

Let us go back to the presenting-problems interview with Alfonso and Maria, cited in chapter 9. Some bugs in the family's information-processing system can be inferred from this interview. Apparently, the core of the conflict between Alfonso and his son Carmelo was their dispute about Carmelo's going out in the evening to spend time with his friends. Alfonso was worried about this habit of Carmelo's, and he disapproved of Carmelo's friends. He thought they had a bad influence on Carmelo. However, Carmelo did not respect what Alfonso said. Alfonso felt that he was losing his authority over Carmelo. Carmelo, for his part, thought his father did not make any effort to understand him and his needs, but, instead, used arbitrary commands, accompanied by threats. This mutual interaction pattern was culturally naive both ways. Alfonso did not try to learn anything about Carmelo's social world. He did not understand how his own attempts to impose harsh discipline provoked Carmelo's extreme responses. Carmelo, for his part, did not understand Alfonso's fears and concerns. The symptoms of violence were direct consequences of these bugs.

To illustrate the main features of the diagnostic analysis, let me analyze the following case, whose description was written by Dr. Florence Kaslow.

Case 32: The Hernandez Family. Mr. Pedro Hernandez's family emigrated from Cuba to the United States when Rogerio was twelve years of age. The family settled in the Miami area in 1967. The parents maintained deep emotional ties to their homeland and to the family and friends who remained in Cuba. Mr. Hernandez often talked nostalgically about Cuba and his longing to return there some day. The family spoke Spanish, as did their neighbors and friends. They send the children to a private, predominantly Cuban Catholic school in their community.

Rogerio was a good student and quickly learned English. He acquired many North American mannerisms. He became a wild, rebellious teenager. He got into weekend partying and beer drinking and was dismissed from his high school football team because of his outrageous, flamboyant, sometimes "stoned" behavior.

His family of origin tried to keep him within bounds and sent him to a Catholic College, with strict instructions not to dishonor the family. He behaved well for about one year and liked his courses in Business Administration.

Then, he gravitated toward a partying crowd at the university and became a campus "Latin lover." He majored in wine, women and heavy-duty drugs, and flunked out by the end of his sophomore year. The family told him: "Now you have to make it on your own." But he was expected and permitted to move home and not to pay anything toward expenses.

He went to work for a manufacturing company and due to his intelligence and affability, he rose rapidly into management. He learned to "play the game well." He studied how to invest wisely and was determined to become a young tycoon. By age thirty, he was married to a beautiful Cuban dancer, had two daughters and was dreadfully unhappy. By age thirty-five, he had become embroiled in a horrendous divorce and custody battle. His exotic, volatile wife had left him for someone else and had moved to Mexico with their two daughters. He fought for several years to gain custody. During this time he rarely saw the girls. Eventually he triumphed, and the two girls, Ileana and Maria, came to live with him when they were twelve and ten years old. Ileana was obstreperous and defiant; Maria was silent and taciturn.

When the family entered therapy in 1995, Ileana was a beautiful sixteen-year-old girl and a junior in a private, special school for adolescents with learning difficulties. She was chronically discontent and pushing the limits. She had been expelled from her boarding school for violating rules such as drinking on campus and breaking curfews. Her grades were poor. Upon returning to the family home in the Palm Beach area, her attitude and behavior created chaos and dissension in the family.

Rogerio's second wife of five years, Diana, came from a midwestern farm family. She had down-to-earth, solid values and wanted the girls to be more stable and to work hard at school. Rogerio's volatility and passion initially were new and challenging to Diana. By the time they entered therapy, she was tired of his screaming matches with Ileana. After several years of trying to intervene, she now attempted to smooth over the easily ruffled feelings, while detaching herself from the stormy interactions. Since Rogerio's numerous business ventures took him out of town for most of the week, Diana handled the day-to-day parenting and tried to set clear rules for the children. She appeared patient, considerate and firm, in contrast with her husband, who exhibited high expressed emotions and frequently sabotaged implementation of the rules either of them set. Thus, the household was reasonably calm when he was away and became explosive when he was home as a catalyst.

Living within a two-block radius were Rogerio's two sisters and their respective families of creation and his mother. The family was close. Discussion about and with Ileana and Maria had to take into account the thinking of the entire extended family.

Rogerio expected to have complete obedience from his daughters and thought respect (*respeto*) should be automatic from child to parent. He believed the family of origin should play a large role in rearing his children. He railed against the American way of allowing teenagers to speak out, hang out and "do their own thing." He was unprepared to have his daughters negotiate the rules, so he became infuriated with them.

Ileana was in danger of failing at school and was "running around with a bad crowd." She had gotten drunk a few times and didn't know "what the big deal is," since dad and his family "always got loaded" when they were together. Dad was enraged when the idea of adults serving as role models was raised. He couldn't even consider asking his relatives or himself to modify their drinking habits, nor did he like it when his wife told him he was objecting to his daughter behaving very much like he had as an adolescent. He preferred to say she had inherited her wild pursuit of pleasure from her mother.

At one point, Ileana was causing so much turbulence and dissension at home, and her own behavior seemed so self-destructive, that the parents reported the situation was beyond their control and they were totally exasperated. When Ileana indicated she did not want to live at home any more, nor did she want again to reside with her mom, I suggested they consider an excellent residential treatment center school that would provide Ileana with the structure and education she needed. It would provide the rest of the family with a chance to get off their roller coaster and settle down and would give the family an opportunity to give Maria more attention, since all of the focus was on Ileana.

Ileana told her teacher she didn't want to go. Her aunts got involved, saying "no child in this family should be sent away." So Ileana remained at home.

Analysis

Following immigration, the family protected itself against cultural shocks and acculturation stresses by *fixating* itself, to the extent that this was possible, to previous programs. This was achieved by the following means: Settling in a predominantly Hispanic area, keeping intensive connections with the old country, conducting a Cuban style of life, conserving previous values, beliefs and attitudes and cultivating a myth of return to the homeland.

The role of making it in America was subtly allocated to Rogerio. As the only male son, his duty toward the family, dictated by tradition, was to succeed, earn money, provide the family with financial security, serve as its messenger to the new society and enhance its honor and respect in the Hispanic community. As a dutiful son, Rogerio began to gear himself toward this role. He learned English, assumed local mannerisms and acquired various North American teenager status symbols and modes of behavior. His active, energetic, temperamental character, his good looks and his extrovert "Latin" mannerisms concorded with his culturally prescribed goals. In the language of the model presented in this book, he attempted to restore simplicity by deriving new adaptive programs from his family's programs. Here, however, his information-processing system failed. His two worlds—the world of his family and Cuban community and the world of his peers at school—were sources of bugs that prevented his information-processing system from readjusting itself. Restoring simplicity by becoming fully acculturated would have caused intolerable distress because it would have contradicted his family's values and way of life and invited pressures to conform and clash with his own internalized values. His system became flooded with unfamiliar information incompatible with his family's programs. It reacted by disorganization, shuttling randomly between contradictory programs (foregoing consistency). He was exposed to a new culture, but had lost some of the controls of the old culture and had not yet internalized the subtle regulative mechanisms of the new culture. He behaved like "a Latin WASP," who did not distinguish between the permissible behavior at parties and the proper behavior of the classroom or football training sessions. His interpretation of the partying behavior of his peers was *culturally naive*. He confused their finely controlled excesses with the limitless hedonism often found in the society he came from.

Rogerio's behavior in school was considered disrespectful and dishonorable by his family. This family placed a very high premium on education, but, for them, education served the goal of remaining respectable and a part of their social class. For Rogerio, education served a different goal: becoming a success in America. Schooling, which did not seem to him to serve this goal, was irrelevant to him. The communication between him and his family was *culturally naive* in this respect. He and his family conceived of schooling in different ways.

Rogerio's family attempted to solve the problems presented by Rogerio by placing him in a Catholic school. This was a regressive move; an attempt to restore simplicity by removing him from the acculturation agents he was exposed to. This move was successful. Simplicity was restored for Rogerio. He was now in one world only, the world of tradition. During that period, he conformed, was relaxed, behaved well, was asymptomatic. Furthermore, he continued working toward his family's goal of making it in America by doing well in business classes. When he finished school, however, and went to university, the whole story of high school repeated itself. He became chaotic and disorganized again and dropped out. At this point, his family withdrew financial support but did not expel him from their midst. This was a kind of rite of passage for him. Withdrawing support could be conceived as a punishment, but it could also be construed as an act of unbinding, of partly releasing him from his duties toward his family.

Afterward, he progressed on the acculturation course. He became more individualistic in his thinking and behavior and went through a process of cultural learning that enabled him to become a social and financial success. His acculturation process was not complete, however. The centrality of his traditional *familismo* became apparent from the moment he decided to marry a wife and start a family. He married endogamously, a Cuban woman. Being the male, he attempted to control her, but she was uncontrollable, and a power struggle developed. His persistent efforts to gain custody of the children also attest to the centrality of the value of *familismo* in his spiritual make-up. Apparently, he was not motivated by emotional attachment to his daughters, because later, once he won the custody battle, he was detached from them and let the women in his family—his mother, sisters and, later, his second wife and the nannies—see to their upbringing. The daughters belonged to his extended family; to his father's lineage. That is why custody was to be acquired at all costs. But it was the women's job to do the rest, not the man's. The man's role was to be the provider and the head of the household.

At that stage, the family system was not bugged. There were no acculturation conflicts. The whole family system, including Rogerio, behaved according to tradition. For Rogerio, as for his parents, education of the daughters was again a primary goal. However, for him, education now, again, served the traditional function of bringing respect to the family and preserving its social status. The girls, being women, did not have the role of becoming providers and "making it in America." Their role was to preserve Rogerio's achievements. During this period, the whole family, including Rogerio, coped with acculturation stresses by *regressing* to previous cultural patterns.

Rogerio's second marriage was exogamous. This should not, however, be interpreted as a sign of progress along the path of acculturation. He married a woman from a midwestern farm family whose values were the traditional North American WASP values of individualism, tolerance, industriousness and respect for law and order. Apparently, he felt that Diana would not make demands on him, would fit well into his own extended family and would know how to deal with everybody, especially the children, in a benign manner. Bringing such a wife into the family would not expose him to new intercultural challenges or require him to change. He was right. Diana fit well into his own scheme of things.

The family system became bugged, again, when Ileana reached adolescence and, even more so, when she was expelled from boarding school and returned home. Heredity cannot be ruled out as a factor in Ileana's functioning and in her conflict with Rogerio. She had her parents' good looks, volatile and impulsive character and disinterest in academic pursuits. However, family-cultural factors should be taken into consideration, too. Ileana was a second-generation Cuban American. She had already partly internalized some current urban North American values such as individualism, intergenerational equality, feminism, a teenager's independence and rights and personal achievement. Whereas for Rogerio, at her age, the stay at a Catholic school had a calming effect, because it helped him restore simplicity; for her, being placed in a boarding school was a source of ambivalence and confusion. On the one hand, this was a refuge from home and from all the pressures applied to her there. On the other hand, the boarding school itself was an environment that partly contradicted her acquired values. Both at home and in school, she was unable to restore simplicity. She could not derive, from her existing repertoire of programs, a new consistent, complete and parsimonious set of programs that would introduce order into her confusing world. At home, she could not reconcile her above-mentioned North American values with the collectivism and *familismo* of her father's extended family (she still was considered the property of the family). She could not tolerate her father's sexism and *machismo*, his putting her in a position of inequality, his double standards concerning drinking and smoking, his inconsistency and the differences between him and Diana. At school, she could not reconcile her acquired values with the strict rules imposed on her. Her communication with her father and his sisters was culturally naive. The generation gap could not be bridged. She reacted with insubordination, fight and flight.

For Rogerio, Ileana's attitudes and behavior were confusing and distressing. On the one hand, she was like her mother; on the other, she was a typical North American teenager. This shook his world again. His programs became both disorganized and rigid.

For the therapy in this case to succeed, the parties involved, mainly Ileana and Rogerio, should be helped to derive, from their existing repertoires, programs that will enable their respective systems to change and restore their simplicity. One possible strategy is to help Ileana derive, from values endorsed by her (such as individualism, independence, equality and utilitarianism), an attitude of tolerance and respect toward her family's traditional values. This does not mean that she has to hold these values, conform or blindly obey her father's orders. She can choose her own lifestyle. When she is at home, however, in direct contact with her father and aunts, she should avoid provoking them and should play the game according to their, rather than her, rules. Her new programs will be context dependent. This is likely to lead to lifting the pressure applied on her. For Rogerio, his daughter's independence can be reframed as a tangible proof of his own success. His mission, dictated by his parents, had been to lead his family along the road toward success in the United States and integration. His daughter's character and values give evidence to the fact that this goal has actually been reached.

SUMMARY

This chapter concentrates on analysis of the diagnostic data collected with the instruments described in chapter 9. The analysis leads to an idiographic theory of the case, which provides the therapist with a solid basis for designing a culturally competent therapy with the family. A technique of semiotic microanalysis of observations and interviews is proposed. The stream of transcribed behavior is divided into activity units. Each activity unit or sequence of such units is assigned a semantic and a pragmatic interpretation.

Microananalyzed observations are macroanalyzed semantically and pragmatically. That is, generalized semantic patterns and pragmatic structures are inferred from the discrete semantically and pragmatically analyzed units. Techniques of semantic analysis, which reveal the main culturally determined meaning patterns the family imposes on its world of experience, are proposed in Tyler (1969). A particular technique, an adaptation of *componential analysis*, designed to reveal and describe the family's main emotional concerns, is presented. A particular pragmatic technique is also presented. Its purpose is to expose the family members' proximity and control goal with respect to each other and to the external environment, along with their strategic plans for reaching the goals, despite obstacles.

It is explained how the main culturally relevant family programs can be revealed and described, using the semantically and pragmatically analyzed observations and the other, unanalyzed diagnostic data. It is shown how bugs in the family programs can be identified. One has to search for the new unfamiliar information encountered by the system, the difficulties in processing this information experienced by the system and the errors in attempting to process this information. It is explained how the history of the case is described: One describes the major family programs at each stage of its development. Special attention will be given to transitional periods, during which the family encountered unfamiliar information. One describes how bugs emerged at such stages and how they were expressed in symptoms. Then, it is shown how the symptoms created environmental reactions that also provide new information to be dealt with. Symptoms are explained by relating the semantically and pragmatically analyzed problematic behaviors to the bugs in the information-processing system. This method of diagnostic analysis is illustrated by a number of cases.

PART V

THERAPY

The subject of this part of the book is the principles, processes and techniques of culturally competent family therapy. Chapter 11 includes a discussion concerning the special nature of the therapeutic alliance in culturally competent family therapy. Cross-cultural communications between therapist and family are often subject to suspicion, ethnocentric prejudices and misunderstandings. These are particularly prominent in communication between therapists who represent the advantaged mainstream and families that represent disadvantaged minorities. The problems are even graver when the therapist represents organizations that symbolize political, social and economic power. Methods for overcoming these difficulties are suggested. Using intermediaries is recommended.

Chapter 12 concentrates on the question of how culturally competent therapeutic strategies and tactics are planned on the basis of the assessment. General principles for constructing a strategy are proposed. The components of a good strategy are listed and discussed. The main component specifies the principles and mechanisms for effecting therapeutic change. The choice of tactics and techniques of intervention should take into consideration the cultural-specific family programs and the stage of the therapeutic process. The therapist's analysis of the family's culture is not necessarily shared with the family. What is shared is determined by the family's cultural characteristics and by the goals of therapy. Techniques are borrowed from various sources and adapted to the needs of culturally competent therapy. Major sources are various schools of family therapy and traditional healing methods.

Chapter 13 discusses the structure and dynamics of the overall therapeutic process. It includes also one complete case description.

11

The Therapeutic Alliance in Culturally Competent Family Therapy

Establishing and maintaining a good therapeutic alliance in culturally competent family therapy is a thorny problem. Cross-cultural communication in general—and the context of therapy is no exception—is often fraught with ethnocentric prejudices, suspicion and misunderstandings. The difficulties are particularly great if the therapist and the family are unfamiliar with each other's culture: The therapist represents the dominant culture, and the family belongs or believes itself to belong to a disadvantaged minority. Some of the main problems arising in such situations are discussed in this chapter. Ways for solving the problems and overcoming the difficulties are proposed.

CULTURALLY DETERMINED CONCEPTIONS OF THERAPY

As specified in chapter 6, families of different cultures differ in their conceptions of and attitudes toward symptoms, problems and therapy. The differences are related to questions such as what constitutes a symptom, which situations are considered stressors, how all these are explained, what is considered help, what cures, how cure is explained and what the roles of traditional and modern therapists are.

Cultural differences between the therapist's and the family's conceptions and attitudes concerning all these questions can have a decisive influence on the nature and effectiveness of the therapeutic alliance. This is illustrated in the following example. Shosh, a participant in a culturally competent family therapy course for social workers (which will be cited throughout this chapter as SW) had this to say about the characteristic attitudes of clients of the Ethiopian Jewish community in Israel toward therapy.

It is difficult to bring them to therapy. They don't understand the concept "thera-peutic process." Straight away they want to get a divorce. This, for them, is the only possible solution for their marital difficulties. . . .

They also don't know what a commitment to something means. You make an appointment for 8 o'clock, and they come at 10. This happens at lot. "How strange are you Whites!" they say. They find it hard to understand why if I say 10 it should be 10. People come to me like one comes to a doctor, according to the pain and the immediate problems and not according to the appointed time. With regard to this I should be more flexible. If something has not changed for ten years and I face two thousand people then it is I who I should change.

BUGGED THERAPEUTIC COMMUNICATION

In chapter 8, the conditions under which bugs in the family's information-processing system are created have been discussed and the bugs themselves listed. The therapeutic encounter between a therapist, the organization he represents and the family may be considered as an occasion on which both sides, as cultural systems, face a new situation and unfamiliar information. In some circumstances, bugs of the same kinds as listed and discussed in chapter 8 can invade both the therapist's and the family's information-processing systems. Such bugs can cause dysfunction in the therapeutic al-liance. A bugged therapeutic relationship is often characterized by prejudices and mutual suspicion. The sides often project their cultural stereotypes on each other.

Orly, another participant of SW, recounted the following episode repre-senting bugged therapeutic communication. The bug in this example is cul-tural naiveté.

We tried to help a family of immigrants from Iran. They had only tattered clothes. We wanted to give them second-hand clothes that we had collected. Extremely good condition. They refused. We could not understand why. Later, the wife told us that second-hand clothes can bring bad luck. The clothes carry over their original owners' misfortunes with them. For instance, if a man divorces his wife, the wife burns her clothes and never gives them to other people, because they can bring bad luck.

LIMITATIONS ON THE RELIABILITY OF CLIENT-PROVIDED INFORMATION

It is more usual than not that families in therapy with a therapist repre-senting another culture withhold information or deliberately give false in-formation about themselves. Many cultures ban imparting inside information to strangers. What members of the culture know about themselves is con-sidered a kept secret, often a sacred secret, not to be shared with others. The different attitudes of different cultures toward the notion "telling the truth" have been discussed and illustrated in chapter 5. Families of disadvantaged minorities are often reluctant to impart information about themselves to members of the dominant culture, lest this information be used against them or misused in some way.

Boyd-Franklin (1989b) mentions characteristic subjects that African Americans often prefer to keep as secrets, especially from strangers. These include, among others, secrets about parenthood and about informal adoption. Gwaltney (1981) cites statements made by some of his African American informants, which provide a vivid picture of their reservations with regard to disclosing information about themselves to whites.

White men do not worry much about my troubles. . . . See, if they can figure out how somebody thinks then they can figure how to gitover with that person, . . . Now we would be some fancy fools to tell this man anything that would help him to sock it to us. I'll talk to the dude all day long if he'll pay me, but he won't know as much about me when we finish as he knows now and let me tell you that's not a hell of a lot. . . .

ARE FAMILIES BENEFICIARIES OR VICTIMS OF THE SYSTEM?

More often than one would like to admit, the difficulties in cross-cultural therapeutic alliance reflect a harsh reality of institutional oppression, racism and discrimination or just inflexibility and indifference. Such phenomena are well documented in McGoldrick (1998). Boyd-Franklin (1989b) discusses the problematic relations between low-income black families and the agencies in charge of helping them. "Many fear that they will be "reported" in these agencies if they share personal information. . . . Black therapists are often surprised to discover that they are also perceived as part of 'the system' and are not trusted initially" (p. 162).

PRINCIPLES FOR EFFECTIVE CROSS-CULTURAL THERAPEUTIC ALLIANCE

If cross-cultural family therapy is administered in accordance with certain principles, to be listed below, there are good chances for the obstacles cited above to be at least partly removed. Putting these principles into practice is not an easy task. It requires changing established norms, ideas and habits concerning what is considered the right way of performing therapy and overcoming personal and institutional prejudices. Here are some such principles.

Know Your Own Culture

People tend to take their own culture for granted. In order to form a good cross-cultural therapeutic alliance, the therapist should be consciously aware of his or her own culture and of how it differs from the family's. A good way to gain a conscious awareness of your own culture is by trying to apply all the categories and constructs introduced in this book to oneself and one's own family.

Avoid an Ethnocentric Attitude

An ethnocentric attitude is one whereby other cultures are seen through the lenses of one's own culture. Holders of such an attitude usually see their culture as superior to others. A culturally competent family therapist must learn to see the client family's subjective reality as the family sees it and not impose his or her own culturally determined world-view on it. The values, cultural rules and norms of the family should never be seen, at least in the context of therapy, as intellectually or morally inferior, even if they are radically different from the therapist's. To illustrate, let us go back to the participants in SW.

In response to my question about whether the participants had encountered norms of thinking and behavior in their work, which they found intellectually and morally objectionable, they mentioned the following: adolescent marriages, treating women as inferior, tolerance of violence within the family, indifference to dirt and low standards of hygiene and rejection of deviations such as homosexuality or mental illness.

Omer shared his experience with a client of his from Iran, who had been married off when she was fourteen. He said that when girls reached puberty, some men kidnapped them, so they had to find a protector, a husband.

I summarized this part of the discussion by saying: This shows us that sometimes there are good reasons why a certain culture has certain customs, even if these customs appear objectionable to us. I am not denying that a fourteen-year-old girl is not ripe for marriage. But if she is not married the consequences for her can be grave.

Later in the discussion, the participants were shocked by what Saleema told about her society's attitude toward deviants: In our community, if someone is an addict or a homosexual, all his brothers and the rest of his family mobilize against him. They drive him out of the family. A woman who goes out with a boy against her parents' will, they exclude her from the family. They declare publicly, print it in the local newspaper, that she is not their daughter any longer. In some cases, the reaction is more extreme. A man burned his sister to death because she went out with a boy.

In response to the participants' horrified reactions, Saleema said: I also reject these norms. But I must admit I am split inside. I was brought up to believe that this is how things should be. Only later did I adopt the more modern attitude. I can still identify with both sides, although now I am much more on your side than on my own society's side in these matters.

At that point I felt that I had to share my own ambivalence. I said: I also find it extremely difficult to adhere to my principle of nonethnocentricity where such atrocities are concerned. Adopting a nonethnocentric attitude does not mean that in your own personal life and in your own mind you must give up the moral, aesthetic or intellectual norms that you had been brought up to view as the right ones. It only means that, at least in your professional work you have to suspend judgment, try to relate to all these things through the eyes of your clients, adopt a tolerant attitude and attempt to understand the background.

Adopt the Truly Humble Position of a Learner: Admit Ignorance

Being nonethnocentric implies also admitting one's own ignorance of the other culture and being curious and open to learn. In most cases, it will benefit the therapeutic alliance if the therapist admits his ignorance openly and asks the family to teach him about their own culture.

This principle was discussed in SW. Some participants expressed their concern that taking this position could undermine the therapist's professional authority. My response was: "Your clients know that you are ignorant of their culture. You can't deceive them. If you don't admit your ignorance openly they are likely to think of you as insensitive, conceited, dishonest or pretentious. The position of an open-minded learner is a very respectable one."

Learn the Family's Modes of Communication

To be able to communicate with the family, one should learn their language, in the wide sense of the term, and be able to decipher and use it, at least partly.

Respect the Family's Norms, Values and Customs

Assuming a nonethnocentric attitude also means that, at least in the context of therapy, the therapist accepts and, to a certain extent, behaves according to the family's own cultural codes. This requirement also excited some debate in SW. Participants shared their difficulty of putting this principle into practice when they had encountered culture-bound attitudes or practices that they considered offensive or objectionable.

Be Empathetic to the Disadvantaged

People who consider themselves oppressed, persecuted or otherwise disadvantaged are not always easy to understand or empathize with. They can be angry or bitter, or overly servile and submissive or evasive. They can arouse in the therapist fear, guilt, anger, overprotectiveness or other undesirable attitudes. The therapist should be on guard against such responses and try to relate to such people on a common human level of equality.

Let the Family Define Its Own Identity and Respect It

People tend to classify and define other people who do not always define and classify themselves in the same way. People are offended if an identity is attributed to them that they refuse to own.

In SW, Dina shared her feelings about a situation in which she and her husband had been classified by a foreigner:

My husband is a businessman. Once we were invited to dinner with a business associate of his in Amsterdam. The host prepared a surprise for us. He invited us to a Jewish restaurant with traditional Eastern European Jewish food. During the dinner he kept talking with us about things Jewish. He said something like "Jews are intellectual." My husband said: "I am not sure I concur with this generalization." Our host said: "You are a living proof." My husband is a well-read man. This was a very unpleasant experience. We consider ourselves Israelis, not Jews. We are atheists. Our Jewishness is not a significant aspect of our spiritual world. Eastern European Jewish food means nothing to us. Both of us are fifth generation Israelis of Syrian and Iraqi origins. My husband is well read, but he did not grow up in an intellectual home. In fact both his parents were uneducated manual laborers. We would have preferred to be addressed as us, as individuals, and not as representatives of some nation or religion.

Try to Create a Common Cultural Ground with the Family

The achievement of insider status does not mean that the therapist has lost his or her own cultural identity and has become a full member of the family's culture. The therapeutic alliance can be benefited if the therapist associates with the family through those parts of their respective cultures that are shared by both. Furthermore, the therapist can strive to create a new cultural common ground out of elements of the two cultures and their derivatives.

Orly (of SW) believed that having adopted this principle helped her establish a good therapeutic alliance with the couple who were Kurdish doctors (see Case 30):

I emphasized the cultural characteristics shared by them and me: The fact that both they and I belong to helping professions with a strong commitment to community service, the fact that both they and I are members of small nations struggling to preserve their identity and independence in a hostile nationalistic Arab and Muslim fundamentalistic surroundings; and many other things related to our common Near Eastern heritage (my parents came from Yemen), like the kind of food and music we like and the importance we attach to the extended family.

Identify and Acknowledge Differences between Your Own and the Family's Conceptions of Therapy

The general awareness of the fact that people of different cultures have different conceptions of therapy should lead one to find out what these differences are in each particular case. Reena of SW listed some common attitudes to therapy she had witnessed in her client families.

I find that most of our clients have a different conception of therapy than we do. Many see us as providers of material goods—money, housing, etc. Or, if they have a problem that cannot be solved by material aid, they want us to do some magic trick and make the problem disappear. For instance, to tell the children to behave in a way that will stop all their conduct problems. Other families see us as some kind of teacher. They want us to teach them efficient ways of solving their problems. Some take us to be their "wailing walls." They come to us to cry and get things off their chests. It is interesting that none of the conceptions mentioned is remotely similar to what we conceive as psychotherapy or family therapy.

Achieve Insider Status

To be able to form a satisfactory alliance, the therapist should do the impossible: Somehow manage to cross the cultural barrier and be accepted by the family not as a complete stranger, but, at least partly, as "one of us." Some other principles in the above list are preconditions for achieving insider status.

Identify and Analyze Bugs in the Therapeutic Communication with the Family

If the therapist feels confused, unable to make out what's going on or is misunderstood, these may be signs that the therapeutic communication with the family is bugged. At this point, it is advisable for the therapist to stop and try to identify and define the bugs.

Do Not Believe Blindly in the Information Imparted by the Family

Because of the reliability problem, one should not be naive about the information provided by the family. This principle should not be misinterpreted and taken to mean that the therapist must impart to the family an attitude of suspicion and disbelief. However, if the therapist naively accepts everything the family tells him, he is apt to misinterpret the family's culture and make false steps. If the therapist receives inconsistent or incredible information, it is legitimate for him to share his being puzzled about it with the family in a friendly way, try to clarify the reasons for it with the family and look, together with the family, for ways of correcting it.

Share Your Own Self and Life with the Family

In many cases, if one wants to be a culturally competent family therapist, one should become a part of the family's life and let them be a part of his or her own life. The therapist should bring his or her true self into the therapy. This seems to run counter to some time-honored norms about how to do therapy. This question, like any question in culturally sensitive therapy, should not however be approached dogmatically. There will be families who would regard the therapist as a distant authority figure. They would be embarrassed if the therapist involved his own self or his own personal life in the therapy. However, therapists must realize that their ideas about the psychotherapeutic relationship will be alien to many clients representing other cultures. Some are likely to take customary professional attitude as a sign of indifference, aloofness or conceit.

Montalvo and Gutierrez (1983) commented that many South American clients would show what could look to a North American therapist as a prying interest in his or her personal affairs. This is due to the deeply rooted cultural value of *familismo*. These people can be hurt if the therapist evades their efforts at familiarity.

This principle, too, aroused some controversy among the SW participants. Some expressed their concern about breaching their privacy, breaking the boundaries between their private and professional worlds. Others felt that adopting this principle would undermine their professional authority. My response was: "I see that some of you are worried about the problem of boundaries. I did not mean to turn your clients into your personal friends. Just, within clearly set limits, be your own self and don't hesitate to share a slice of your real life with your clients."

Use Intermediaries

Due to the linguistic and cultural barriers it is often difficult or even impossible to form a therapeutic contract and good alliance without the use of go-betweens. Characteristically, go-betweens are at least partly bicultural, for example, a university-trained social worker who comes from the extended family or the community represented by the clients, an authority figure in the community who is used to external contacts, and so forth.

Try to Influence within the Frame of Reference of the Family's Own Culture

The therapist's attempts to achieve a position of influence in the family and effect change should take into account the family's own culturally prescribed ways of influencing people and inducing them to change. A good example of this is included in the following citation from Omer of SW.

I treated a battering husband of Caucasian origin with a talisman. These people use all kinds of talismans against the Evil Eye and other harmful powers. I wrote some charms on a piece of paper, for example,

> "Let this arm be dead
> If violent thoughts come into my head."

I asked him to memorize the verses. Then I folded the paper, and placed it in a tiny metal container attached to a bracelet, which he had to wear on his wrist. And it worked!

Consider How to Empower the Family

Therapists should look for the family's strengths and use them as levers for change. They should mobilize the family's natural support systems. This is well illustrated in the following case, recounted by Reena of SW.

All too often, we are quick to remove a child from his family, rather than fortify those elements of the family or its environment that contribute to his healthy development. This seven-year-old kid, his father was in jail. The boy will finish university before he sees him out and free. His mother walks the streets and does not care whether he is alive or dead. Put in residential care three times and ran away, at most, by the second day. Tikva, my colleague who was in charge of the case, failed to pay attention to the fact that his aunt, his father's sister, and his twenty-five-year-old cousin were absolutely determined to keep this child out of trouble. They cared for him jointly, kept him off any bad influences and saw to it that he went to school regularly and did his homework. I managed to persuade Tikva to work with these two figures; to encourage them, give them feedback and guidance. They fully cooperated and were grateful. I believe this boy has a good chance, although you can never be really sure in such circumstances.

SUMMARY

This chapter is devoted to the therapeutic alliance in culturally competent family therapy. Some obstacles to reaching optimal alliance are discussed:

differences in culturally determined conceptions of therapy, bugged therapeutic communication, limitations on information exchange, prejudices and
an abusive attitude on the part of of service givers. A number of principles
for achieving good alliances are offered and discussed.

12

Planning the Therapy: Strategies, Tactics and Techniques

WHAT IS A STRATEGY?

Strategies for the whole therapy can be constructed on the basis of the overall diagnostic assessment. It is not implied that the therapist necessarily shares his diagnostic theory with the family. The therapist's decisions as to what to say to the family or what to do with it will be influenced by his therapeutic goals, by the nature of the therapeutic alliance and by characteristics of the family's culture. Such decisions will be included in the strategy and tactics.

The concept "strategy," as it is used in this text, refers to the general approach to solving therapeutic problems. In other words, it is a general plan for removing or weakening the culture-bound bugs in the family system's information-processing programs that breed the presenting problems, so that these problems are likely to be solved or disappear, spontaneously. Bugs will be eliminated if the conditions that brought them into being and are nourishing and protecting them are changed.

A good strategy specifies the shortest, simplest and least costly way of removing or weakening bugs. When the therapist designs a strategy he or she should ask the following questions: (1) What are the alternative approaches for changing the bug inducers? and (2) How costly is each alternative in terms of obstacles, resources required and possible complications? Then she will choose the best alternative, that is, the one that is the least costly. A preferable strategy is one whereby the intervention will not be met with unbending, insurmountable resistance and will not require excessive efforts, complicated operations, time and financial resources. Furthermore, with such a strategy, changes effected by the intervention sow the seeds for other significant desirable changes and for a minimum of undesirable side effects.

THE COMPONENTS OF A STRATEGY

Each of the alternative approaches to changing the bug inducers can be broken down into the following subcomponents.

Objectives of the Whole Therapy

- Which bugs should the intervention be particularly directed at?
- What kinds of changes in these bugs will the intervention attempt to achieve?
- What is the rationale for the answer given to these questions? The rationale will refer to the costs of each alternative, as explained above.

Priorities among These Objectives

- Which of the above targets of change will be given the first and highest priority?
- Which of them will be tackled first and which later?

In other words, what will the sequential order of the goals and subclass be? What is the rationale of these decisions in terms of costs?

Mechanisms by Which These Objectives Will Be Achieved

- What kinds of *mutations* will the therapist attempt to effect in each stage of the therapy? *Mutations* should be distinguished from *goals* or *change targets*. In this book, the term *mutation* refers to small changes which, hopefully, lead, step by step, to the attainment of a particular goal or change target.
- What kinds of change mechanisms will be activated in attempting to effect these mutations? Change mechanisms are listed and discussed below.
- How are these change mechanisms related to the family's existing repertoire of programs?

Manners by Which These Mechanisms Will Be Put into Practice

- How will the therapist use himself and the means available to him to facilitate the activation of the change mechanism chosen?

- What kinds of difficulties in carrying out this strategy (technical difficulties, resistance, limitations in family members, cross-cultural difficulties) are expected? How does the therapist plan to detour or overcome them?
- What is the rationale for each of these decisions? The rationale will take into account the therapist's idiographic theory about the family's culture.

THERAPEUTIC TACTICS AND TECHNIQUES

The term *tactic* refers, in this text, to the plan for a particular culturally competent family therapeutic intervention. A tactic is a particular stage in the overall therapeutic strategy. It may be viewed as a ministrategy, with all the considerations and components listed and discussed earlier. In each tactic, specific therapeutic techniques are employed. Each technique is designed to effect a mutation, a small change.

Considerations for Choosing Therapeutic Techniques

The choice of a particular therapeutic technique will be directed by the following questions.

1. *What is the entity to be changed?* (briefly, *entity*) Entities can be defined by the information-processing terminology proposed in this book. An entity can be an item of information included in the input or the output, or stored in memory; an information-processing instruction (e.g., *select, compare, transform, attribute properties*) or an operator (e.g., AND, NOT, OR, IF ... THEN).

The following examples are from the case of Beatrice and her family (Case 31, chapter 10):

The entity to be changed is *input*: The input into Beatrice's system consists mainly of the aggressive elements in her family members' behavior. In other words, she selectively attends to these elements. This should be changed.

The entity to be changed is *output*: Gloria produces mainly aggressive behaviors with respect to Karen. This has to be changed.

The entity to be changed is *information stored in memory*: James' memory with respect to Beatrice includes mainly painful episodes of neglect and rejection.

The entity to be changed is *instructions*: Gloria's program *attributes* to Karen *properties* such as "conceited," "racist," etc.

The entity to be changed is *operators*: Beatrice's program includes an IF ... THEN operation connecting a memory and output:

AND IF Aj is the memory of James' having actually assaulted Karen when she was sixteen,

THEN *Select output*—Appease Karen.

The conditioning relation expressed by this operator should be changed.

2. *What is the desired mutation in this entity?* (briefly, *mutation*) Mutations can also be defined by our information-processing terminology. Examples are from the case of Beatrice's family: Drawing Beatrice's attention to co-operative and nonaggressive elements in her family's behavior; inducing Gloria to produce nonaggressive behaviors with respect to Karen.

3. *What is the mechanism of change?* (briefly, *mechanism*) The concept *mechanism of change* refers to the process that makes the change actually happen. Mechanisms of change can be characterized by our information-processing language, too. Generally speaking, a mechanism of change consists of feeding some kind of input into the system and, subsequently, activating some instructions and operations. The input is different from the kind of input the family has been accustomed to taking in, but not radically different. The instructions and operations are partly derived from the family's existing repertoire of programs. These are designed to remove or weaken particular bugs.

In Gloria's program, she *selects*, as input, certain aspects of Karen's behavior, *compares* them with certain images and concepts stored in her memory concerning conceited, racially prejudiced persons, *treats* Karen's behavior and the behavior of these people *as equivalent* and *attributes* all these *properties* to Karen. To avoid doing this and get close to Karen would be extremely objectionable from her viewpoint. She would never associate with such people; only fight them. To change this bugged program, the therapist can feed some new input into Gloria's system. The new input includes some stories of Karen's past and present and a fuller discussion of Karen's political opinions. This is designed to emphasize the similarities, rather than the differences between Karen's and Gloria's fates and sociopolitical identifications. The mechanism of change, here, includes *introducing new input* and directing Gloria to use different information-processing instructions: *select* different aspects of Karen's behavior; *compare* them with different images and concepts stored in her memory; *treat* Karen's behavior and world-view as *partly equivalent to* her own and those of the people she identifies with, and *attribute* different *properties* to her.

4. *By what means will the mechanism of change be activated?* (briefly, *means*) Means include the therapist's verbal and nonverbal actions *(moves)*, their sequential order *(procedure)* and any aids or props she uses. For example, the therapist feeds new input into the family by conducting a semiformal family meeting. The therapist presides over the meeting. His moves include seating the family around a table, opening the meeting by uttering some characteristic formulas, according or denying the right to speak, commenting, and so forth. He uses a wooden mallet as a prop.

SOURCES OF CULTURALLY COMPETENT THERAPEUTIC TECHNIQUES

Once the therapist has mastered the theoretical language, concepts and principles presented above, he can design his own intervention techniques and tailor them to the needs of any phase of the therapy. Culturally competent family therapy, however, makes systematically eclectic use of ready-made techniques borrowed from various schools of family therapy and other genres of psychotherapy. Another major source is traditional healing and problem-solving methods existing in various cultures. The techniques design and their manner of application are adapted to the special needs of culturally sensitive therapy. "Adapting," in this context, means taking into account the culturally coded family programs, the bugs and the special nature of the intercultural therapeutic alliance.

A TYPOLOGY OF TRADITIONAL AND MODERN THERAPEUTIC TECHNIQUES

Techniques will be classified according to *means* of change, with *entities* and *mutations* and *mechanisms* of change as subclassifications. The following typology will include the following categories of change means.

(a) Facilitating communication (presiding over a discussion, circular questioning, mediating, leading negotiations, evaluating the quality of communications, and so forth)

(b) Clarifying information (commenting, interpreting, exposing, explaining, integrating, narrating, reframing, etc.)

(c) Providing support (nurturing, giving warmth, enlisting support of other people or deities, reinforcing, providing positive feedback, giving gifts, taking sides, taking a one-down position)

(d) Instructing (e.g., teaching, informing, training in problem-solving skills, modeling, rehearsing, using teaching aids, e.g., genograms)

(e) Giving directives (e.g., paradoxical injunctions, conditioning)

(f) Communicating with the supernatural (mediating between the family and supernatural powers, seeking supernatural advice, invoking spirits, prayer, reciting sacred texts, formulas or names, using magic, charms, talismans, fetishism, exorcising)

(g) Inducing an emotional experience or an altered state of mind (creating a new experience, confronting, shocking, testing, acting crazy, inducing a trance state or hypnosis, using humor, invoking catharsis, escalating, cooling down)

(h) Concretization (e.g., sculpting, symbolizing, role playing, dramatizing, story-telling, telling fables and allegories, using metaphors, songs, etc.)

(i) Dream interpretation and dream induction

(j) Creating or using rituals

(k) Substance and physical therapy (massage, using medication and other substances)

The subclassification by *entities* to be changed and *mutations* will be done according to the content areas discussed part II above, for example, techniques for changing the family's interpretation of the constraints on reaching its proximity goals with respect to the ecological environment, techniques for changing a family's myth about itself, techniques for changing the family's modes of emotional experience or techniques for changing the family's structure.

The subclassification according to change mechanisms will include the following subcategories:

1. Techniques designed to adjust the amount of unfamiliar information the system is exposed to (by introducing new input, removing available input, opening or closing input channels)

2. Techniques designed to help the system interpret the information it is exposed to correctly and consistently (by adding, deleting or changing instructions and operations)

3. Techniques designed to reduce distress caused by change (by activating dormant ameliorative programs or creating homeostatic metaprogram)

Following is a sample of family therapeutic and traditional techniques. These are classified according to the categories and subcategories specified above. Some will be illustrated by cases. It should be stated, however, that the classification is rough and crude. Many of the techniques listed are too complex and multifaceted to be classified in a clear-cut, clean and unambiguous manner.

(a) Facilitating Communication

1. Techniques Designed to Improve the Quality of the Family's Communication

The main mechanism of change in this technique is adding, deleting or changing information-processing instructions and operations.

Holtzworth-Munroe and Jacobson (1991) and Falloon (1991) propose various behavioristic techniques for improving family communication, for example, providing diary rates and doing cost-benefit analysis of positive versus negative exchanges, communication-skills training and conflict-resolution training. In the facilitation of the communication-skills model, family members are invited to describe and reenact their attempts to communicate their feelings; they receive supportive coaching from therapists and from other, more competent family members. Stress is placed upon the person's strengths. Congruent verbal and nonverbal expression is emphasized. Specific home tasks are assigned. Performance is monitored by worksheets and feedback during the next session.

Reichelt and Sveaass (1994) list characteristics of poor conversations: parallel talk, tangential talk (eluding concerns), past misery flows on, repeated demands for help, being stuck in perspective and resentment at clarifying questions. The therapist's role is to point out these inadequacies and propose alternative conversation strategies.

Ellis, Duran and Kelly (1994) discuss discourse strategies of competent communicators. Competent communicators use meaning-based versus text-based processing strategies. Meaning-based strategies reach deeper, more elaborate meanings in a conversation. Deep, meaning-based processing strategies have a map covering a large territory of the linguistic and communicative context. Competent communicators monitor the flow of conversation and take into account extended and complex syntactical and semantic turns.

The therapist's role in enhancing competent communication is helping the family acquire deep-processing strategies by directing them to explore the verbal and situational context more widely than they are accustomed.

2. Conflict-Resolution Techniques

Sager (1981) asserts that conflicts between marriage partners often center around unexpressed and often unconscious and contradictory expectations that have been inadequately explored and not brought to full awareness of both partners. These expectations have to do with a variety of subjects, for example, dependence-independence, power, emotional support or intimacy. The therapist's roles are to help the couple become aware of these expectations and facilitate negotiations toward explicit compromise agreements. The change mechanism is, again, adding or changing instructions and operations.

Most societies have developed conflict-resolution techniques. "Among the Ainu, an ancient people in Japan, family disputes often were settled by having the parties debate the issue before the assembled villagers. A winner was declared if one contestant gave up or collapsed or if one speaker was judged the victor by the village leaders" (Oswalt, 1972, pp. 180–188).

The Jewish community in Ethiopia had many alternative avenues for solving family conflicts. In the early stages of marriage, the young wife could ask her fictional brother (beker mizeh) who was also a close friend of her husband, to exercise his influence over the latter. She could also ask her mother-in-law to intervene. The couple could also consult with the religious leader (kes) who performed the marriage ceremony. Each of these people was allowed to hold sessions of consensual arbitration (shimglena) with the couple. If this did not solve the problems, a formal session (irk) was held with an ad-hoc group of elders, called shimagleotz. In the irk, the elders heard both sides, tried to identify the sources of the conflict, and attempted to work out a compromise or an agreement. The agreement, if reached, was written on a parchment, signed by the parties and by the elders as witnesses, and kept by the village head (Bodovsky and Eran, 1989).

3. Techniques Designed to Create a Better Balance between the Collective and the Individual Identities of Family Members

One of the techniques employed in Bowen's family therapy, as well as in Nagy's, is rejunction; that is reworking family cutoffs through encouragement of open negotiations among family members. The negotiations center around questions of personal autonomy and differentiation, loyalty vs. independence, relational commitments and balances of fairness (see Friedman, 1991; Boszormenyi-Nagy and Urich, 1981).

The mechanisms of change employed in these techniques are adjusting the amount of information the system is exposed to, opening input-output channels, adding and changing instructions and operations.

(b) Clarifying Information

1. Techniques Designed to Integrate Interpersonal and Intrapersonal Programs

Bentovim and Kinston (1991) describe their method of focal family therapy in which they systematically explore, with the family, the interrelations of their complaints, the current structure and functioning of the family system, past events and the structure and functioning of the families of origin. The main mechanism of change activated in these techniques is adding, deleting or changing instructions and operations.

2. Narrative Techniques

These techniques are based on the idea that family problems are maintained by narratives depicting and explaining the family's past and present, which have been constructed by the family. Therapy involves restorying, helping the family change its subjective reality by constructing different, alternative narratives.

Eron and Lund (1993) propose an integration of narrative and strategic techniques, for example, widening the strategic technique of reframing to restorying. Restorying helps the family create a story that provides an alternative explanation to the origins of their problem.

Parry (1991) suggests narrative techniques designed to help the individual in the family find his or her own voice, his or her own story. People find themselves living out a story to which they have been recruited. Each person is a character not only in his or her own story, but also in the stories of others. The first stage of therapy is deconstruction of established family myths, questioning and challenging them and testing their validity. Then, the family is encouraged to create a common story, which, however, should not proceed at the expense of the stories of each of its members. Each person composes his or her story, but also plays a supportive role in the stories of others.

Sluzki (1992) proposed an ingenious technique for transforming a family's narrative by selective questioning. The answers to the questions introduce small but significant change in the family's original story, which changes its perspective. The transformations are in:

time (from static to dynamic, from noun to verb, from an ahistoric view to historic one)

space (from noncontextual to contextual space)

causality (from noncausal to causal)

interactions (from intrapersonal to interpersonal, from intentions to effect, from symptoms to conflicts, from roles to rules)

values (From bad intents to good intents, from insane to sane, from illegitimate to legitimate)

manner of telling (from passive to active, from interpretations to descriptions, from incompetence to competence)

Other narrative techniques, useful for being specific, have been proposed by Penn and Frankfurt (1994). The family is encouraged to produce oral or written texts: journals, letters to persons living or dead, notes between sessions, personal biographies, dreams, poetry and dialogues. Then, the text can be rewritten or edited in various ways: changes of tense, inclusion of other relevant viewpoints, reordering of paragraphs, layering of ideas, clarifying meanings, introducing internal voices and internal dialogues.

Similar techniques have been offered by Zimmerman and Dickerson (1994). Madanes (1991) proposed narrative-like strategic techniques: Every time a bad memory of parenthood comes to mind, counteract by evoking the memory of a good parental figure; change the family's version of its life history; forecast a better future; arrange deeds of reparation.

In all the narrative techniques, the main mechanisms of change are adding, deleting or changing instructions and operations and activating dormant ameliorative programs or creating homeostatic metaprograms.

(c) Providing Support

1. Techniques Designed to Help Family Members Define Their Rights and Commitments with Respect to Each Other.

In Bowen's therapy and Boszormenyi-Nagy's therapy (see Friedman, 1991 and Boszormenyi-Nagy and Ulrich, 1981), the therapist applies multidirectional partiality, a flexible, sequential side-taking for everybody's entitlements and, also, their obligations. She searches for evidences of corruption. Family members are led by the therapist to talk about their relational commitments and balances of fairness. In Contextual Family Therapy (Boszormenyi-Nagy and Ulrich, 1991), the therapist encourages family members to negotiate in order to reach a balance of fairness in their relationships. In the process the therapist takes such moves as blocking, forcing people to listen and siding with each family member in turn.

2. Techniques Designed to Support and Empower the Family and Its Members

Holzworth-Munroe and Jacobson (1991) propose various behavioral techniques for providing emotional nurturing and increasing the frequency of positive interactions within the family. Behaviors described as desirable by one or more spouses are pinpointed and reinforced by both partners and the therapist. The couple is instructed to increase the rate of beneficial exchanges. In Ethiopia and Somalia, women who feel neglected by their husbands can be visited by a spirit called *Zar*. The Zar is believed to give the woman attention, support, and, sometimes, sexual satisfaction. The treatment for exorcising the *Zar* includes instructing the woman's husband to give her attention, support and gifts (Arieli and Seffefe, 1994). The main mechanisms of change employed in techniques of this category are introducing new input, opening or closing input channels, adding and changing instructions and operations.

(d) Instructing

1. Techniques Designed to Improve Family Members' Skills and Abilities to Perform their Familial Tasks

Falloon (1991) proposes a series of behavioral family-therapy techniques. These include:

Education about developmental milestones and aging

Child-rearing techniques (e.g., consulting the child about possible solutions to his or her behavioral problems, letting the child suggest various solutions and rehearse them)

Stress-management techniques (e.g., examining irrational thoughts that increase, rather than decrease, stress)

Contingency contracting (contracts about desirable responses, including rewards)

Operant conditioning (shaping, time out, keeping a record of specific behaviors, providing verbal and nonverbal reinforcers)

Communication-skills training (e.g., listening and providing feedback)

Problem-solving strategies (defining the problem and the goals in a clear manner, brainstorming a wide range of potential solutions, examining costs and benefits of each proposed solution, choosing the solution that better fits the current needs and resources of the family, planning how to implement the chosen solution and reviewing implementation efforts)

2. Techniques Designed to Enhance the Family's Ability to Cope with Stresses and Problems Coming from Outside or Inside the Family

Some strategic techniques are designed to enhance coping abilities. For example, various techniques developed in the Mental Research Institute (Segal, 1991) are designed to change the family's inadequate problem-solving efforts. For instance, a wife who pays her husband's gambling debts reinforces, rather than reduces, his compulsion to gamble. A paradoxical injunction, for example, to give him all her savings, can lead her to stop her inadequate problem-solving attempts. Various cognitive-behavioral techniques have been proposed for empowering family members and increasing their stress-management and problem-solving abilities (see Holtworth-Munroe and Jacobson, 1991; Falloon, 1991).

3. Techniques Designed to Increase the Family's Awareness of its Dysfunctional Patterns

Many techniques of the Milan school are geared toward making the family aware of the systemic nature of their problems. The method of circular questioning guides the interview by feeding hypotheses into the family about its systemic nature. Questions about behavior, beliefs and relationships turn the family members' attention to the interactional nature of their difficulties (see Campbell, Draper and Crutchley, 1991). The main mechanisms of change activated in techniques of this category are introducing new input by adding, deleting or changing instructions and operations, activating dormant ameliorative programs and creating homeostatic metaprograms.

(e) Giving Directives

1. Techniques Designed to Change the Patterns of Information Flow within the Family

These techniques change the family's structure, because family structure can be defined as the sum total of the family's patterns of information flow. Colapinto (1991) lists a variety of structural family therapeutic techniques that change the patterns of information flow within the family: starting and stopping interactional sequences; making enactments; reordering sequences; interrupting and reframing interactions; exaggerating or ignoring particular items of data; confirmation (of family's expressions); maintenance (respect for family rules); selective joining by nonverbal imitation of member's mood, tone of voice, posture or behavior and sitting close to peripheral members; intensification of specific interactions by repetitions or playing the protagonist; boundary making by changing special positions; turning some members into spectators; prolonging interactions and blocking gestures; crisis induction by facing a chronically avoided conflict; challenging the family's world-view. The main mechanisms of change activated in these techniques are introducing new input, removing available input, opening or closing input channels.

Strategic techniques also change patterns of information flow within the family. Madanes (1991) proposes many ingenious strategic techniques. As an example: For children who parentify their parents—parentify them to independence. The children will be instructed, for example, to educate the parents to act independently. A depressive parent presents himself or herself as worthless, as a person whose life is meaningless. The therapist accepts this self-presentation but uses it as a lever for change: OK, you are worthless, so give your life over to people whose life is not worthless. The depressed parent is then encouraged to do anonymous good deeds for people toward whom he or she bears guilt feelings. When family members hurt each other, create an atmosphere of higher emotions, find protectors for the victim and elicit repentance, forgiveness, compassion and a sense of unity from the others.

Sluzki (1992) proposed the following schematic formulas for strategic interventions designed to change information-processing patterns: If A and B concur in defining A as a victim and B as victimizer, then find a way of reversing the roles/labels and state the reversal forcefully. If A and B describe a sequence of events that leads to conflict or to the emergence of symptoms, then search for the events or steps that precede what has been described as the first step in the sequence. If you cannot specify it, state its existence, nonetheless. If it has been detected, and has been accepted by A and B as possible, then repeat the cycle (e.g., search for a previous step or, at least, assert its existence).

Many strategic techniques have been developed in the framework of the Milan school (see Campbell, Draper and Crutchley, 1991). Here are some:

Asking a third person to describe the relationship between two others.

Reframing everything, including symptoms, as positive or good because they contribute to the preservation of the system.

Ritualizing the prescribed behavior (e.g., on alternate days, one parent decides, alone, how to deal with a troublesome child while, the other parent behaves as if he or she is not there).

Holding one part of the system still while the rest of the members and the rules revolve around it and readjust to the new point of fixture.

Siding with the parents against a child who tries to divide and rule.

Separating overinvolved parents from the rest of the family and then reuniting them.

Positioning, that is, accepting and exaggerating a family position. For example, a family member's position is pessimism, complementing or counteracting an over-optimistic position of other family members by an optimistic or encouraging response from significant others. The therapist may "undo" the client's pessimism by defining the situation as even more dismal than the client has originally held it to be.

Asking hypothetical questions about future possibilities.

Experimenting with tasks: If certain behaviors are prohibited because of a belief within the family, a task might be suggested that would incorporate that behavior, but in a different context. For example, if an adolescent is denied independence because he is considered incompetent, he is prescribed the task of organizing and leading the family's summer vacation.

Restraining: the therapist does not take credit for change, declares impotence and discourages family members from changing. She overestimates the efforts required for change and attributes noble motives to resistance to change.

Duplicating an experience the client reports in the session.

Agreeing with the client's self-derogatory attitude.

Following the client's recommendations for treatment by directing the client to have a relapse; teasing, minimizing the prospect of success; illusion of alternatives—for example—do you want to stop abusing your wife immediately or take your time and stop abusing her later?

2. Symptom Removal Techniques

Strategic and other techniques have been designed to get rid of outward symptoms of dysfunctional family information processing. The following techniques are included in Madanes (1991):

Interactional ordeals. For example, a husband suffers from headaches. This is ana-lyzed by the therapist as a response to pressure applied on him by other family members (e.g., excessive financial demands). He is instructed to give a present or money to the people who cause him the headaches, such as his wife or his mother-in-law, every time the headaches appear.

Prescribing the pretending of the symptom. For example, the husband is instructed to pretend to have a headache whenever an excessive demand is made on him.

Prescribing a symbolic representation of the symptom. For example, a bulimic client was instructed to mash up food at the dinner table, then throw it down the toilet. The person the bulimic loves most is the only one who is allowed to unclog the toilet. This is both an ordeal and a symbolic representation of the stress caused by the symptom to the family.

Prescribing where, when and how the symptom will appear. Scripting communica-tions about the symptom.

Engaging people with each other in issues other than the symptom.

Transferring the symptoms: Different family members will be instructed to have the symptom in turn.

Sluzki (1992) proposed schematic formulas for removing symptoms, too. For example, if A and B describe a sequence of events that leads to the emergence of symptoms, then search for the events or steps that precede what has been described as the first step in the sequence. If you cannot specify it, nonetheless state its existence. If it has been detected, and is accepted by A and B as possible, then repeat the cycle. If A has a symptom that fluctuated within the day or the week, then instruct A to select times when the symptom improves and tell B that it is worse.

Most cognitive-behavioral techniques are aimed at symptom removal. Here is a sampling: systematic desensitization; massed practice (repeatedly evoking problematic behavior until such contrasting factors as fatigue set in and make it aversive); flooding (evoking feared stimuli in the clients' imagination without resulting in the dreaded consequences); implosion (flooding plus evocation of dreaded consequences) and abreaction (a form of catharsis); cognitive restructing (interpreting the symptom differently) (see Goldfried, 1994).

(f) Communicating with the Supernatural

In numerous cultures all over the world, physical and mental disturbances are attributed to supernatural causes, such as witchcraft and sorcery, spirit intrusion or possession, evil eye or a curse by deities. Treatment requires communication with the responsible supernatural beings. The conceptual basis for diagnosis and treatment is culture bound. Before listing some specific techniques, let me refer briefly to the following two general theoretical studies.

Morley and Wallis (1978) distinguish between *endogenous* (centrifugal or subtractive) and *exogenous* concepts with respect to supernatural causes of disturbances. Endogenous concepts attribute illness to magical capture of the individual's soul. Treatment requires magical intervention to recapture the soul and restore the balance of spiritual forces within the individual. Exogenous concepts attribute illness to the intrusion of a real or symbolic object into the body. Even if the object is real (e.g., a thorn), magical powers are attributed to it or to forces that caused its intrusion. Treatment consists of exorcising or propriation through ritual. The intruding spirit also can be disposed of by sweating it out, by dietary measures or trepanation.

Bourguignon (1976) asserts that the relationships between the supernatural, the victims and the curers reflect selective cultural patterns. The more complex the society, the more likely it is to have possession trance, which requires exorcism, or coming to terms with the spirits (e.g., "marriage" of the shaman with the spirit). The less complex the society, the more likely it is to have just trance. Mediumistic possession trance is more likely to exist in more rigid societies than in more flexible ones. Peripheral cults provide means of supernatural vengeance for the downtrodden. The medium, acting as a spirit, may make it possible for the individual to be provided with solutions to some of his problems in ways that circumvent the rigid demands of his society. Yet, it follows the social constraints in that he relies on an external authority, a spirit speaking through the medium, to get authorization for his actions. By playing the role of spirits, the individual may be able to modify social constraints and the behavior of others and, thus, enlarge the scope of actions open to himself. Trance with hallucinations in front of an audience is a dramatic way of loosening social constraints.

Simpler societies are more likely to use dreams to seek the control of supernatural powers. These societies also use trance, rather than a possession trance. Possession involves dependence and compliance, more than just trance. Possession trance is more widespread among women and trance among men (see also Dow, 1986; Hippler, 1976).

Let me now present a classified list of specific techniques:

1. Techniques Designed to Remove Possession that Causes Disturbances (Exorcism)

Arieli and Seffefe (1994) describe exorcism techniques for getting rid of the *Zar* spirit in Ethiopia and Somalia.

The exorcism ceremony is directed by a shaman (*belezar*). . . . Many members of the extended family and neighbors gather in the patient's home. They sing and beat drums. The patient begins to dance a rhythmic dance called *gurri* . . . and goes into a trance. . . . The *belezar* . . . asks the *zar* to state what his wishes or demands are. The most common requests expressed by possessed women are gifts such as clothes or pieces of jewelry. The woman's husband makes a pledge to provide these items, then the *zar* agrees to leave the patient's body. (P. 637)

Suwanlert (1976) discusses exorcising techniques for expelling a spirit called *Phii Pob* in rural Thailand.

One case described is that of a woman who was possessed by a female *Phii Pob* after her husband had a long talk with a young woman. The shaman talked with the *Phii Pob* through the possessed woman's mouth. The *Phii Pob* asked many questions about the possessed woman's husband. . . . Then the shaman recited *Ghata*, sacred verses and spells, derived from Buddhist texts in Pali or Sanskrit. He blew three times across the crown of the patient's head. He pricked parts of her body, especially bifurcations, with needles, until the area where the spirit was located. Then he burned chilli peppers to drive out the spirit. (P. 76)

Freed and Freed (1964) describe a case of spirit possession in a north Indian village.

The victim was a newly married young woman who, as prescribed by custom, had just left her father's home village and was moved to her husband's parents' home. Her symptoms included loss of consciousness, shivering and convulsions, dizziness and a sensation as if her stomach were swelling. The treatment was performed by a local shaman. The latter gathered the young girl's husband's mother and sisters around her bed and instructed them to sing verses expressing their love and support. She also took measures to make the ghost uncomfortable by beating parts of the young woman's body with straw, cursing and smoking burning dung. (P. 78)

2. Techniques Designed to Appease Angered Supernatural Beings and Persuade Them to Alleviate Punishment

Villagers in Thailand appoint a priest to look after the *puu ta*, the guardian spirit of a village. If *puu ta* is not taken care of, the villagers are exposed to physical and mental disease (Suwanlert, 1976). Lee (1988) describes the *kut* ceremony, which includes rites and prayers to various deities and spirits for protection against physical or mental affliction.

In a study of folk psychotherapy in Taiwan, Tseng (1976) describes practices used to please the deities and keep away evil forces:

For example, the shaman gives the client a piece of paper on which he has written some characters and symbols. He orders the client to affix this charmed paper to the top of his door to prevent the devil's entrance, to carry it on his body as a charm, or to burn it and put the ashes into water to drink as medicine. The characters and symbols reaffirm the patient's union with the divine. (P. 166)

This is very similar to the Jewish *mezuzah*, a parchment scroll inscribed with biblical verses and the name of God, inserted in a case and attached to doorposts as protection against the entrance of evil forces.

3. Techniques Designed to Restore Harmony among the Family, Society and Deities

Hyden (1995) asserts that the main therapeutic method used by native healers is reaffirming the solidarity of the community and the deities with the patient. Healing ceremonies show concerned goodwill and serve to reintegrate the sick person into the social group. Tseng (1976) describes Chinese customs, designed to heal by restoring balance:

In Chinese temples, people who come to seek advice about their personal misfortunes can get answers to their questions, written on a piece of paper called *Chien*. People also consult fortunetellers, who place their stalls on street corners or in market places. The answers . . . are usually based on the following principles: Certain universal rules and principles of nature determine one's destiny. Something is wrong because something relating to the balance between *yang* and *yin* is amiss in a person's predisposition, or the timing of events has gone against the basic laws of nature. The person should be made aware of his or her own predisposition, to learn what the chances are for the attainment of his or her goals. To obtain a more harmonious combination of factors to improve life, great concern is expressed for time, order, relationship and harmony. (Pp. 167–168)

A culture-bound syndrome called *Malgri* is discussed in Cawte (1976):

Its symptoms include headaches and distended abdomen. . . . It affects a person who enters the sea without washing his hands after handling land food. This syndrome is found only among the Lardil people of the Wellesley Islands of the Gulf of Carpentariain Australia. The locals attribute this disease to spirit intrusion, linked with the totemic organization of the people and their territory. A central theme underlying this explanation is mutual antipathy between land and sea. If precautions are neglected, the totemic spirit that is guardian of that particular littoral is believed to invade the body "like a bullet." Offending the sea can lead to other misfortunes: engulfment, failure of food supply, or attack by sea entities. (Pp. 23–24)

Cawte hypothesizes that *Malgri* serves the functional purpose of social regulation by contributing to the maintenance of territorial boundaries. *Malgri* is a sickness of intruders. The traditional treatment for a *Malgri* attack goes as follows:

When a victim is found . . . a grass or hair belt is unraveled to provide a long cord that is tied by one end to the victim's foot while the other end is run down to the water, to point the way home for the intruding spirit. (P. 24)

4. Techniques Designed to Change Interpersonal Programs that Cause Stress

Traditional Chinese therapists use metaphors in treating relationship programs. For example, such a therapist can say to a nagging woman: Your tongue has been replaced by a male tiger's tongue (Tseng, 1976).

Unfinished family business is acted out in a form of therapeutic drama called *nŏkchŏng-gori* (invocation of spirits), practiced in Korea. The dialogue is spoken between a dead man, represented by a shaman, and his living family. A seance of *nŏkchŏng-gori* is performed:

The shaman, wearing a paper image on her head . . . goes into a trance, and then, supported and [then] . . . begins to assume the role of the deceased. "He" grasps his widowed wife and sympathizes with her by saying "What will become of you alone in the future?" He consoles her in her sorrow. . . . The widow weeps bitterly, grasping the deceased, then mournful messages continue. The deceased says: "I did not inherit from my parents and tried hard to make a living, so we had little leisure time." In response to the message, the widow irritably screams: "Don't you remember what I said? I said I wanted to die first. Why did you die first?" Again, the message: "Well, a widow is better than a widower. You whelp; what made you so hot-tempered? Oh, this is the last time to get hot-tempered!" As if the deceased were alive, a quarrel takes place between the couple. They are then parted, drink together, smoke cigarettes, and reconcile with each other. Turning to his daughters-in-law, the deceased says: "Live your lives happily. You sisters in-law, have affection to each other." And then, turning to his wife again: "Please take good care of the housekeeping in my absence." Hearing the message, the family of the deceased embrace each other and weep. Then a comic skit takes place. The deceased asks for digestive aid for his stomach pain. His wife answers, "You've already died. Isn't that enough? Why you, a dead person, want medicine?" The relatives ask the deceased to leave, saying: "Why don't you stop complaining, rather than commenting on the diseases of your wife? Please give help to your sons and daughters, and please stop grieving your family and fly away without any lingering attachment." In response to that, the deceased says: "I'll give you no more grief. Don't worry about me, but take good care of your lives. And now I'm leaving." (Lee, D. H., 1988, pp. 155–156)

5. Techniques Designed to Complete a Psychodynamic Process

Bourguignon (1976) refers to ritual drama as a way of rendering some aspects of society symbolically, at the same time bringing out the intrapsychic state of the visionary. The trancer recounts his visions dramatically to others. Since trance is a private state, it tends to stress the individual and his separation from others. Reid (1983) recounts that, among the Yirrkala of aboriginal Australia, death sets in motion an elaborate sequence of rituals that continues for days or weeks. It provides a vehicle for the expression of anger and grief and a means of dealing with the loss.

Bilu and Witztum (1993) describe a number of cases in which psychodynamic principles were combined with traditional popular religious concepts and practices in the treatment of ultra-Orthodox Jewish patients in Jerusalem. In one of these cases they tell about a young repentant Orthodox Jew who felt guilty for his father's death some years earlier. His father was an alcoholic. This young man blamed himself for having neglected him.

He began to hear voices coming from a vengeful angel, telling him to fast and to abstain from sexual intercourse with his wife. He began to perform nightly religious rituals and to visit sanctuaries of popular holy people, but these measures did not help. The therapists, employing a culturally sensitive form of therapy, suggested that he send a letter to his dead father, asking for his forgiveness. They also quoted classic Jewish sources forbidding excessive mourning and self-neglect. (Pp. 203–210)

(g) Inducing an Emotional Experience or an Altered State of Mind

The techniques of Gestalt therapy lead the client to full awareness of the present, uncontaminated by blocks and resistance. The client is instructed to continue to identify a feeling, for example, "stay with the tightness," "go into the fear." *Reductio ad absurdum* is one way of changing the emotional experience. The client continues experiencing until she begins laughing at herself. Oswalt (1972) reports that Caribou Eskimos shame offenders by singing ridicule songs against them.

Symbolic-experiential family therapy makes use of various techniques designed to produce specific emotional experiences (Roberto, 1991). These include:

Fantasy alternatives to real stress (using absurdity to increase flexible problem solving). For example, if a man says that his son does not listen to him, the therapist says: "Tie him to the bed, get a loudspeaker and shout into his ear."

Separating interpersonal stress from internal stress. For example, if a wife says: "My husband degrades me," the therapist says: "Tell me about all those parts of yourself that you consider inferior."

Augmenting family despair. For example, saying: "I believe your problems are unsolvable. You should either prepare yourselves to be miserable for the rest of your life or commit suicide."

Using self (sharing dreams, primitive thoughts, personal emotions and even touch with the family).

Reversing roles with family members.

Using humor and joking.

(h) Concretization

1. Techniques Designed to Help the Family Become Aware of Certain Programs

Family sculpting techniques are a way of making emotions, structural organizations and other abstract constructs concrete and, therefore, immediately available for the family. Onnis et al. (1994) propose sculpting techniques representing the family's present structure and potential changes in it. Duhl, Kantor and Duhl (1973) are a primer of sculpting techniques.

Papp (1982) describes an approach to couples therapy based on defining the reciprocal positions of each spouse in relation to a central theme. These positions and the theme around which they are organized are crystallized into visible forms through stage metaphors. When studied in relation to one another, the metaphors provide a holistic view of the relationship and are used as an artifice for change.

Seltzer and Seltzer (1983) propose techniques imitating magic rituals in non-Western societies.

A widow who functioned as both a mother and a father to her children was called "witch" by her children. The therapist arranged a ceremony . . . in which the mother wore a witch mask and her children danced around her. (see pp. 6–7)

A couple that complained about difficulties in their sexual relationship were led by the therapist to conduct a mock funeral, in which their bad sex was buried. (see pp. 8–9)

Similar techniques are offered in O'Connor (1984) and O'Connor and Hoorwitz (1984). Some of these techniques are akin to the family play therapeutic techniques proposed in Ariel (1994). The Greek chorus (Papp, 1980; Hoffman, 1981) is a concrete way of helping the family become aware of the structure and functioning of their system.

2. Techniques Designed to Change Programs

Many of the techniques connecting humans with supernatural beings belong to this category too. Bourguignon (1976) lists many such techniques, for example, mock marriage between the shaman and an invading spirit; the shaman acting as a medium; role-playing and ritual drama. Butler and Harper (1994) tell about the use of God as a co-therapist in work with religious couples. When therapy is stuck, the therapist and the clients consult God through visual imagery and prayer.

(i) Dream Interpretation and Dream Induction

At least since Freud, dreams have been considered a biopsychological phenomenon. Traditionally, however, dreams have been considered as omens reflecting messages from God or other supernatural entities. They have been viewed as coming from a source external to the dreamer, situated on a cosmological, rather than a psychological, plane.

Bilu and Witztum (1993) note the following: A traditional belief in Jewish mysticism is that, while the person is asleep, the soul departs from the body and commences a nightly voyage to heaven. Its destination is the *Shekhina*, the female counterpart of God, with whom it yearns to unite. Dreams reflect the experiences of the wandering soul, and their character and outcome derive from the nature of the entities encountered on the way. As such, dreams are taken very seriously by religious Jews, and a lot of effort may be invested in discerning the moral standing of the protagonists in the dream plot. Special attention is given to visitation dreams in which messages from deceased relatives are conveyed. The notion that most dreams are meaningful and decipherable, and that their messages spill over to and affect reality, has given rise to many written texts of dream interpretation techniques. Most of these methods rely heavily on religiously based cultural vocabularies of symbols.

Here is a case described in Bilu and Witztum (1993).

Sarah . . . lost her husband one year prior to treatment. She responded to the death with a severe mourning reaction, which soon developed into a full-blown depression. She reported the following dream:

First dream: She was walking to the pharmacy to buy an important medication, but got stranded in a closed bazaar with the gatekeeper until nightfall. . . . Sarah herself interpreted the day and the bazaar as symbols of life and the night and the gatekeeper as symbols of death. But she looked at the dream not as a psychological entity but as a sinister communication from the world of the dead. . . .

The therapists instructed Sarah to write her husband a letter, telling him that she has not forgotten him, but asking him to let her live her life without ghastly dreams. Then she was to prostrate herself on her husband's grave and read the letter aloud. . . .

Following these, Sarah's husband appeared in person in her dream. He sent her to bring him wine for *Havdala* [a religious ritual conducted on Saturday evening, to separate between the holiness of the departing Sabbath and the mundane quality of the coming week]. This was interpreted by Sarah as permission from her husband to go on with her normal life. (Pp. 216–218)

(j) Creating or Using Rituals

Many of the techniques listed above include rituals. Rituals are a major therapeutic tool in many cultures as well as in modern psychotherapy. Bennett, Wolin and McAvity (1988) recommend the construction of new rituals with the family, for demarcating rites of passage and for resolving particular family problems. They also suggest reinstating lost rituals, redirecting rituals back to usefulness and modifying current rituals. Madanes (1991) proposes various rituals within the framework of strategic family therapy: a birthday party; a trip to visit relatives; a transition ceremony; renewal of marital vows and peace rituals.

(k) Substance and Physical Therapy (Massage, Using Medication and Other Substances)

Many of the techniques described above include the use of various substances, natural objects and physical touch.

ADAPTING TRADITIONAL AND MODERN TECHNIQUES

As stated earlier, the choice of techniques to be employed in any culturally competent family treatment can be subject to the principle of *technical eclecticism* (see Lazarus, 1995). According to this principle, techniques developed in various schools of therapy can be borrowed and employed in the treatment of any single case. The choice of particular techniques will be subject to various considerations, such as the kinds of problems to be solved, the stage of the therapeutic process and the personality characteristics of the therapist and the clients. In culturally competent family therapy, other considerations will be added: the culturally relevant family programs (entities) to be changed, other culturally relevant family programs that are likely to influence the results of the intervention and the nature of the cross-cultural therapeutic alliance. These considerations will determine the suitability of a technique to the task at hand. If it is found unsuitable, it should be discarded or modified.

The choice and adaptation of techniques should take into account culturally determined difficulties in restoring simplicity. The following are the main kinds of puzzles discussed in chapter 8, some directions for how to take these into account in technique adaptation and some relevant examples.

The System's Inability to Settle on a Single Interpretation

Many therapeutic techniques presuppose a clear, unambiguous understanding of some key cultural concepts or customs, which is shared by both the therapist and the client family. For example, both Bowen's and Boszormenyi-Nagy's techniques presuppose a reasonably unambiguous understanding of such key concepts as individualism, autonomy, fair play or equality. Whitaker's techniques of symbolic-experiential therapy presuppose a clear understanding of notions, figures of speech and communicational attitudes such as irony, playfulness, the absurd and nonsense. If there is a danger that the family will not be able to settle on one single interpretation of these key concepts or customs, the use of the technique in question is likely to introduce bugs into the therapeutic alliance. Therefore, the technique should be either discarded or modified. The modification should remove the possible ambiguity by providing a single interpretation that can be accommodated easily by the clients' culturally determined information-processing system.

In chapter 8, the family's inability to settle on a single interpretation of the input was illustrated by the case of Jewish immigrants from Ethiopia to Israel. Due to the ambiguous attitudes of the Israeli authorities and general public toward these immigrants, many families and individuals could not make up their minds whether the Israelis were friends or enemies, whether Israel was really the Holy Land they had dreamed about or an unholy, profane society. The choice and remolding of therapeutic techniques to be used with Ethiopian immigrant families should take into consideration this state of mind.

A set of narrative family therapeutic techniques was briefly summarized above. The application of such techniques requires deconstruction of established family myths, questioning them and testing their validity. At the same time, the family is encouraged to create a common story. The new or revised stories constitute a more adequate, more useful representation of reality than the previous stories or the former versions.

Can these techniques be used with Ethiopian immigrant families whose state of mind is as described above? It is not easy to give a clear answer to this question. On the one hand, challenging the validity of the family's current views of reality is apt to increase the family's confusion and insecurity.

On the other hand, creating a common family story, while preserving individual stories can help them interpret their new reality more consistently.

It seems that, in principle, these techniques can prove useful, but they should be employed with extreme caution. They must be re-tailored to the special needs of such families. The main revision required is deleting the first part of the intervention. That is, the deconstruction, questioning and challenging of the family's existing stories are moves that must be avoided. However, the second part of the intervention, encouraging the family to create a new common story, can be safely applied. The family can be helped to derive a new, consistent narrative, depicting and interpreting its current reality, from its existing repertoire of programs. Such a revision was attempted in the following case.

Case 33: A family of Ethiopian Jews was referred to the social services department in the city of Arad after a suicide attempt by its oldest son, twenty-five-year-old Marahu. The boy cut his wrists after the Israeli rabbinical authorities questioned the Jewishness of the mother, and, therefore, of her sons. The case was referred to Haiim, a social worker of Ethiopian Jewish origin. During the beginning sessions, the family members told Haiim their own personal stories, which expressed their utter confusion and disappointment with respect to the reality they had been exposed to since their arrival in Israel.

After hearing the stories, Haiim suggested reading, together with the family, some stories of the Bible and finding analogies to the family's own stories in them. The biblical stories could serve as fables that would help the family interpret its life experiences in Israel in consistent, comprehensible manners and find solutions to its problems.

The choice of biblical stories for this purpose was not coincidental. This family, like most other Ethiopian Jewish families, was deeply attached to the Old Testament and had complete faith in it. Unlike most other Jewish communities, which lead their everyday lives in accordance with Talmudic and rabbinical laws, the Ethiopian community still views the Bible as their chief guide. Another consideration was that stories and fables had traditionally been a common way of transmitting knowledge and wisdom in this community.

One story Haiim read with the family was the story of Sodom and Gomorah (Genesis 18). In this story, the Lord told Abraham that He would destroy Sodom and Gomorah because the people there were wicked and sinful. Then Abraham said to the Lord: "Will you sweep away the righteous with the wicked?" As expected, the family interpreted this story as a message that they should not blame the whole of Israeli society for the bad attitude of some of its members. Then Haiim read with the family some verses from the book of the prophet Isaiah, for example: "Oh, sinful nation, people loaded with guilt, a brood of evildoers, children given to corruption. . . . Hear the word of the Lord, you rulers of Sodom, listen to the law of our God, you people of Gomorah! [Sodom and Gomorah are used in these verse as symbols of evil-doing—S.A.]. Stop bringing meaningless offerings! . . . When you spread out your hands in prayers, I will not listen, your hands are full of blood! . . . Stop doing wrong, learn to do right, seek justice, encourage the oppressed, defend the cause of the fatherless, plead the case of the widow!" Through these verses, the family was helped to see that false religious ceremonies and corruption existed in Israeli society in biblical times, too. Their disappointment was turned into identification with Isaiah's sermon, calling for social justice and the return to true religion. Isaiah's courage and integrity were adopted by them as a model to be identified with and followed.

Situations Where Restoring Simplicity Can Cause Distress

Many therapeutic techniques are designed to reduce distress in the clients. For example, evicting low-income families from inadequate houses and providing them with better housing, as well as instructing them in the appropriate use of available public resources and services, are designed to improve their quality of life and reduce their distress. Structural family therapeutic interventions that aim at turning a rigid, authoritarian family structure into a flexible, democratic one are geared toward improving its functioning, thereby reducing the distress experienced by the family members. However, such moves are apt to cause more distress in families of certain cultures. If this is the case, the therapist should refrain from using these techniques or modify them to suit the family's culture. Modifications must predict and prevent any distressful consequences likely to be produced by the application of the technique at hand.

Let me illustrate this with another Ethiopian example: (see Case 13).

Case 34: The case of Boaz, the homeless Ethiopian Jewish immigrant, was described in chapter 4. The social workers in charge of Boaz's case, before it was transferred to Shosh, attempted to rehabilitate him by providing him with a low-cost one-room apartment, arranging a simple job for him, and applying techniques of the kind listed above under *instructing*, for example, informing him about various social services and guiding him in proper ways of dealing with them, offering him a vocational training course. Although Boaz seemed to be grateful and cooperative, he, in fact, systematically sabotaged all attempts to help him. Soon after he had moved into the apartment given to him, he disappeared and was found living on the street again. He made appointments with some social agencies he was referred to but failed to show up.

This case was discussed in SW. The hypothesis was put forward that Boaz undermined all attempts to rehabilitate him because these attempts, while easing the distress caused to him by his homelessness, brought on him even greater distress. Boaz brought his miserable condition upon himself in order to punish himself for what in his own subjective mind was his betrayal of his father and his family. Other people of his community would have committed suicide if they felt guilty of such sins. Boaz's choice was to remain alive but to lead a life that resembled death. Cooperating with the attempts to rehabilitate him would reawaken in him intolerable guilt feelings.

The participants in the discussion came up with the idea to resume the efforts to rehabilitate Boaz, but to modify the intervention techniques in ways that would take into account Boaz's need to punish himself and atone for his sins. Some of the ideas proposed included: Establishing a memorial place for the Ethiopian immigrants who died on their way to Israel, which could also serve as a charity and aid center for their living relatives. Boaz could live in that place and work there as a caretaker.

Boaz's rehabilitation program will be reframed as punishment for his sins. He will be obliged to cooperate, because he is not entitled to enjoy the privilege of getting away with what he had done by choosing the easy penalty of being a homeless person. He should lead a normal life and carry his guilt inside him. He will be required to atone for his sins in a different way: By devoting his life to helping the living members of his family and community. He should learn some vocation that will enable him to take this course, for example, become a teacher, a nurse or a religious leader.

Unfortunately, we were unable to find out whether any of these ideas actually worked, because, soon after this discussion, Boaz broke off all contacts with social services and left the town.

Situations Where the System Has Become Fixated, Regressed, or Has Been Functioning Randomly

When the family system is flooded with new, confusing or stressful information, it is unable to restore its simplicity. It can respond by fixating itself to its current state, by regressing to a previous state or by attempting to restore simplicity in a random, disorganized manner (forgoing consistency).

Some existing therapeutic techniques flood the family system with new or confusing information. Other techniques induce crisis on purpose. For example, certain training and guidance programs for immigrant families can overwhelm them with unfamiliar information. Some narrative techniques attempt to introduce many changes into the family's subjective construction of reality. Gestalt therapy and symbolic-experiential therapy include forceful shock and crisis-inducing techniques. Again, with families that are already flooded with stressful and unfamiliar information the therapist should either avoid using such techniques or modify them appropriately.

Modifications must reduce the amount of unfamiliar information conveyed by the technique at hand and remove any sources of confusion or stress induction from it. Case 3 (Chapter 3) tells the story of a family of immigrants from a North African Muslim country to France. The husband accused his wife of being "a whore" for wearing modern clothes and working out of the home. Although this man encouraged his wife to work, and although he knew that most French women wore modern clothes, he could not develop new programs or change his previous ones. He became fixated on his previous programs concerning attitudes toward women and many other areas of life. This was due to the cultural shock he had gone through. Life in France was different in many respects from life in his home country and was very different from his expectations. He found himself in many humiliating situations: unemployment, loss of social status, alienation, and the like. The dysfunctional strategy used by the system in this case was foregoing completeness and parsimony. The information-processing system was exposed to too much new and distressing information to fully restore simplicity.

This couple was referred to therapy in a local social service agency. The husband was told that beating his wife was illegal and that he could be charged for this offense. Then, couple therapy was attempted, applying behavioristic techniques for improving marital communication of the kinds proposed in Holzworth-Munroe and Jacobson (1991) and Falloon (1991), for example, doing a cost-benefit analysis of positive versus negative exchanges, communication-skills training and conflict-resolution training. However, the accusations and beatings did not stop. The failure of the therapeutic intervention can be explained as follows: The choice of techniques failed to take into consideration the husband's fixation due to cultural shock. The warning issued to him, though justified, only intensified his confusion and worsened the shock. The therapeutic techniques were alien to the couple's culturally prescribed programs. Therefore their employment overloaded the couple's already-overburdened information-processing system. The therapeutic strategy should have included measures for softening this couple's, especially the husband's, cultural shock. Behavioristic techniques for improving marital communications could be used, but they should be modified to suit the couple's cultural programs.

Traditional Muslim family law can be interpreted (if necessary, by a *kadi* [a Muslim judge] whose authority is accepted by both husband and wife) in a manner designed to reduce the husband and wife's confusion. According to Muslim law, a husband may prevent his wife from taking a job, but may not compel her to work (see Hodkinson, 1984; Pearl, 1987). The therapist or the *kadi* can explain to the husband that he could have prevented his wife from working outside of the home, but he chose to let her or even compelled her to do it. She did not violate Muslim law. He did. Therefore she is not a *nashuz* (a rebel), and he has no right to reprimand or beat her. A cost-benefit analysis of positive exchanges should take into account traditional Muslim concepts of marital rights and duties. It can be explained to the wife that, if she provokes her husband she will be declared a *nashuz*, disqualifying her from spousal support and bringing shame upon her own family. The husband can be told that, if he wants to control his wife and guide her in the right way, he should encourage her to continue working and to dress and behave like a French woman when she is at work. Having a diligent wife who is treated with respect by the French will increase his own power and status and bring him honor.

Situations Where Cultural Naiveté Prevents Approximation of Target Programs

As was said earlier, many therapeutic techniques presuppose a knowledge base that is shared by therapist and clients. When the common knowledge base is meager, the application of certain techniques can inadvertently cause the introduction of bugs attesting to cultural naiveté into the client's system. When deciding to employ a certain technique, the therapist should make sure the clients are not ignorant of some explicit or implicit key elements connoted in the technique, which might lead to the production of culturally naive bugs. If such elements are found, they should be either removed or explained to the clients.

Case 35: A Chinese American family was referred to therapy, with the presenting complaint of acute chest pains in the father. The symptoms set on after the father was fired from his job as an accountant in a paper factory. The therapist, whose orientation was eclectic but strongly influenced by both psychoanalysis and Gestalt, encouraged the family members, especially the father, to let out their feelings and emotions and "stay with them." This intervention was chosen because the therapist diagnosed the pains as resulting from repressed, inwardly directed feelings of shame for the failure, loss of face and social status and fear for the future. Although this diagnosis was accurate, the family disengaged themselves from the therapy after the first session. The therapist called the father and spoke with him over the phone. The father dismissed it with some polite, but vague, excuses.

What the therapist was not aware of was that his intervention reinforced, rather than reduced, the very emotions that produced the symptoms. This family's information-processing programs included the code that exposing emotions such as those noted was a disgraceful, socially unacceptable indulgence in one's own private self. The therapist's moves were viewed almost like an encouragement to indulge in obscenity. The intervention introduced a culturally naive bug into the therapeutic communication. This bug could not be identified and removed, because another program espoused by the family qualified discussing such offenses with the offender as an unacceptable form of behavior (see Lee, 1982; Lawson and Thompson, 1995).

The Special Nature of the Therapeutic Alliance

In choosing and adapting techniques, the therapist should take into account the special nature of the therapeutic alliance in culturally competent family therapy, as discussed in chapter 11. Relevant considerations are:

Differences in Culturally Determined Conceptions of Therapy

The choice of techniques should suit the family's conception of therapy. If techniques based on insight must be resorted to with a family that conceives of therapy as magic, the techniques should be modified in such a way–that the insight comes to the family through magic-like means. This is exactly what happens in some of the "exotic" healing techniques detailed earlier. Techniques involving communication with the supernatural should not be used with clients who view therapy as rational problem solving.

Suspected Bugs in the Therapeutic Communication

If the therapist encounters excessive resistance, lack of cooperation or other signs of dissatisfaction on the part of the family, he should explore the possibility that his choice of techniques has inadvertently introduced bugs into the therapeutic communication. An example is the bugged communication with the Chinese family described in Case 35. If the family does not cooperate with the therapist in his attempts to identify bugs, the therapist can attempt to communicate with the family through an intermediary (see below).

Possible Limitations on Information Exchange

In choosing a technique, the therapist should be aware of the possibility that the family withholds crucial information or gives misleading information. Suppose, for instance, that the therapist wants to use techniques taken from Boszormenyi-Nagy's therapy. In this form of therapy family members are led by the therapist to talk about their relational commitments and balances of fairness. The application of these techniques is apt to lead to more unfairness if the family withholds information or lies about abuse or injustice perpetrated against certain family members. It should be recalled that, in such cases, the victims often cooperate in keeping what had been done to them secret.

If the therapist suspects the information given to her by the family, she should avoid using techniques that are based on the availability of reliable information. Other possibilities are double-checking the information given, or raising the problem of limitations on information exchange with the family itself or with an intermediary.

Private and Institutional Prejudices and Misconceptions with Respect to the Other Side

Techniques that require a high degree of mutual trust cannot be applied successfully in a situation infested with mutual prejudices and misconceptions among the family, the therapist and the social setting in which the therapy is conducted. In such situations, the therapist should choose techniques that are not based on mutual trust, for example, directing the family to use its own traditional problem-solving techniques.

The list of principles for achieving good alliance offered in chapter 11 should also guide the choice and adaptation of techniques. When the therapist selects a particular technique, he is advised to go through this list, examine the technique with respect to all these principles and then decide to go ahead, applying the technique, discarding it or modifying it in accordance with these principles. This can be illustrated with Case 35 of the Chinese American family. Before the therapist applied the technique of encouraging the family members to let out their emotions and "stay with them," he should have asked considered the following:

Question: What is there in my own culture that makes the application of this technique acceptable and effective? (Principle: Know your own culture).

Answer: In my own culture, people distinguish between a person's behavior and his or her inner world of thoughts and feelings. We consider thoughts and emotions, different, distinct entities. We believe that when emotions are pent up inside a person this causes him or her suffering. We believe that a person's emotions affect his or her physical condition. We view ourselves as distinct, interacting, individual entities. We think it advisable to open up and share emotions.

Question: Considering this family's culture, will the application of this technique be as acceptable and effective as in my own culture?

Answer: I don't know. (Admit ignorance; avoid an ethnocentric attitude; adopt the truly humble position of a learner.)

At this point, the therapist should have refrained from applying these techniques until he learned more about the family's culture, achieved an insider status and created a common cultural ground with it. Afterward, he should have replaced or modified the techniques to suit the family's own modes of communication, norms, values and customs. The techniques to be used should have built on the family's strengths and enlisted its own support system. The therapist could begin by showing interest in culture-free human concerns, being empathetic and sharing his own self and life with the family. He could have told them, for instance, about an uncle who developed similar symptoms after he was fired from his job. The uncle showed self-control and tenacity. He continued leading the family and giving good counsel. The whole family showed solidarity and supported each other through the difficult times. The uncle decided to establish his own business. With his skill, diligence and the support of the family, he soon became very successful and prosperous.

SUMMARY

This chapter is devoted to the actual practice of culturally competent family therapy, that is, the planning and execution of each particular therapeutic move. The term *strategy* refers to the overall therapeutic plan. A good strategy is an effective and economical approach to the problems posed by the case in hand. The strategy identifies the information-processing bugs underlying the presenting complaints, specifies mechanisms and means for removing or weakening these bugs and sets an order of priorities among the therapeutic moves.

The term *tactic* refers to the plan for a particular culturally competent family therapeutic intervention. A tactic is a particular stage in the overall therapeutic strategy. It may be viewed as a ministrategy. In each tactic specific therapeutic *techniques* are employed. Each technique is designed to effect a *mutation*: a small change.

The choice of specific techniques is directed by the following questions: What is the *entity* to be changed? What is the desired *mutation* in this entity?

What are the activated *mechanisms of change*? By what *means* will the mechanism of change be activated?

Techniques can be designed by the therapist. However, culturally competent family therapy makes a systematically eclectic use of ready-made techniques borrowed from various schools of family therapy and other genres of psychotherapy. Another major source is traditional healing and problem-solving methods existing in various cultures. The techniques' design and their manner of application are adapted to the special needs of culturally sensitive therapy. "Adapting," in this context, means taking into account the culturally coded family programs, the culturally determined dysfunctional attempts to restore simplicity, the ensuing bugs and the special nature of the intercultural therapeutic alliance.

A typology of existing techniques is proposed. The techniques are classified according to the means of change and subclassified according to the entities to be changed and the change mechanisms.

13

The Therapeutic Process

STAGES IN CULTURALLY COMPETENT FAMILY THERAPY

First Contact

The first contact between therapist and family in this form of therapy is often different from the first contact in ordinary therapy. Disadvantaged minorities are overrepresented in culturally competent family therapy. In many cases, the family is compelled to go to therapy by court order, administrative pressure or the like. Frequently, the therapist will have to reach out to the family, going to look for the family at home or on the street. In many cases there will be little common ground between the therapist and the family. The family's conception of what therapy is about, their understanding of the nature of their relationship and their expectations will be radically different. Often, the family and the therapist will not understand each other's language. All the problems and difficulties discussed in chapters 6 and 11 are likely to appear from the very first moment. The therapist cannot avoid acting immediately and according to all the principles listed there.

Intake and Assessment

After an initial understanding has been reached between the therapist and the family, the therapist begins the intake process, which includes naturalistic observations in various settings, a presenting-problems interview and a case-history interview. As emphasized in chapter 9, in this form of therapy the observations and the interviews should not be conducted in a standardized, formal manner. The timing, location, setting, techniques of execution and therapist's verbal and nonverbal behavior should be chosen with great sensitivity and flexibility, with all the principles governing the nature of the therapeutic alliance in culturally competent family therapy kept in mind.

The observation and interview protocols will be analyzed according to the guidelines presented and discussed in chapter 10. The result of the analysis is an overall idiographic theory of the case, including its history, the current system of culturally relevant family information-processing programs, bugs in these programs and systematic explanations for the presenting problems.

Planning a Strategy

An overall strategy, or a number of alternative strategies for the whole therapy, will now be designed on the basis of the general diagnostic assessment. Guidelines for constructing a strategy are presented in chapter 12.

Therapeutic Contract

At this stage, the therapist shares with the family some central elements of the strategy and attempts to reach an agreement with them to proceed with the therapy according to this strategy. If the family objects to some components of the strategy, the therapist is advised to replace or modify these components. In culturally competent family therapy it is often not enough to reach a therapeutic contract with the family alone. Some key figures or social bodies in the community—religious leaders, elders, school authorities, social agencies and other bodies should be involved and agree to cooperate too.

Carrying out the Strategy

Therapy will proceed roughly according to the strategy. Tactics for particular interventions will be planned ahead of time. Techniques will be created, chosen and, if necessary, modified according to the considerations discussed in chapter 12. The key words in culturally competent family therapy are sensitivity and flexibility. The therapist should continuously monitor the therapeutic process and watch for any sign of dissatisfaction and lack of cooperation. She must be alert to any symptoms of negative side effects of her interventions. This is advisable in any form of therapy but is crucial in culturally competent family therapy because the therapist's skills and intuitions are underfunctioning.

Termination

The timing and procedure of termination in culturally competent family therapy should be suited to the family's culturally determined conception of therapy and of the nature of the therapeutic alliance.

CASE 36: ISTIKLAL

Let me illustrate the above stages through the following case description. This case was described and discussed intensively in the culturally competent family therapy course for social workers (SW), referred to many times in this text. The description below was recorded verbatim from Saleema, the social worker in charge of this case. The names of people and places have been changed, to disguise their identity.

Saleema: I would like to bring the case of Istiklal, thirty-two-year-old Muslim woman of my home town Madgd-El-Krum, four years divorced, with four children. The name Istiklal means in our language "independence." And indeed, Istiklal is an independent person, a rebel and an outcast in our society, as will become amply clear from her and her family's case history.

First Contact

Saleema: My first contact with Istiklal and her family had a dramatic and frightening nature. Istiklal and her nine brothers and sisters invaded the social services department, where I work, and made a commotion, yelling, kicking doors, smashing windows, throwing chairs against the wall and making loud threats. This was four years ago, shortly before the divorce. The scene was made as a reaction against a report written by Ikhlas, our Welfare Officer for Legal Affairs [a social worker with some law enforcement authority]. It was submitted to the *kadi* [traditional Muslim judge] of the *shar'i* [traditional Muslim religious] court, at his request. The report was ordained to help the *kadi* decide whether to accord Istiklal's husband full custody of the children, except for the baby, after the divorce takes effect.

In the report, Ikhlas questioned Istiklal's competence as a parent. She claimed that Istiklal and her family were breaking social norms and setting a bad example for the children. She wrote that all the women in Istiklal's family used to break norms. Istiklal's husband Ali would make a better father to the children. He does not break social and religious norms. He has a house and other assets. He loves the children.

What upset Istiklal and mobilized her brothers and sisters was not the very fact that Ikhlas recommended denying Istiklal custody of the children and property rights, but what they considered a slanderous attack on their family, besmirching its honor. After this event, our department head asked me to take the case. I was considered a "modern Muslim" who understands both sides. The purpose of the referral was to reevaluate the decision to transfer full custody of the children to their father and to help Istiklal and her children establish good relationships with each other.

Intake and Assessment

Saleema continued: I had entered into this case before I participated in this course. Therefore I had not conducted the intake procedure according to the guidelines and the methods I learned here. However, I collected a great deal of information informally, from all the people involved in the case.

History of the Family

Istiklal comes from a family of eight sisters and two brothers. She is the fourth-born. Her mother used to break norms. She was one of the first women in town who got a driving license. Her daughters followed her lead. All of them departed from the traditional Muslim way of life in one way or another.

Both Istiklal's mother and her father are of a lower social class. They have never owned land of their own. Uneducated, too; illiterate. However, her mother is an intelligent woman. Istiklal's father comes from a weak, quiet family. He works as a garbage collector. Istiklal was married off by her family. Her mother and her husband's mother arranged the marriage.

Istiklal was very pretty. Her husband's mother wanted a beautiful, fair, blue-eyed wife for him. Many wanted her and asked for her. She was not very good at school, though. She was married when she was sixteen. Her husband Ali was thirteen years her senior. He is the first-born in his family. His background is not higher than hers. He also had a dominant mother who ruled in her home.

Istiklal's husband, Ali, managed to raise his economic status higher. He purchased a bus and established a transportation business, which was based outside of Madgd-El-Krum, in the neighboring Jewish town of Karmiel. Most of his customers were Jewish. He earned enough money to purchase a house, furniture and everything needed for a household. Istiklal's mother had wanted to secure her daughter's economic status. This was why she agreed to give her daughter to this man, Ali.

Istiklal became pregnant soon after the marriage, giving birth to a son, Taher, now sixteen years old. Ali liked going out, seeing people, having a good time in the big city. He showed his young, pretty wife the good, sparkling life of the Jewish Israeli city. On the other hand, he forbade her to work, study or meet people outside of the home. He wanted children, many children—a new child every one or two years. Istiklal did not want all these pregnancies and home duties. Ali discovered that she was using contraceptives, so they started fighting. Following each such fight, Istiklal would run away to her mother. Her mother would talk with Ali's mother. This only aggravated the situation, and conflict developed between the mothers. The other family members soon got involved. It was now a struggle between two *hamulas*, extended families. Still, Istiklal kept getting pregnant and giving birth to children: Waleed, now fourteen, Yasmeen, now thirteen, and Faisal, now five years old.

Istiklal did not demonstrate respect to her mother-in-law and did not visit her. The norm in our society is that the bride either moves with her husband to her mother-in-law's house or at least visits her regularly and helps her with house duties. Istiklal had never done this.

Istiklal began to wear modern clothes. When Ali was at work, she used to go out without letting him know or asking for his permission. She would leave the children with a neighbor, asking her not to tell anybody. When Ali found out he shouted and threatened her. Maybe he even beat her up. I'm not sure. Istiklal left their home a number of times and went back to her mother's home. The latter would persuade her to go back home, until the next time. Once, Ali went to a *shar'i* court and complained that his wife was rebellious. The kadi issued a *Ta'a* (a decree of discipline), which demanded of Istiklal to go back home and obey her husband.

After almost thirteen years of marriage, Ali divorced Istiklal. There was a rumor that she was dating a young man. Ali drove her out of the home. She went to her parents. By Muslim law, a husband has a right to expel his wife if she has committed adultery. The *shar'i* court confirmed the divorce and gave Ali full custody of the children, except the baby boy, Faisal, who had just been born. It is a norm in this society that, if a woman leaves home, she does not take the children with her, unless they are very young. The court also accorded Ali all the rights over the house and the family's property. By *shari'ah* law, a divorced wife does not have any rights over her husband's property, because he either brought the property with him to the marriage or earned it after the marriage. In our community, men never marry unless they already have a house with all the furniture and everything else ready.

I took the case shortly after the divorce. After the divorce, Ali's mother took the children to her home. When I spoke with her, I learned that she had objected to the divorce. She told me, crying, how she felt when her father married a second woman. She will never forget it. Although Istiklal did not treat her well, she did not want her son to divorce her.

Shortly after the divorce, Istiklal began to fight for the custody of the children. She came to realize that she had gotten the worst part of the deal. She was blamed twice—for being a bad mother and for giving up her children. She wanted the children, but the children did not want to have anything to do with her. Her second son, Waleed, told her: You are not my mother. My older brother Taher, he brought me up. We explained to her that her chances of winning her case in a *shar'i* court were dim, and she gave up.

After the divorce, Istiklal went to Haifa to study hairdressing. Then, she took a job as a hairdresser in Karmiel. The hairdressing shop she works in serves both women and men. In our town, women do women's hair and men get their haircut in men's barber shops. Istiklal changed her hairstyle and began to wear short, tight skirts and blouses with an open neck line, like young Jewish women. For her family and the general social milieu in our town this looked extremely cheap and provocative. There have been rumors that she has been seen with both married and unmarried men. She also got a driving license.

Last year, Istiklal got engaged to a young man, Fahed, twelve years her junior. His parents objected to the union. They drove him out of their home. They denied him his rights over the house and property. He lived in Istiklal's parents home. They are now married. A feud developed between his extended family and Istiklal's. Last month there was big a brawl, with sticks and knives. Some gunshots were heard too. The police intervened. Some had to be taken to the hospital.

Last year, Ali, Istiklal's ex-husband, married Fareeda. His new wife was of the same age as Istiklal and belonged to his own extended family. Fareeda is the opposite of Istiklal in outward appearance. She is plain. She wears traditional, modest clothes and is a good housewife, conservative in her views and behavior, but a bitter, aggressive, impulsive person; single until a relatively advanced age. She lived with her parents.

After the marriage, Istiklal called Ali's home and congratulated the couple on the marriage, wishing them good luck. This is not customary in our society. The divorced wife is not supposed to have any contact whatsoever with her ex-husband. Fareeda, Ali's new wife, interpreted this phone call as an expression of jealousy, with a disruptive intention. She got very upset and angry.

Shortly after Ali's marriage, Istiklal herself married her fiancee. This was a fancy wedding in a luxurious hall. Istiklal's family invited the police and an ambulance was on standby. Her groom's family had threatened to attack him during the wedding and break it up. However, the wedding was concluded peacefully. They now live in their own apartment, away from her parents and near the children's school. At this point Istiklal demanded to see her children again. Occasionally, she would visit her daughter Yasmeen at school. Istiklal's little son, Faisal, now five years old, remained in Istiklal's mother's home. He has no contact whatsoever with his father or siblings.

Treatment History

I'll tell you what I've done with this family up to now. I would like to reevaluate the whole case, including the treatment so far, and, with your help, develop a more effective strategy.

After this case was transferred to me, shortly after Ali divorced Istiklal, we held a team discussion. We decided to hold a meeting with Istiklal and her children in my office every week, in my presence. Already in the first meeting, it became obvious that the rift between Istiklal and her children was unbridgeable. Taher, her eldest son, then ten years old, said: "How am I going to spend time with this woman, when she dyes and blows her hair, wears tight skirts, with a cigarette packet stuck in her pocket? This is not what I call a mother."

After two such meetings, the children refused to come. Ali, their father, and his family did not want the children, especially the girl, to be close to Istiklal and come under her influence.

I tried to persuade Istiklal to adopt a more flexible attitude toward our community in general and toward the children, Ali and his parents in particular. I tried to make her aware of her errors of judgment and of the destructive elements in her behavior. However, she was very rigid. After the divorce, she kept calling her ex-husband and talking about the children. When I pointed out the unacceptability of this behavior, she was not willing to understand. She said: "So what? Jewish women do this and that."

Since I saw that my intervention was leading nowhere, I stopped the treatment and did not have any contact with this family until after Ali's and Istiklal's second marriages. From time to time, Istiklal would visit her daughter in school. At that time, Istiklal came to me and asked me to use my influence on Ali and his family and have them let the children have regular contact with her. At the same time, Ali and his wife came to me with the opposite purpose. Ali complained that, since Istiklal had come back into the picture, his daughter had become nervous, restless and disobedient. His wife said that, since then, she has begun to ask embarrassing questions, such as: "Why do you sleep in my father's bed?" I told her to shut up and mind her own business. Her so-called "mother" gets ideas into her head.

One day, the school counselor called and asked me to tell Istiklal to stop visiting her daughter at the school. She said these visits were disruptive. Once, Ali's wife went to see the teacher and saw Istiklal with her daughter in the school yard. The two women started a loud, violent row in front of the pupils.

I have to admit, I have failed in my efforts to mediate among all these warring parties. All of them lost faith in me and left the treatment. Istiklal thought I was judging and criticizing her. She could not understand my efforts to help her become more flexible. Ali and his wife believed I had incited Istiklal to undermine their and the school's authority. The school had the same impression. On the other side, my department head pressures me to continue the treatment. I am at a loss for what to do with this case.

Diagnostic Evaluation

At this point, the students were asked to propose a diagnostic evaluation of the case, based on the data provided by Saleema, however incomplete.

They were instructed to attempt to formulate their idiographic theory of the case in the language of the model they had learned in the course. They were not however required to use all the formalisms and technical details of this language, just to apply the main concepts and terms. Below is the summary of the main ideas expressed in the conjoint discussion.

Unlike the modern urban Jewish society of Israel, the Israeli Arab society is highly stratified. Social class, based on the owning of inherited land by extended families, plays a central role in the lives of people and in their psychology. This society, however, has been going through a period of rapid transition. The lower classes are upwardly mobile. Many people attempt to reach a position of social advantage by doing business and making money or by getting formal education. The influence of the modern, capitalistic, achievement-oriented Jewish society is seen everywhere.

The proximity and control goals of the various members of the family described in this case have been derivatives of these characteristics of their society. Istiklal and her first husband, Ali, belonged to a low social class. Istiklal's father's goal was to remain a part of his low social class. He made do with a humble job: a garbage collector. He himself was uneducated and never attempted to give his children more than minimal education. Istiklal's mother on the other hand had different goals. She wanted personal freedom and higher socioeconomic status. However, her ability to reach these goals was limited by social and economical constraints. She could not actually reach her goals. She could only display some small tokens of freedom and independence, such as receiving a driving license. What she was able to achieve was partly to reach her goals through her children, particularly her daughters. She could not provide them with more than a minimum of formal education, but she brought them up to be open-minded, rebellious and stubborn. She could endow them with higher socioeconomic status by having them marry up, if not to high-class men, at least to rich men.

Ali, Istiklal's first husband, also came from a humble social class. However, he was a diligent man who established his own successful transportation business. Istiklal's mother used Istiklal's beauty as a bargaining chip for getting a higher socioeconomic status.

Ali's family also belonged to a low social class. They seem to be more traditionally minded than Istiklal's mother. One would say their goals have been to raise their socioeconomic status but remain an integral part of traditional Muslim society. Ali was the first-born son. His mother wanted a beautiful young wife for him, apparently a status symbol: The first-born deserves the best, and he needs a wife who can serve as a sparkling showcase.

Istiklal and Ali entered the marriage with different sets of values and expectations. Istiklal's internal programs, adopted from her mother's verbalized fantasies, included values such as hedonism, having the good life, personal freedom and independence. Maybe she believed her mother had chosen for her a liberal, "modern" man. Ali also liked having a good time, enjoying night life in the Jewish city. However, in every other respect he adhered to the traditional Muslim code concerning marriage and family life.

In the terms of the model learned in SW, some of Ali and Istiklal's programs were dysfunctional, bugged. Ali expected Istiklal to behave like a Jewish girl in dance clubs in Haifa and like a traditional Muslim woman at home. Istiklal expected Ali to treat her like an equal partner. Both of them wore *blinders*. Both failed to see the complete picture. Istiklal did not take into account her mother's real purposes in marrying her off to Ali, Ali's values and the expectations of the social environment. Ali on his side was not aware of Istiklal's expectations. Another bug was *cultural naiveté*. Due to a misinterpretation of some superficial features of the other person's behavior, each partner blindly attributed to the other programs that were taken from his or her own rather than the other's repertoire.

All the people involved in this case, to various degrees, had been massively exposed to the influence of the modern urban Jewish society that surrounds them. This influence, however, has not been evenly distributed. For most modern secular Israelis, the owning of land does not make a social difference. A woman can wear provocative clothes at a party and still be faithful and modest as a wife. Most husbands and wives consider themselves equal partners and respect each other as free, independent individuals. For the people in Madgd-El-Krum, however, some of these values and modes of behavior seem confusing and self-contradictory. In our terms, this cultural information-processing system lost its simplicity without being able to restore it. This family did not know what to take of the Israeli way of life and what not to take, and how to interpret and react to what the other person had taken. Istiklal gave up *completeness* and took just the hedonistic, irresponsible parts. Ali gave up *consistency* and tried to live in two worlds at the same time. Everybody expected the other people to understand or accept his or her choice. Nobody could understand or tolerate the other party's choice.

As the marriage proceeded, the bugs in Istiklal's and Ali's programs were not removed or weakened. Quite the contrary. They had become chronic dysfunctional elements. Instead of getting close, Ali and Istiklal grew more and more apart. Their systems became polarized. Istiklal did the opposite of what was expected of her. Ali refused to compromise. For all we know, he used to beat her up, restrain her physically and force her to pregnancies.

Neither Istiklal nor Ali was successful in reaching their goals. When they could not take it any more they used the traditional channels for getting help and support. Each of them turned to their own immediate family, first of all the mothers, for help. Later other members of the nuclear and extended families were drawn in and eventually the court. Both became extremely stubborn and inflexible. This was due to the fact that both of them were flooded with bewildering and stress-inducing information, and they responded by rigidly fixating themselves on their premarriage programs. The metaprograms restoring simplicity by changing programs were paralyzed; could not work.

Istiklal's family and Ali's family began a feud, but in fact both families collaborated in attempting to keep the couple in a traditional Muslim marriage. Istiklal began to realize that her fate was going to be like her mother's fate. She expected her mother to protect her against such a future, but her mother did not. Ali realized that his young wife was not going to be the prize his mother promised him.

Maybe without all the pressures of the extended families and the court, Ali and Istiklal could have continued living unhappily ever after, had Istiklal not been suspected of having committed adultery. This was the ultimate offense against the honor of the man and the family. Divorce was the only choice left to Ali, to save what had remained of his honor.

After the divorce, Ali regressed. His marriage to Fareeda, a conservative Muslim woman, shows that he could not deal with the confusing information he was exposed to in his life with Istiklal. He chose to restore simplicity by regressing to a fully traditional way of life.

Istiklal, in her own way, regressed, too. She went to an ever-greater length in rebelling against everything her society stands for and mobilizing her whole family to go along with her. This may be called "regression," because it can be analyzed as taking her previous programs to a rigid extreme. She breached every taboo in the book. It was more foolhardiness than courage. It was regression to an oversimplified, rigid and restricted view of her environment and to inflexible, self-defeating modes of behavior. As a result she, her second husband and her immediate family became outcasts, hated and despised by the whole community in which they lived.

Istiklal's approach to her children reflected an inconsistent, random, disorganized attempt to restore simplicity. One day she could decide that she was going to give them up and forget about them, and the next day she would decide to fight for them to the bitter end.

Istiklal's children faced a major bug-inducing situation. They could not settle on a single interpretation of their mother's behavior. On the one hand, she was the good mother. On the other hand, she was a sinner, a bad woman, a whore. Any attempt to reconcile these two images would have caused them distress. All the boys restored simplicity by *restricting completeness*, putting *blinders* on, choosing one narrow interpretation that depicts Istiklal as unworthy of being a mother.

The girl, Yasmeen, maybe because she was a girl and younger, solved the confusion by forgoing *consistency*. She was ambivalent, fluctuating between getting closer to her mother and keeping her at a distance, accepting her as she is and letting herself be influenced by her and criticizing her.

Following this discussion, Saleema told the group: I tried to analyze what I had done in this case, and I think I understand which mistakes I had made and why I had failed in my efforts to help this family. I began the therapy without attempting to do an overall diagnostic evaluation and without planning a strategy. I tried to mediate between Istiklal and her children directly, without taking all the complexities of the situation into account. It was a mistake to ignore all the bodies involved with the children's life. Their cooperation should have been secured. It was necessary to remove or weaken the bugs in the system of each of the parties separately, before attempting to put them together in the same room. I did try to work with Istiklal separately, but, instead of addressing the emotional forces that kept her system bugged, I tried to use logic on her.

To this, Galeela commented: I think, also, that you were not sufficiently aware of how you yourself were perceived by all the people involved in the case. You are "a modern Muslim," and that is why your department head thought you were the right person to do the job. I also think you are the right person, but your image in the eyes of the polarized, hostile opponents can be different. For Istiklal and her family, you represented the social services that denied them rights over Istiklal's children and property and defiled the honor of their family. You are "modern" but still a member of the Muslim establishment, so you belong to the enemy. For the other side, Ali's side, the school and the court you are "modern" and "liberal." You do not respect tradition, and you challenge the authority of the traditional centers of power. Many of the factors that stand in the way of good therapeutic alliance, discussed in this course, are present in your case.

Saleema responded: You are right. It is not easy for me to admit that I am seen in this way, but I probably am.

Planning a Strategy

The group went on, attempting to construct a strategy, based on the above diagnostic evaluation.

Goals

Saleema was asked to define her therapeutic goals. She said: Officially, I was assigned by my department head to help Istiklal and her children resume normal relationships, although they are in their father's custody. What lies behind this insistence? Maybe a belief in the central importance of the biological mother in children's development, maybe guilt, maybe politics. I am not sure that most of my colleagues share his concern about Istiklal's parenthood. We learned in this course that different cultures qualify different states of affairs as "a problem."

It is easier for me to say what motivates me to continue investing in this case. I think this family, particularly the children, are victims of the rapid cultural transitions societies like ours have been going through in recent years. I have found ways of bridging over the unavoidable conflicts that come with progress. Therefore, I am at peace with myself and with the social world that surrounds me. I want to share this achievement with families I work with.

Target Bugs

In the diagnostic evaluation a number of bugs in the information-processing systems of the main heroes in this drama—Istiklal, her children and Ali—had been identified. One should not forget the other people involved. Istiklal is still *blinded* and culturally naive with respect to the children, Ali and his new wife and Israeli-Arab and Jewish societies. The male children are *blinded* with respect to Istiklal, and Yasmeen is *ambivalent* toward her. Ali, his new wife and almost everybody else are *blinded* with respect to Istiklal. In their eyes, she is the devil himself. The goal of therapy is to free these people of these bugs so that they can restore simplicity with respect to the other parties.

Priorities

The therapy should concentrate, first and foremost, on changing Istiklal's rigid programs. If she does not change her attitudes and behavior, nobody else will move in her direction, certainly not her children. Saleema is advised to try to reestablish contact with Istiklal and work with her individually and only then involve other people in the therapy. If the adults cooperate, the children will cooperate too.

Mechanisms and Means of Change

Here are the change mechanisms mentioned in chapter 12:

1. Adjusting the amount of unfamiliar information the system is exposed to, by introducing new input, removing available input, opening or closing input channels.
2. Helping the system interpret the information it is exposed to correctly and consistently, by adding, deleting or changing instructions and operations.
3. Reducing distress caused by change, by activating dormant ameliorative programs or creating homeostatic metaprograms.

Beginning with 1.—adjusting the amount of unfamiliar information—one can see two main sources of unfamiliar or confusing information that influence people's behavior in this case. One is the confusing influence of the Jewish sector, to which Istiklal is still exposed. Another is Istiklal's provocative behavior, to which Ali's new wife and the children are exposed. As to the influence of modern Jewish society, it is impossible to remove or close down input channels. What can be done is introduce new input that will help Istiklal form a fuller, more balanced picture of both Jewish and Muslim Arab society. This is 2.—interpreting the information. Ways should be found of persuading Istiklal to stop her provocations, so that the other side will not be exposed to this information.

These change mechanisms will be derived from the system's existing repertoire of programs. Saleema can achieve this, for instance, by explaining to Istiklal that being "modern," "liberal," etc., includes also being tolerant toward cultural differences and respectful toward people's beliefs and traditions. At the same time she can attempt to convince the other side that a less-defensive interpretation of Istiklal's behavior may be derived from Muslim traditions. As to 3.—activating dormant ameliorative programs or creating homeostatic metaprograms—all sides in this case can be assisted to derive constructive programs of action out of their current negative and destructive programs. For example, Saleema can persuade Istiklal to become a sociopolitical activist. She can start or join organizations that protect Muslim women's rights and help Muslim women in distress. Saleema can use herself as a model. She is a Muslim woman whose style of life is traditional and yet, as a social worker, she has introduced many social and political reforms in Madgd-El-Krum.

Saleema came up with an idea. She told the group about a day-care center for working women of low-income families she had established in a neighboring Arab town. She suggested asking Istiklal to volunteer giving the children a haircut every week. For the purpose of helping Istiklal get a more balanced view of Jewish society, it was suggested that Istiklal would meet with the participants of SW.

Carrying out the Strategy

Below are some highlights in the therapeutic process, as discussed by the participants.

First discussion. Saleema reported about her first success with Istiklal. Saleema called her at home. At first Istiklal sounded surprised. But when Saleema asked her to volunteer to do haircuts in the day-care center in the neighboring town Sakhnin, she mellowed down and became very curious. She agreed to meet at Saleema's home. She spoke willingly about herself. She said she was happy with her new husband. He was very considerate, understanding and liberal in his mind. But then she said she missed her children and began to cry. She expressed her resentment and bitterness over the rejection and hostility she and her husband had been suffering from everybody in the town except her own family of origin. Saleema just listened empathetically and did not say a word; did not try to preach to her or change her.

At this point, some members of the group commented that these moves were in line with some of the principles for establishing good therapeutic alliance they had learned: Share your own self and life with the family; be empathetic with the disadvantaged; think how to empower the family; look for its strengths; show interest in culture-free human concerns.

Saleema said: "I told Istiklal 'We are neighbors, and we know each other for a long time, and yet we don't know much about each other. I would like to tell you about my own background and would like to know more about yours. And then I told her about myself. My grandparents were *fallaheen*, peasants. They did not have land of their own, they were poor and uneducated and they worked hard. But, whatever they managed to save, they spent on their children's education. My father, their first-born, studied agronomy at the Hebrew University of Jerusalem. After he got his B.A. degree, he got a job in the Israeli Ministry of Agriculture. His Jewish colleagues liked him and used to invite us to family celebrations. Yet, my parents have always remained observant Muslims and led a traditional lifestyle. When I studied social work at Haifa University, I lived with a Jewish family who treated me like a daughter and I had many Jewish friends; knew many boys too, but I would never see them alone, because I was engaged to be married. When I got married, we built our home on top of my husband's parents' home, as customary. I lead a traditional Muslim life out of choice, although I am not ignorant of Jewish society and the modern world.'

"When Istiklal heard my story, she expressed her surprise and incomprehension of my being a Muslim out of free choice, despite my high status in both Jewish and Arab society. I realize that this was an important moment in our conversation, because she seemed to be open to influence and curious to learn the formula that would extricate her out of her entanglement. However, I myself felt at a loss. If I had the formula at all, I was totally unable to spell it out."

Reena said: "I think the key word is education. Both your father's family and your own family are highly educated. Your family's contact with the Jewish world has always been with the academic, political and social elites. Istiklal's family is uneducated. Their contacts with the Jewish world is with the lower social strata. This means that your vista is much longer and wider than hers and that you have more power and enjoy greater freedom of choice."

Saleema completed these ideas: "The bottom line is then a wider perspective, power and freedom of choice. I can help her gain a wider and deeper view of her reality and, in this way, achieve more power and greater freedom of choice. This will be in line with her own programs."

Second discussion. Saleema reported about her progress with Istiklal. She said: "I told Istiklal that I had chosen my way of life not despite my high status, but because of my high status. And contrariwise: This choice had given me power and status. And then I explained to her how my knowledge of both Jewish and Muslim cultures and my decision to take the best of both worlds give me a sense of identity, continuity and significance, power, status and freedom of choice. I invited her to join my world, learn more about it and share my secrets. I decided to attempt achieving these purposes by the following means: Continuing meeting with Istiklal individually and answering her queries; inviting Istiklal to a dinner with my family to learn about the way of life of a 'modern Muslim' family and starting a study and discussion group for women, entitled Being a Muslim Woman in the Modern World, which will meet regularly in my home.

"In one of the individual sessions, Istiklal complained about people being hostile to the way she dresses. I expressed my empathy but was afraid to go into this sensitive subject."

Some of the participants commented that in Jewish society dress and makeup are also a way of furthering one's interests. People change their outfit according to the occasion and their self-interests. At this point Saleema suggested to arrange a meeting between Istiklal and some of the participants, to talk about dress codes. I concluded this discussion by saying: "Through the central concepts of power, status and freedom of choice, which seem to be her core values and her goals with respect to the environment, you are going to remove the *blinders* from her eyes and gain a more complete and balanced picture of the world she lives in."

Third discussion. Reena began the discussion by telling the group: "I'm sure you are curious to hear about our meeting with Istiklal. There were three of us: Saleema, Orly and myself. It was fun. We turned it into a fancy-dress party. We role-played various kinds of situations in which one needs to wear different kinds of 'uniforms' to further one's own interests. We kept changing clothes and makeup. I played as if I were doing a home visit with an Orthodox Jewish family. I made myself look like I was one of these people, to show them my respect. I said this was a way of becoming accepted and gaining a position of power and influence. We explained to Istiklal that we don't always need to look attractive, because we have many other things to impress people with—our knowledge, our skill, our compassion. We played a game in which each of us, in her turn, wore unflattering clothes and made herself look as unattractive as possible. Then each of us had to find ways of impressing the other three, not with her physical appearance, but with her other assets."

Fourth discussion. Saleema started the meeting by reporting, all excited, that Istiklal was beginning to change. When she goes out she wears standard conservative clothes, like Saleema's. She sounds less bitter and defiant and seems to be more mellow and open to other people's point of view. There was a setback, however. Somebody from Madgd-El-Krum talked about her in Sakhnin, and then the director of the day-care center told Saleema that parents and other people in the community didn't want her there. When Istiklal heard about this, she became extremely upset and angry again. Saleema told her that one cannot erase one's public image in one day. She should work hard for it. However, she was fully cooperating in the therapy and was coming to the sessions regularly. She was also a very active and stimulating participant in Saleema's home discussion and study group. To make up for her loss in the day-care center, Saleema asked her if she wanted to help her, on a voluntary basis, in her social work with women and children in distress in Madgd-El-Krum, and she agreed.

Fifth discussion. Saleema said: "Istiklal helps me in my work with some women and children, and she does this with an admirable combination of enthusiasm and modesty. She provides some primary care for children who were neglected because their mothers are ill, or hospitalized or depressed, or unable to cope. She encourages such women by improving their physical appearance, by doing their hair and makeup. She never incites them to look or behave in an immodest way. The word has begun to spread in Madgd-El-Krum that Istiklal has been reformed. Some colleagues of mine have told me people have begun talk about her in positive terms. That is what I wanted to happen. I wanted Ali and Istiklal's children to hear about the changes she has gone through, before I intervene."

The other participants suggested that this was the right moment to involve Istiklal's husband in the therapy, because, if Saleema was going to reintroduce the children to the therapy, Istiklal would need his support and cooperation.

Sixth discussion. Saleema told about a session she had with Istiklal and her husband Fahed. He was very cooperative, but did not seem to have an opinion of his own. He admires Istiklal and—at least openly—agrees with everything she was saying or doing. Saleema suspected that he kept his thoughts to himself. This was usual in that community. People were not always open, especially not a man with a woman. When Saleema suggested to attempt reconnecting Istiklal with her children, he said he would go along with what Istiklal wanted. If she thought it would do her and the children good, he would be the last one to object.

Participants suggested that Saleema would ask Ikhlas, the welfare officer who wrote the report against Istiklal, to suggest to Ali and his wife Fareeda the possibility of involving the children in the therapy again. They would listen to Ikhlas more than to Saleema. Saleema agreed that the time was ripe for such a move.

Seventh discussion. Saleema told the group that she had given Ikhlas a full report about the course of the therapy. Ikhlas was impressed. She agreed to speak with Ali, Fareeda and the school. Ali and the school headmaster agreed for the children to go back to therapy, but they asked not to arrange an early meeting with Istiklal. The stumbling block was Fareeda, who objected vehemently to any connection between the children and the social services department. Participants thought that both Fareeda's strict traditional codes and her feelings of being threatened by Istiklal should be taken into account. They observed that Fareeda did not feel secure in her role of surrogate mother to the children and was afraid of whatever authority she had being undermined.

It was decided to ask Ikhlas to meet Fareeda again and enlist her cooperation. Ikhlas would be advised to commend Fareeda for the good traditional education she gives the children and acknowledge her authority over them. Then she could ask her to describe the history of her relationships with them; an adaptation of narrative techniques. This will perhaps lead her to describing the problems and difficulties and spell out her own worries and ambivalent feelings. Such a conversation is likely to create a motivation in her to continue.

Eight discussion. Ikhlas spoke with Fareeda along the lines suggested in the latter discussion. Fareeda did mellow down, but when the idea of having the children meet Istiklal was mentioned, she became very agitated. She cursed Istiklal and said that she would destroy everything she, Fareeda, had built through years of persistent efforts. Ali, on the other hand, said he would not object to such meetings. He suggested, however, that the first meetings be with Yasmeen, his daughter, who is attached to Istiklal and misses her. He asked Ikhlas to be present at the meetings. Fareeda had no choice. She obeyed him grudgingly.

Saleema wanted to prepare both Istiklal and Yasmeen for their first meeting. She invited Yasmeen to a play-therapy session, with Ikhlas as an observer, as the issues involved were too sensitive to discuss directly with a thirteen-year-old girl. Saleema prepared dolls representing people and animals. Yasmeen played eagerly. She did not consider playing with dolls too childish for her age. Her game represented her relationships with Fareeda and Istiklal symbolically. Fareeda was represented as a woman who treats the girl figure harshly and orders her around. Istiklal was represented as an evasive person, who comes and suddenly disappears.

Saleema introduced new themes into the play, whose purpose was to change the image of the two women in Yasmeen's eyes. She made "Fareeda" speak to a male figure, saying that she is worried about the girl. She wants her to grow up and become a healthy person and a loved and respected member of her society. Because she is worried, she is sometimes hard on her and impatient, but this is not because she does not lover her or care for her. Then Saleema changed "Istiklal"'s clothes into more traditional ones, introduced her husband and little boy into the game and made her help people and speak nicely. She put into "Istiklal"'s mouth words that express her love of the little girl, her longing for her and her being concerned about her. At this point Yasmeen made the girl doll approach "Istiklal," hugged her and demonstrated her wish to become her friend. Apparently, the play session helped her develop a more consistent and benign view of both Istiklal and Fareeda. This reduced her loyalty conflict. Ikhlas videotaped this session and showed the tape to Istiklal. The latter was deeply moved by it. Saleema suggested that she join her, Ikhlas and Yasmeen for conjoined play sessions in the social services department and she agreed. It was suggested that the same tape be shown to Fareeda. Then she could be invited to meet Yasmeen and do a parallel doll-play session.

Ninth discussion. Saleema said: "Surprise! Fareeda agreed to do play-therapy sessions with Yasmeen! The doll-play session with Istiklal and Yasmeen went very well. There was no tension in the air and no accusations. They spoke through dolls, told each other about one another's lives and exchanged many expressions of affection.

"Encouraged by this success, I asked Ali to arrange a meeting between me and Istiklal's oldest son, sixteen-year-old Taher. My tactic with Taher was restorying his life history and helping him restore simplicity by acquiring a less-confusing picture of his current family situation and of his mother's personality and way of life. This tactic worked. I filled him in with information about his mother's family of origin and the circumstances of her marriage. I helped him place the history of his family in the wider context of the current sociopolitical situation of the Muslim Arab community in Israel. I also told him about the changes his mother has been going through. I told Istiklal about this conversation, and both of them were ready to meet. In the meeting, both of them were reserved and kept a distance from each other. The conversation was mainly polite. But this was just the first meeting.

"The doll-play meeting between Fareeda and Yasmeen was also good. They fought playfully through the dolls and kept giggling. This session helped release the tension between them. After this session, Fareeda was much less hostile and defensive. Her attitude toward me became one of friendly respect."

Tenth discussion: termination. Saleema began the meeting with a declaration: "I think we are ready for termination. Istiklal has become a normal "modern Muslim" married woman in Madgd-El-Krum. People gradually are forgetting her past. She is appreciated as a constructive person in the community. She meets her children regularly, once a week. They come to her home and enjoy an afternoon with their mother, her new husband and her brother. Istiklal is now pregnant. The children look forward to meet their new half sibling."

SUMMARY

This chapter is devoted to the therapeutic process and its stages: First contact, diagnostic assessment, designing a strategy, carrying out the therapy and termination. The stages are illustrated by a detailed description of the case of Istiklal and her family.

Epilogue

One of the stations in my life journey was the School of Oriental and African Studies of London University, where I taught anthropological linguistics for several years. In the basement of the old red-brick building was housed a most magnificent collection of ethnic African musical instruments, which had come into existence thanks to the life-long efforts of a man whose name I have forgotten, a Anglican priest and an indefatigable student of African music. I used to spend many enjoyable hours with him in that basement, listening to his stories and explanations.

One of the instruments that impressed me most was a xylophone made of rosewood. It was a very simple construction that could produce unusual resonating clicks. I decided that it would be easy enough for me to attempt to build such a xylophone for myself. But where would I get rosewood? No timber store in London stocked such wood. I looked feverishly through various directories until I came across the typically English title, The Royal Timber Society. The secretary directed me, in the King's English to a far-away dock on the banks of the River Thames, where redwood was to be found. I somehow managed to find the place. The man in charge Cockneyed to me that they had two leftover chips that I could purchase for a negligible price. He led me to two unimpressive, coarse and quite ugly logs, which he agreed to sell to me for fifty pounds each. I was shocked by the price, but it was too late to withdraw. I somehow carried the exceedingly heavy logs home and set myself to work. It should have been simple enough—cutting pieces of wood to shape and size and tying them together with a rope. The rosewood, however, did not think so. It refused to be cut at all. It defied saws, knives, hammers and even glazier's diamonds. I felt mounting frustration. The rosewood simply refused to become the xylophone I dreamt about.

Finally, I gave up the idea of making a xylophone out of these logs. Instead, I bought strings and made a kind of primitive harp, which, surprisingly enough, did produce some discernible sounds.

Writing this book has been a similar experience. Every line in it refused to be written in the way I intended and obstinately formulated itself into something different. At a certain point along the way, I gave up and let the book take the shape that it wanted to take. At least, I thought, it would teach me something new, something different from what I had led myself to believe I had already known and was ready to impart to the rest of humanity.

As I am writing these last lines of this book, I am asking myself. What have I learned from the process of having written it? In what ways has writing it been changing me? Again, the answers compel themselves upon me. They belong more to the realm of feelings and emotions than to the domain of knowledge or information. I have not become much richer in facts, figures or ideas. I have, however, been becoming growingly and sometimes painfully aware of the narrowness of my perspective, of my being a product of my own cultural traditions. I have been learning that people differ in many more dimensions than I had ever realized. I have been becoming increasingly more sharply aware of the fact that human psychopathology is a normal reaction to novelty. And I have been gradually becoming more and more tolerant, more and more patient, less and less judgmental in my encounters with other people.

Appendix: A Classified List of References

Below is a classified list of selected published books, chapters of books and articles in the field of culturally competent family therapy. It covers the years 1980 to 1998. The literature's search was aided by computerized data bases covering the fields of psychology, psychiatry, sociology and anthropology, linguistics and education. It tracked down nearly four hundred relevant items.

PROGRAMMATIC WORKS

Characteristically, works of this kind have the nature of a manifesto, persuading the readers of the importance of the new pursuit and sketching a rough plan for its further development. Most of these contributions start by expressing discontent at the omission of cultural relativity from current theories and methods of family therapy. They point out the ethnocentric nature of family therapy: "Research, theories and therapeutic techniques are consistently based on a monocultural, Eurocentric approach, which continually highlights American mainstream values" (Gardano, Davis and Jones, 1994). The argument is put forward, that both theory and techniques should be varied to accommodate the needs of families of various ethnic, religious and socioeconomic communities. Then the main categories of data that should be included in a culturally sensitive diagnostic family evaluation are listed. This is followed by attempts to identify the major culturally influenced sources of dysfunction. Finally, the principal considerations in designing and carrying out culturally sensitive interventions are specified.

Sources: McGoldrick, Pearce and Giordano, 1982; Schwartzman, 1982; Spiegel, 1982; McGill, 1983; London and Devore, 1988; Karrer, 1989; Ramondo, 1991; Anderson, 1992; Comas-Diaz, 1993; Gardano, Davis and Jones, 1994; Martinez, 1994; Kaslow, Celano and Dreelin, 1995; Fontes and Thomas, 1996; Pare, 1996; DiNicola, 1997; Gopaul-McNicol, 1997.

THEORETICAL WORKS

In works of this kind, concepts and propositions introduced in programmatic works above have been worked out and elaborated in some depth and detail. Here are succinct classified summaries of some prominent contributions in this category.

Defining Key Concepts

Studies of this kind attempt to grapple with the problem of how to define basic concepts such as family, culture, ethnicity, race, value systems or sociocultural change in the context of family therapy. The major lesson taught by these studies is to my mind that the meaning and range of application of none of these concepts is self-evident. The problem of how to define them has been worked at extensively by sociologists, anthropologists and social psychologists. The results of this work can and should be incorporated into models of culturally competent family therapy.

Sources: Barot, 1988; Ponterotto and Pedersen, 1993; Bradby, 1995; DiNicola, 1997; Gopaul-McNicol, 1997; Pedersen, 1997.

Culture as an Explanatory Construct

The idea of using culture as an explanatory construct in family systems theory and therapy is not at all self-evident, nor universally endorsed. Studies in this subclass discuss the pros and cons of incorporating culture into existing theories.

Sources: Montalvo and Gutierrez, 1983; DiNicola, 1986; Barot, 1988; Hodes, 1989; DiNicola, 1997; Gopaul-McNicol, 1997; Pedersen, 1997; Richeport-Haley, 1997; Waldegrave, 1998.

Functional and Dysfunctional Adaptation to Human and Nonhuman Ecological Pressures

Most of the studies in this category refer to the problems produced by the encounter between families of cultural minorities and various aspects of the dominant culture.

Sources: Sluzki, 1979; Serrano, 1985; Baptiste, 1987; Pinderhughes, 1987; Bemak, 1989; Chambon, 1989; Ganesan, Fine and Lin, 1989; Roijen, 1991; Turner, 1991; Guernina, 1992; Baptiste, 1993; Scandariato, 1993; DiNicola, 1997.

Intermarriage and Intergenerational Relations

The most interesting studies in this subcategory have attempted to identify conditions contributing toward the preservation of the family's cultural identify under circumstances conducive to horizontal (same generation) and vertical (intergenerational) acculturation gaps. Conditions identified have been shared family myths and family rituals and rites.

Sources: Spiegel, 1982; Bernal and Alvarez, 1983; Faulkner and Kich, 1983; Montalvo and Gutierrez, 1983; Andolfi and Angelo, 1985; Quinn, Newfield and Protinsky,

1985; Sebring, 1985; Waidron et al., 1986; Newfield et al., 1990; Zulueta, 1990; Fiese, 1992; Hines et al., 1992; Baptiste, 1993; Blount and Curry, 1993; Gushue, 1993; Martinez, 1994; DiNicola, 1998.

The Family's Structure

The most important achievement of studies of this subcategory is to my mind that of highlighting the cultural relativity of the notions of structural family therapy. Hodes, 1985 argues that concepts used by family therapists to describe family structures are ethnocentric. Fisek, 1991 reports the results of a cross-cultural examination of proximity and hierarchy as dimensions of family structure. The author concludes that proximity is a universal dimension but hierarchy is not. Wood, 1992 concurs with Fisek's suggestion for testing family models cross-culturally to see if they maintain their reliability and validity. Falicov and Brudner-White, 1983 claim that the same types of family triangles can be dysfunctional in some cultures and both normative and functional in others. This implies that family dysfunction is itself a culturally relative concept. A similar argument was put forward by Lappin, 1982 with respect to interpersonal distance in families.

Other sources: Bernal and Alvarez, 1983; Goldner, 1985; Flores and Sprenkle, 1988; Woehrer, 1988; Ford, 1992; Ravich, 1992.

The Family's World-view (Values, Beliefs and Meaning Systems)

There are two kinds of studies in this subcategory: Classification systems for describing the dimensional structure of the family's subjective world-view and ecological theories specifying the conditions for the emergence of specific types of values, beliefs and semantic structures in families.

A work of the first kind is Spiegel, 1982. In this work the following typology of families' value orientations is proposed:

Time (past, present, future)

Interpersonal activity (doing, being, being in becoming)

Relations with groups (individual, collateral, lineal)

Man-nature relations (harmony, mastery, subjugation)

Basic nature of man (neutral/mixed, good, evil)

Other sources: Aponte, 1985; Stein, 1985; Karrer, 1989; Newfield et al., 1990; and McGill, 1992.

Another group of studies that may be placed under this heading deals with linguistic relativity and the role of language in structuring the family's world-view.

Sources: Stein, 1985; McGill, 1987; Ibrahim and Schroeder, 1990; Newfield et al., 1990; Zulueta, 1990; Sciarra and Ponterotto, 1991.

A representative of the second kind, ecological studies, is Bernal and Alvarez, 1983.

Functioning and Lifestyle

An interesting group of works in this subcategory deals with family rituals, their structure and content and their functions in sustaining the family's identify and continuity.

Sources: Schwartzman, 1982; Bennett, Wolin and McAvity, 1988; Fiese, 1992.

METHODOLOGICAL WORKS

This category includes general principles for culturally competent family therapy as well as diagnostic and therapeutic methods and techniques.

Guiding Principles and Techniques for a Culturally Sensitive Family Diagnosis

One kind of study in this subcategory concentrates on those aspects of the family process that a culturally sensitive family diagnosis should focus on. The main question referred to is how the family, as a carrier of a particular cultural tradition, copes with new circumstances that are incongruent with this tradition. This question is a direct derivative of the theoretical discussions of this issue, summarized above.

Sources: Schwartzman, 1982; Falicov and Brudner-White, 1983; McGill, 1987; Roijen, 1991.

Another class of studies in this subcategory offers a variety of culturally sensitive diagnostic techniques, for example, genograms, folk stories, ethnographic interviews.

Sources: Newfield et al., 1990; Todd et al., 1990; Laureano and Poliandro, 1991; Mazurova and Rozin, 1991; McGill, 1992; Solomon, 1992; Lashley, 1993; Mailick and Vigilante, 1997.

Therapeutic Intervention Principles and Techniques

Principles

One kind of work in this subcategory offers general guiding principles for culturally competent interventions. These principles have to do with the following question: How does change take effect in culturally competent family therapy? Change mechanisms touched on are:

1. The healing power of fantasy, symbols, metaphors and rituals.
    Sources: Kobac and Waters, 1984; Ito, 1985; Colman, 1986; Jackson, 1988; Tafoya, 1989; Bright, 1990; Tomm, Suzuki and Suzuki, 1990; Roijen, 1991; Olson, 1993; DiNicola, 1997.

2. Empowerment means tapping the family's own resources for coping effectively with the stresses generated by acculturation or ecological pressures. Therapists are advised to watch against disempowering attitudes and practices such as disqualifying professional discourse, overprotection and institutional racism. Empowering therapeutic strategies mentioned are reinforcing the family's own support

systems, use of cultural knowledge and skills and tapping the family's cultural coping repertoire.

Sources: Ibrahim and Schroeder, 1990; Larner, 1990; Berg and Miller, 1992; McGill, 1992; MacKinnon, 1993; Martinez, 1994; Pedersen, 1997.

Principles also have to do with this question: How is the therapeutic alliance established and maintained in culturally competent family therapy?

1. For cultural compatibility between therapist and family, a number of studies demonstrate that cultural compatibility contributes to therapy effectiveness.

    Sources: Gwaltney, 1981; Flaskerud, 1986; Herrerias, 1988; Ibrahim and Schroeder, 1990; Lau, 1992; Guernina, 1993; Moro and Mazet, 1993.

2. Joining the family's culture is important: cultural incompatibility can be bridged over if the therapist learns the family's culture and joins it.

    Sources: Yahyaoui, 1988; Hodes, 1989; Tafoya, 1989; Ibrahim and Schroeder, 1990; Keitner et al., 1990; Newfield et al., 1990; Seedat and Nell, 1990; Todd et al., 1990; Berg and Miller, 1992; Pinsoff, 1992; Tamura and Lau, 1992; Watts-Jones, 1992; Tamasese and Waldegrave, 1996; McGoldrick, 1998.

3. The therapist should acknowledge differences. A number of writers urge therapists to openly discuss difficulties related to cross-cultural barriers with their client families. Therapists are advised to admit ignorance and preconceptions.

    Sources: Sykes, 1987; Tafoya, 1989; David and Erickson, 1990; Keitner et al., 1990; Newfield et al., 1990; Todd et al., 1990.

Techniques

One type of technique includes traditional ethnic healing methods, borrowed directly or in a modified form into family therapy. Such methods often involve the use of exorcism, faith healing, cultural symbols, images and metaphors.

Sources: Ito, 1985; Waters, 1986; Jackson, 1988; Karrer, 1989; Bright, 1990; Jacobs, 1990.

Another type includes traditional family therapeutic techniques, modified to suit work with families of various cultures.

Sources: Falicov and Brudner-White, 1983; Herrerias, 1988; Hines et al., 1989; Kurtines and Szapocznik, 1996.

FAMILY THERAPY WITH SPECIFIC SOCIOCULTURAL GROUPS

Most of these studies are dedicated to family therapy with specific ethnic groups, mainly in the United States. Culture-specific, therapy-relevant traits distinguishing families in each community are listed and described, for example, help-seeking behavior, problem-solving and ways of coping with stress, sources of support within the nuclear or extended family and values and attitudes related to marriage and parenting. Often speculations are offered concerning the origins of these traits in the group's distant and recent past. This is followed by practical suggestions as to how to take this information into account in diagnosis and treatment. Many studies focus on specific types of problem areas in families of the particular community under discussion, for example, alcoholism in African American families, child abuse in Hispanic American families, etc. (see the section on culturally sensitive family therapy with particular types of families or specific family problems below). Following is a classification of these works, according to the specific communities they refer to.

African American

Most works about family therapy with this community debate the deficit model applied to black families in the past and call for a form of therapy that draws on the strengths of such families, which are strong kinship bonds, a marked work orientation, flexible family roles, high achievement orientation and strong commitment to religious values.

Sources: Hines and Boyd-Franklin, 1982; Grevious, 1985; Fullilove, Carter and Eversley, 1986; Knox, 1986; Lawson, 1986; Lloyd, 1986; Boyd-Franklin, 1987; Fischgrund, 1987; Morris, 1987; Sykes, 1987; Ziter, 1987; Franklin, 1988; Kaufman and Borders, 1988; Lindblad-Goldberg, Dukes and Lasley, 1988; Willis, 1988; Boyd-Franklin, 1989a and b; Hines et al., 1989; Anderson, 1990; Baptiste, 1990; Lewis and Ford, 1990; O'Brian, 1990; Spaights, 1990; Thomas, 1990; Bell and Chance-Hill, 1991; Roberts, 1991; Wilson and Stith, 1991; Hines, et al., 1992; Williams and Wright, 1992; Mohanan, 1993; Black, 1996; Watson, 1998.

Appalachian

Boynton, 1987 and Lemon, Newfield and Dobbins, 1993 discuss specialized family therapeutic techniques for working with Appalachian families.

Asian American

Most works in this subclass advise therapists to take into account traditional values espoused by families in this community. Values often mentioned are academic achievement orientation, familism and respect for family hierarchy, collectivism and holism.

Sources: Lee, E., 1982; Kaufman and Borders, 1988; Hong, 1989; Man Keung, 1989; Hines et al., 1992; Yalung, 1992; Berg and Jaya, 1993; Wang, 1994.

Hispanic

Studies in this category also advise therapists to take into account culture-specific values in their work. Traditional values adhered to in this community are *familismo, personalismo, fatalismo, marianismo* and *machismo, respeto* and *dignidad* (which make it difficult for men to seek help).

Sources: Vazquez-Nuttall, Avila-Vivas and Morales-Barreto, 1984; Szapocznik et al., 1986; Baptiste, 1987; Boynton, 1987; Fischgrund, 1987; Herrerias, 1988; Kaufman and Borders, 1988; Schensul, 1988; Singer, 1988; Zayas and Palleja, 1988; Flores-Ortiz and Bernal, 1989; Steinberger, 1989; Baptiste, 1990; Szapocznik et al.,

1990; Laureano and Poliandro, 1991; Martinez, 1991; Sciarra and Ponterroto, 1991; Hines, et al., 1992; McGill, 1992; Baptiste, 1993; Barkley and Mosher, 1995; Santisteban et al., 1996.

Italian American

Yaccarino, 1993 proposes various adaptations of Minuchin's structural family therapy techniques in work with Italian American families. See also Genoni and Erlanger, 1985.

Irish American

Works devoted to this community emphasize the centrality of shame and guilt proneness in this culture.
Sources: Miller, 1987; Hines et al., 1992.

Jewish American

Studies in this subcategory describe Jewish families as holding a strong community orientation. Values attributed to Jewish families are centrality of the family, suffering as a shared value and intellectual and financial achievement orientation. It is asserted that Jewish families tend to express their feelings verbally. Typical problems in such families are mild neurotic symptoms and triangulation of a child. Their preferred style of therapy is verbal, insight therapy. Jewish families often express a negative attitude toward intermarriage with other ethnic groups.
Sources: Hertz and Rosen, 1982; Friedman, 1982; McGoldrick, Pearce and Giordano, 1982; Miller, 1987; Gleckman and Streicher, 1990; Wieselberg, 1992; Feigin, 1996; Schlossberger and Hecker, 1998.

Native American

Values attributed to Native Americans are collectivism and traditionalism.
Sources: Long, 1986; Kaufman and Borders, 1988; London and Devore, 1988; Gonzalez-Santin and Lewis, 1989; Schacht, Tafoya and Mirabla, 1989; Anderson, 1992.

Other Communities

Africans

Bott and Hodes, 1989 suggest that structural family therapy may be suitable as a treatment technique for nonindividualistic societies such as those in West Africa, in which the individual is constituted through the kinship group; see also Wieselberg, 1992.

Amish

Emery, 1996 attempts to draw the ethnological characteristics of Amish families in the United States.

Australian aboriginal

Brown and Larner, 1992 analyze poetry and painting by Kooris who were removed from their parents and raised in aboriginal children homes.

Bangladeshi in London

Messent, 1992 describes work with Bangladeshi families in the West End of London, England; see also Lau, 1992.

Caribbeans

Dechesnay, 1986 describes types of family structure prevalent in Jamaica. He argues that the patriarchal-patrilocal structure creates problems for working-class Jamaicans; see also Baptiste, Hardy and Lewis, 1998.

Chinese

Hampson and Beavers, 1989 describe cultural and structural changes in Chinese families over the past decade and offer approaches to family systems interventions.

German American

Winawer and Wetzel, 1996 is an attempt to describe the distinct characteristics of such families.

Hungarian American

Smith, 1996 emphasizes the tendency of Hungarian families to extremes and their indomitable nature.

Israeli Muslims

Rubin and Nasser, 1993 present a collaborative work of a supervisor of Jewish and American origin, an Arab Christian therapist in training and a Muslim family in distress.

Israeli Ethiopian Immigrants

Ben David, 1996 discusses characteristics of the Ethiopian Jewish community in Israel. Ben David and Good, 1998 is a comparative study of Ethiopian immigrants in Israel and the Hmong in the United States.

Japanese

Values attributed to Japanese families are other-centeredness and connectedness, authoritarianism and academic achievement orientation. The preferred direction of change for Japanese families is toward a process of integration rather than a process of differentiation.

Sources: Colman, 1986; Isomura, Fines and Lin, 1987; McGill, 1987; Tomm, Suzuki and Suzuki, 1990; Tamura and Lau, 1992.

Pakistanis and Moroccans in Britain

Guernina, 1993 presents work with Pakistani and Moroccan families in London. The families are seen as torn between competing cultural systems: the nurturing environment of the family and the sustaining environment of society.

Singapore

Anderson, 1990 discusses the application of a theory of family cultural reality and value orientation in group work with families in Singapore.

Trinidad and Tobago

Maharajh and Bhugra, 1993 describe family therapy with alcohol-dependent men in Trinidad and Tobago and their families.

Vietnamese

Leung and Boehnlein, 1996 describe the traditional values of Vietnamese families and the changes that have evolved in America.

CULTURALLY SENSITIVE FAMILY THERAPY WITH PARTICULAR TYPES OF FAMILIES OR SPECIFIC FAMILY PROBLEMS

Most of these studies deal with the interface between particular kinds of problems (e.g., acculturation stresses, violence within the family, substance abuse, etc.) and particular cultural characteristics of families of specific social groups. The difficulties and their origins in the families' external and internal environment are discussed. The families' functional and dysfunctional coping styles are characterized. Suitable family therapeutic interventions are proposed.

Special Types of Families

This subclass deals with the problems of atypical families. Mitchell and Cronson, 1987 discuss families in which one member is a celebrity. Such families often enter into a tacit contract, enabling the celebrity to pursue his or her career by relinquishing the parental role to the spouse or to one of the children.

Lesbian couples are discussed in Roth, 1987. It is claimed that these couples are characterized by fusion, that is, the merging of two incomplete people coming together in an attempt to make one more complete whole. Another study of lesbian couples in Rabin, 1992. Aspects emphasized are lack of social recognition and issues of couple boundaries, power imbalances and role differentiation.

"Anti-family families" or alternative families are discussed in Buchholz and Kolle, 1989. Denton, 1990 is a discussion of religious fundamentalist families. Mazurova and Rozin, 1991 discuss family conflicts of countercultural youth in the former USSR.

Adaptation to a New Cultural Environment

Factors emphasized in these studies are loss of extended family connection, intergeneration communication difficulties, "return fantasy" and social isolation.

Sources: Serrano, 1985; Ganesan, Fine and Lin, 1989; Bardin and Porten, 1996.

Parental Problems and Intrafamilial Abuse

Studies in this subcategory investigate the effects of socioeconomic status, intergenerational relations and intrafamilial conflicts on violence and abuse inside the family.

Sources: Long, 1986; Herrerias, 1988; Schensul, 1988; Mullender, 1990; Martinez, 1991; Brown and Larner, 1992.

Children and Adolescents' Problems

In these studies family-cultural factors are interrelated to physical and psychological symptoms in children and adolescents. Conflicting familial and cultural demands and value orientations are claimed to underlie children's depression and aggression.

Sources: Seltzer, 1985; Szapocznik et al., 1986; Singer, 1988; Steinberger, 1989; Yalung, 1992; DiNicola, 1998.

Physical and Mental Health Problems and Handicaps

In these works it is stressed that culturally determined family beliefs about physical and mental handicaps influence coping and prognosis. Family variables mentioned are health locus of control, moral attitude to illness, assumptions about etiology and process versus cure-focused approach.

Sources: Sebring, 1985; Fischgrund, 1987; Rolland, 1987; Ganesan, Fine and Lin, 1989; Furedi, 1991; Rowe and Beamish, 1992; Atwood, 1993; Goldman, Miller and Lee, 1993; Jensen and Shaw, 1993; DiNicola, 1996; Lefley, 1998.

Bereavement

Rubin and Nasser, 1993 discuss cultural and religious experiences affecting bereavement in Muslim families. Shapiro, 1996 emphasizes the culture-bound nature of family bereavement.

Substance Abuse

Some studies in this group investigate the relations between cultural and religious beliefs, addiction tendencies and prognosis.

Sources: Sebring, 1985; Kaufman, 1986; Knox, 1986; Szapocznik et al., 1986; Ziter, 1987; Kaufman and Borders, 1988; Singer, 1988; Newfield et al., 1990; Anderson, 1992; Maharajh and Bhugra, 1993; Friedemann, 1994; Cherry et al., 1998.

Suicide

Aldridge, 1998 discusses the sociocultural context of suicide.

EMPIRICAL RESEARCH

Empirical Validation of Theoretical Premises

Some studies are devoted to the validation of the Circumplex Model. For example, Flores and Sprenkle, 1988 compare Mexican Americans and normative Anglo-Americans by FACES III, based on the Circumplex Model. Results show a modest relationship between acculturation and family structure and a stronger relationship with family income.

Woehrer, 1988 integrates nuclear with extended family systems by comparing extended ethnic families in terms of their dispersion on the cohesion and adaptability dimensions as defined by the Circumplex Model. It was found that rigid, enmeshed families functioned well when they had high expectations for togetherness. It is suggested that enmeshment in extended families increases the resources available for alleviating problems and moderates the effects of low adaptability.

Fisek, 1991 analyzes the cross-cultural validity of the family structure dimensions of proximity, generational hierarchy and boundary permeability. The variable of proximity was found a valid dimension although moderated by demographic and socioeconomic variables. Hierarchy was not found a valid dimension since cultural norms suppress variation in family hierarchy; see also Keitner et al., 1990.

Process and Outcome of Therapy Research

Diagnostic and therapeutic methods, whose efficacy with various cultural communities have been investigated, are genograms (Becker and Lewis, 1992), Bicultural Effectiveness Training and structural family therapy (Szapocznik et al., 1986). Santisteban et al., 1996 report data on the efficacy of Strategic-Structural Systems Engagement in overcoming resistance to engagement in family therapy with Hispanic clients.

Cultural Characteristics of Families

Some studies are devoted to aspects of the therapeutic alliance: McGoldrick and Rohrbaugh, 1987 studied ethnic stereotypes in family therapy. Stereotypes varied according to the ethnic identity of the therapists. Flaskerud, 1986 found that the best predictors of dropping out of therapy were ethnic/racial match between therapists and clients, agency location within or outside the neighborhood and level of education of clients.

Irvine and Stevens, 1985 survey the history of research on black families in the United States. The general trend identified is a transition from a psychologistic or biologistic deficit model to a sociocultural model. Franklin, 1988 is a research review of factors facilitating transition into maternal roles in black adolescents. The main factors found were therapy support, social group support, provision of information and continued schooling.

Thrasher and Anderson, 1988 investigated West Indian families in New York City by a case content analysis. The main findings were: Immigration is uneven. Adults come alone and leave children with relatives. It takes the entire family many years to migrate. Households are multigenerational. Parents hold dual jobs. There are parent-child conflicts. Children are often uncared for. Physical punishment is often used. Lindblad-Goldberg, Dukes and Lasley, 1988 studied stress in low-income, single-parent urban black families in Philadelphia in 1979–1980. Results indicate that dysfunctional families evidence greater stress and that social network characteristics are not significant mediators. The family's internal resources may be the most significant buffer against stress.

Verhoff et al., 1993 compare affective interactions in the narratives of black and white newlywed couples. Luthar and Quinlan, 1993 compared parental images in India and the United States. They found that Indians perceived their parents as more loving and less overprotective. Deference, loyalty and conformity to the family are crucial for Indian women.

TRAINING ISSUES

Works of this class include general principles for training culturally sensitive therapists and also descriptions of particular programs and specific training techniques. Aponte, 1985 and 1991 asserts that multicultural training should address one's own values and culturally relevant emotional and family issues.

Halpern, 1985 focuses on some cross-cultural aspects involved in the process of transposing models of training from one setting to another.

London and Devore, 1988 provide a schematic model to enhance understanding for counseling ethnic minority families with suggested skills and techniques. They suggest the widening of the repertoire of culturally sensitive skills: a wide repertoire of verbal and nonverbal responses, an ability to send and receive verbal and nonverbal messages appropriately and an ability to exercise appropriate institutional intervention skills.

Gonzalez-Santin and Lewis, 1989 is a training textbook for paraprofessionals working with rural Native Americans. Aponte, 1991 proposes an ecostructural model for training workers with low income and minority families. Anderson, 1992 outlines sensitizing concepts to prepare students for family-centered multicultural social work practice. It discusses the family's world-view and value orientation of various ethnic groups and implications for social work with dysfunctional family systems.

Hardy and Laszloffy, 1992 suggest revisions in current curricula for training culturally sensitive family therapists. Educational programs must create a cultural milieu that challenges students to explore the complexities of race, ethnicity and culture. Arnold, 1993 reviews and criticizes the literature on multicultural training. It concludes that this literature is limited, conflicting and not empirically based. Recommendations proposed are adopting an ecological approach, combining didactic and experiential exercises with basic family theory, enhancing ethnic self-awareness in counselors, understanding oppression and racism and reducing resistance to multiculturalism. Exercises are offered for teaching the significance of ethnicity in family functioning.

Speight as cited in Sue, 1994, characterizes the "culture specific" approach to training as "a multicultural cookbook with a recipe" (see Sue, 1994). Preli and Bernard, 1993 claim that prevailing training approaches tend to emphasize understanding of ethnic minorities while deemphasizing the trainees' own ethnic and cultural roots. Specific training activities are outlined. Kalichman, 1994 reviews main problems in multicultural issues in clinical training. Martinez, 1994 recommends graduate school curricula to include substantive culturally responsive training and supervision.

References

Adams, B. N. (1971). *Readings in the sociology of the family*. Chicago: Markham.

Aldridge, D. (1998). *Suicide: The tradgedy of hopelessness*. London: Jessica Kingsley.

Almeida, R. (1996). Hindu, Christian and Muslim families. In M. McGoldrick, J. K. Pearce and J. Giordano (Eds.), *Ethnicity and family therapy* (2nd ed.). New York: Guilford.

Anderson, E. N. (1992). A healing place: Ethnographic notes on a treatment center. *Alcoholism Treatment Quarterly 9, 3–4*, 1–21.

Anderson, J. D. (1990). Group work with families: A multicultural perspective. *Social Work with Groups 13, 4*, 85–101.

Anderson, J. D. (1992). Family-centered practice in the 1990's: A multicultural perspective. *Journal of Multi-Cultural Social Work 1, 4*, 17–29.

Anderson, M. (1971). *Sociology of the family, selected writings*. Middlesex: Penguin Books.

Andolfi, M. and Angelo, C. (1985). Famiglia ed individuo in una prospettiva trigenerazionale [Family and individual in a three-generational perspective]. *Terapia Familiare 19*, 17–23.

Aponte, H. J. (1985). The negotiation of values in therapy. *Family Process 24, 3*, 323–338.

Aponte, H. J. (1991). Training on the person of the therapist for work with the poor and minorities. *Journal of Independent Social Work 5, 3–4*, 23–39.

Aponte, H. J. and VanDeusen, J. M. (1981). Structural family therapy. In A. S. Gurman and D. P. Kniskern (Eds.), *Handbook of family therapy I* (pp. 310–336). New York: Brunner/Mazel.

Ariel, S. (1985). *Touchnotation. A method for transcribing touching* [Hebrew text]. Jerusalem: The Hebrew University.

Ariel, S. (1987). An information-processing theory of family dysfunction. Special issue: Psychotherapy with families. *Psychotherapy 24, 3S*.

230 References

Ariel, S. (1992). *Multi-systemic child therapy* [Hebrew text]. Jerusalem: Ministry of Labor and Social Welfare.

Ariel, S. (1994). *Strategic family play therapy* (2nd ed.). Chichester: Wiley.

Ariel, S. (1996). Restorying family therapy. *Contemporary Family Therapy 18, 1*, 3–17.

Ariel, S., Carel, C. and Tyano, S. (1984). A formal explication of the concept "family homeostasis." *Journal of Marital and Family Therapy 10*, 337–349.

Arieli, A., Gilat, I. and Seffefe, A. (1994). Suicide of Ethiopic Jews—A survey based on psychological autopsy [Hebrew text]. *Ha Refuah 127, 3–4*, 65–70.

Arieli, A. and Seffefe, A. (1994). Psychiatric syndromes related to faith in "Zar" possession [Hebrew text]. *Ha Refuah 126, 11*, 636–642.

Arnold, M. S. (1993). Ethnicity and training marital and family therapists. *Counselor Education and Supervision 33, 2*, 139–47.

Astuti, R. (1995). "The Vezo are not a kind of people": Identity, difference and "ethnicity" among the fishing people of western Madagascar. *American Ethnologist 22, 3*, 464–482.

Atwood, J. D. (1993). AIDS in African American and Hispanic adolescents: A multisystemic approach. *American Journal of Family Therapy 21, 4*, 333–351.

Bachran, M., Lee, S. and Yoo, D. (1995). Holistic approach to family therapy with Asian families. *The Family Psychologist*, 28–29.

Baptiste, D. A. (1987). Family therapy with Spanish-heritage immigrant families in cultural transition. *Contemporary Family Therapy 9, 4*, 229–251.

Baptiste, D. A. (1990). Therapeutic strategies with black-Hispanic families: Identity problems of a neglected minority. *Journal of Family Psychotherapy 1, 3*, 15–38.

Baptiste, D. A. (1993). Immigrant families, adolescents and acculturation: Insights for therapists. *Marriage and Family Review 19, 3–4*, 341–363.

Baptiste, D. A., Hardy, K. V. and Lewis, L. (1998). Clinical practice with Caribbean immigrant families in the United States: The intersection of emigration, immigration, culture and race. In J. C. Roopnarine, and J. Brown (Eds.), *Caribbean families: Diversity among ethnic groups*. Norwood, N. J. Ablex.

Bardin, A. and Porten, D. (1996). Culture change: A training program for recent immigrant professionals from the former Soviet Union. *Contemporary Family Therapy 18*, 61–67.

Barkley, B. H. and Mosher, E. S. (1995). Sexuality and Hispanic culture: Counseling with children and their parents. *Journal of Sex Education and Therapy 24*, 255–267.

Barot, R. (1988). Social anthropology, ethnicity and family therapy. *Journal of Family Therapy 10, 3*, 271–282.

Bateson, G., Jackson, J., Haley J. and Weakland, J. (1971). Toward a theory of schizophrenia. In G. Bateson (Ed.), *Steps to an ecology of mind*. New York: Ballantine.

Becker, L. and Lewis, H. (1992). An exploration of the use of the Genogram with families of different cultural groups. *Maatskaplike Werk [Social work] 28, 2*, 14–21.

Bell, C. M. (1992). *Ritual theory, ritual practice*. New York: Oxford University Press.

Bell, C. C. and Chance-Hill, G. (1991). Treatment of violent families: Annual meeting of the American Family Therapy Association (1988, Montreal, Canada). *Journal of the National Medical Association 83, 3*, 203–208.

Bemak, F. (1989). Cross-cultural family therapy with Southeast Asian refugees. Special issue: Family therapy with immigrant families: Constructing a bridge between different world views. *Journal of Strategic and Systemic Therapies 8*, 22–27.

Ben David, A. (1996). Therapists, perceptions of multicultural assessment and therapy with immigrant families. *Journal of Family Therapy 18*, 23–41.

Ben David, A. and Good, I. J. (1998). Ethiopians and Hmongs: A comparative study in cultural narrative from a family therapy perspective. *Journal of Family Psychotherapy 9*, 31–45.

Bennet, L. A., Wolin, S. J. and McAvity, K. J. (1988). Family identity, ritual and myth: A cultural perspective on life-cycle transitions. In C. J. Falicov (Ed.), *Family transitions, continuity and change over the life cycle* (pp. 211–233). New York: Guilford.

Bennet, P. and Meredith, W. H. (1995). The modern role of the grandmother in China, a departure for the Confucian ideal. *International Journal of the Sociology of the Family 25*, 1–12.

Bentovim, A. and Kinston, W. (1991). Focal family therapy: Joining systems theory and psychodynamic understanding. In A. S. Gurman and D. P. Kniskern (Eds.), *Handbook of family therapy II* (pp. 310–336). New York: Brunner/Mazel.

Berg, I. K. and Jaya, A. (1993). Different and same: Family therapy with Asian American families. *Journal of Marital and Family Therapy 19, 1*, 31–38.

Berg, I. K. and Miller, S. D. (1992). Working with Asian American clients: One person at a time. Special issue: Multicultural practice. *Families in Society 73, 6*, 356–363.

Bermudez, J. M. (1997). Experiential tasks and therapist bias awareness. *Contemporary Family Therapy 19*, 253–267.

Bernal, G. and Alvarez, A. I. (1983). Culture and class in the study of families. In C. J. Falicov (Ed.), *Cultural perspectives in family therapy* (pp. 33–50). Rockville, Md.: Aspen Systems.

Bertalanffy, L. (1973). *General systems theory* (revised ed.). New York: Braziller.

Bilu, Y. and Witztum, E. (1993). Working with ultra-Orthodox patients: Guidelines for culturally-sensitive therapy. *Culture, Medicine and Psychiatry 17*, 197–233.

Biolsi, T. (1995). The birth of the reservation: Making the modern individual among the Lakota. *American Ethnologist 22, 1*, 28–53.

Black, L. (1996). Families of African origin: An overview. In M. McGoldrick, J. K. Pearce and J. Giordano (Eds.), *Ethnicity and family therapy* (2nd ed.). New York: Guilford.

Blount, B. W. and Curry, A. (1993). Caring for the bicultural family: The Korean-American example. *Journal of the American Board of Family Practice 6, 3*, 261–268.

Bodovsky, D. and Eran, Y. (1989). *Household peace and marital conflicts: Family problems in the Ethiopic Jewish community in Israel* [Hebrew text]. Tel Aviv: Bet Achin and Joint Israel.

Bodovsky, D., David, Y., Baruch, A., Eran, Y. and Avni, B. (1994). *The Ethiopic Jewish community in Israel in cultural transition: Family life cycle*. Tel Aviv: Bet Achin and Joint Israel.

Bonvillain, N. (1993). *Language, culture and communication: The meaning of messages*. Englewood Cliffs: Prentice Hall.

Boszormeyi-Nagy, I. and Spark, G. M. (1973). *Invisible loyalties*. New York: Harper & Row.

Boszormenyi-Nagy, I. and Ulrich, D. N. (1981). Contextual family therapy. In A. S. Gurman and D. P. Kniskern (Eds.), *Handbook of family therapy I* (pp. 159–186). New York: Brunner/Mazel.

Bott, D. and Hodes, M. (1989). Structural therapy for a West African family. *Journal of Family Therapy 11*, 2, 169–179.

Bourguignon, E. (1976). Possession and trance in cross-cultural studies of mental health. In W. P. Lebra (Ed.), *Culture-bound syndromes, ethnopsychiatry and alternative therapies* (pp. 47–55). Honolulu: University of Hawaii Press.

Bowen, M. (1976). Theory in the practice of psychotherapy. In P. J. Guerin (Ed.), *Family therapy*. New York: Garden Press.

Bowen, M. (1978). *Family therapy in clinical practice*. New York: Jason Aronson.

Boyd-Franklin, N. (1987). The contribution of family therapy models to the treatment of black families. Special issue: Psychotherapy with families. *Psychotherapy 24*, 3S, 621–629.

Boyd-Franklin, N. (1989a). Five key factors in the treatment of black families. *Journal of Psychotherapy and the Family 6*, 1–2, 53–69.

Boyd-Franklin, N. (1989b). *Black families in therapy: A multisystems approach*. New York: Guilford.

Boynton, G. (1987). Cross-cultural family therapy. The ESCAPE model. *American Journal of Family Therapy 15*, 2, 122–130.

Bradby, H. (1995). Ethnicity: Not a black and white issue. *Sociology of Health and Illness 17*, 3, 405–417.

Bright, M. A. (1990). Therapeutic ritual: Helping families grow. *Journal of Psychosocial Nursing and Mental Health Services 28*, 12, 24–29.

Brown, C. and Larner, G. (1992). Every dot has a meaning. *Australian and New Zealand Journal of Family Therapy 13*, 4, 175–184.

Brown, R. (1988). *Group processes—dynamics within and between groups*. Oxford: Blackwell.

Buchholz, M. B. and Kolle, U. (1989). Familien in der Moderne-anti familie-familien? [Families in the modern, anti-family families?] *Prax-Kinderpsychol-Kindierpsychiatr 38*, 2, 42–52.

Butler, M. H. and Harper, J. M. (1994). The divine triangle: God in the marital system of religious couples. *Family Process 33*, 277–286.

Campbell, D., Draper R. and Crutchley, E. (1991). The Milan systemic approach to family therapy. In A. S. Gurman and D. P. Kniskern (Eds.), *Handbook of family therapy II* (pp. 325–362). New York: Brunner Mazel.

Cawte, J. E. (1976). Malgri: A culture-bound syndrome. In W. P. Lebra (Ed.), *Culture-bound syndromes, ethnopsychiatry and alternative therapies* (pp. 22–31). Honolulu: University of Hawaii Press.

Chambon, A. (1989). Refugee families experiences: Three family themes—family disruption, violent trauma and acculturation. *Journal of Strategic and Systemic Therapies 8*, 3–13.

Cherry, V. R., Belgrave, F. Z., Jones, W., Kennon, D. K., Gray, F. S. and Phillips, F. (1998). An Africentric approach to substance abuse prevention among African American youth. *Journal of Primary Prevention 18*, 319–339.

Chomsky, N. (1965). *Aspects of the theory of syntax*. Cambridge, Mass: The MIT Press.

Colapinto, J. (1981). Structural family therapy. In A. S. Gurman, and D. P. Kniskern (Eds.), *Handbook of family therapy II* (pp. 417–443). New York: Brunner/Mazel.

Colman, C. (1986). International family therapy. A view from Kyoto, Japan. *Family Process 25, 4,* 651–664.

Comas-Diaz, L. (1993). Diversifying clinical psychology. *The Clinical Psychologist 46,* 2, 45–49.

Corson, D. (1995). World view, cultural values and discourse norms: The cycle of cultural reproduction. *International Journal of Intercultural Relations 19,* 2, 183–195.

Cranch, M. von and Ploog, D. (Eds.). (1979). *Human ethology.* Cambridge: Cambridge University Press.

Cuff, E. et al. (1990). *Perspectives in sociology.* London: Allen and Unwin.

David, A. B. and Erickson, C. A. (1990). Ethnicity and the therapist's use of self. *Family Therapy 17,* 3, 211–216.

Dechesnay, M. (1986). Jamaican family structure: The paradox of normalcy. *Family Process 25,* 2, 293–300.

Dennis, P. A. (1985). Grisi Siknis in Miskito culture. In R. C. Simons and C. C. Hughes (Eds.), *The culture-bound syndromes: Folk illnesses of psychiatric and anthropological interest* (pp. 289–306). Dordrecht: D. Reidel.

Denton, R. T. (1990). The religiously fundamentalist family: Training for assessment and treatment. *Journal of Social Work Education 26,* 1, 6–14.

Deyhle, D. and Margonis, F. (1995). Navajo mothers and daughters: Schools, jobs and the family. *Anthropology and Education Quarterly 26,* 2, 135–167.

DiNicola, V. F. (1986). Beyond Babel: Family therapy as cultural translation. *International Journal of Family Psychiatry 7,* 2, 179–191.

DiNicola, V. F. (1996). Ethnocultural aspects of PTSD and related disorders among children and adolescents. In A. J. Marsella et al. (Eds.), *Ethnocultural aspects of posttraumatic stress disorder: Issues, research and clinical applications* (pp. 389–414). Washington, D.C.: American Psychological Association.

DiNicola, V. F. (1997). *A stranger in the family: Culture, families and therapy.* New York: Norton.

DiNicola, V. F. (1998). Children and families in cultural transition. In S. O. Okpaku et al. (Eds), *Clinical methods in transcultural psychiatry* (pp. 365–390). Washington, D.C.: American Psychiatric Press.

Dow, J. (1986). Universal aspects of symbolic healing: A theoretical analysis. *American Anthropologist 86,* 56–69.

Duhl, F. S., Kantor, D. and Duhl, B. S. (1973). Learning, space and action in family therapy: A primer of sculpture. In D. Bloch (Ed.), *Techniques of family psychotherapy* (pp. 47–64). New York: Grune and Statton.

Eckhardt, B. (1993). *What is cognitive science?* Cambridge, Mass.: The MIT Press.

Eibl-Eibesfeldt, I. (1989). *Human ethology.* New York: Aldine Gruyter.

Ekman, P. (1978). *Facial action coding system.* Palo Alto: Counseling Psychologists Press.

Ellis, D., Duran, R. L. and Kelly, L. (1994). Discourse strategies of competent communicators: Selected cohesive and linguistic devices. *Research on Language and Social Interaction 27,* 2, 145–170.

Emery, E. (1996). Amish families. In M. McGoldrick, J. K. Pearce and J. Giordano (Eds.), *Ethnicity and family therapy* (2nd ed.). New York: Guilford.

Eron, J. B. and Lund, T. W. (1993). Problems evolve and dissolve: Integrating narrative and strategic concepts. *Family Process 32*, 291–309.

Eshkol, N. and Wachman, A. (1958). *Movement notation*. Tel Aviv: The Movement Notation Society.

Falicov, C. J. (Ed.). (1983). *Cultural perspectives in family therapy*. Rockville, Md.: Aspen Systems.

Falicov, C. J. (Ed.). (1988). *Family transitions, continuity and change over the life cycle*. New York: Guilford.

Falicov, C. J. and Brunder-White, L. (1983). The shifing family triangle: The issue of cultural and contextual relativity. In C. J. Falicov (Ed.), *Cultural perspectives in family therapy* (pp. 51–67). Rockville, Md.: Aspen Systems.

Falloon, I. R. H. (1991). Behavioral family therapy. In A. S. Gurman and D. P. Kniskern (Eds.), *Handbook of family therapy II* (pp. 65–95). New York: Brunner/Mazel.

Faulkner, J. and Kich, G. K. (1983). Assessment and engagement stages in therapy with the interracial family. In C. J. Falicov (Ed.), *Cultural perspectives in family therapy* (pp. 79–90). Rockville, Md: Aspen Systems.

Feigin, I. (1996). Soviet Jewish families. In M. McGoldrick, J. K. Pearce and J. Giordano (Eds.), *Ethnicity and family therapy* (2nd ed.). New York: Guilford.

Ferreira, A. (1966). Family myths. *Psychiatric Research Reports 20*, 85–90.

Festinger, L. (1962). *Cognitive dissonance*. San Francisco: Freeman.

Fiese, B. H. (1992). Dimensions of family rituals across two generations: Relations to adolescent identity. *Family Process 31*, 151–162.

Fisch, R., Weakland, J. H. and Segal, L. (1982). *The tactics of change*. San Francisco: Jossey-Bass.

Fischgrund, J. E. (1987). Hearing-impaired children in black and Hispanic families. *Volta Review 89*, 5, 59–67.

Fisek, G. O. (1991). A cross-cultural examination of proximity and hierarchy as dimensions of family structure. *Family Process 30*, 1, 121–133.

Fish, J. M. (1996). *Culture and therapy: An integrative approach*. Northvale, N.J.: Jason Aronson.

Flaskerud, J. H. (1986). The effects of culture-compatible intervention on the utilization of mental health services by minority clients. *Community Mental Health Journal 22*, 2, 127–141.

Flores, M. T. and Sprenkle, D. H. (1988). Can therapist use FACES III with Mexican Americans? A preliminary analysis. *Journal of Psychotherapy and the Family 4*, 1–2, 239–247.

Flores-Ortiz, Y. and Bernal, G. (1989). Contextual family therapy of addiction with Latinos. *Journal of Psychotherapy and the Family 6*, 1–2, 123–142.

Fontes, L. A. and Thomas, V. (1996). Cultural issues in family therapy. In F. P. Piercy, and D. H. Sprenkle (Eds.), *Family therapy sourcebook* (2nd ed.). New York: Guilford.

Ford, F. (1992). Family typology: The search for language. *Ann-1st Super Sanita 28*, 2, 203–271.

Franklin, D. L. (1988). The impact of early childbearing on developmental outcomes: The case of black adolescent parenting. *Family Relations 37*, 3, 268–274.

Freed, S. A. and Freed, R. S. (1964). Spirit possession as illness in a North Indian village. *Ethnology 3*, 152–171.

Freud, S. (1949). *An outline of psychoanalysis*. London: Hogarth.

Friedmann, M. L. (1994). Evaluation of the Congruence Model with rehabilitating substance abusers. *International Journal of Nursing Studies 31*, 1, 97–108.

Friedman, E. H. (1982). The myth of the Shiksa. In M. McGoldrick, J. K. Pearce and J. Giordano (Eds.), *Etincity and family therapy* (pp. 499–526). New York: Guilford.

Friedman, E. H. (1991). Bowen theory and therapy. In A. S. Gurman and D. P. Kniskern (Eds.), *Handbook of family therapy II* (pp. 134–170). New York: Brunner/Mazel.

Fullilove, M. T., Carter, K. O. and Eversley, R. (1986). Family therapy for black patients. Second Annual Conference of the Black Task Force. The black family: Mental health perspectives (1984, San Francisco, California). *American Journal of Social Psychiatry 6*, 1, 62–68.

Furedi, J. (1991). A case study of an identity crisis from the 70's. *Psychiatria Hungarica 6*, 3, 179–184.

Ganesan, S., Fine, S. and Lin, T. Y. (1989). Psychiatric symptoms in refugee families from South East Asia: Therapeutic challenges. *American Journal of Psychotherapy 43*, 2, 218–228.

Garcia-Preto, N. (1996). Latino families: An overview. In M. McGoldrick, J. K. Pearce, and J. Giordano (Eds.), *Ethnicity and family therapy* (2nd ed.). New York: Guilford.

Gardano, A. C., Davis, R. M. and Jones, E. (1994). Promoting receptivity to issues of cultural diversity in mental health services at health maintenance organizations. *The Family Psychologist 10*, 2, 15–18.

Gardner, H. (1985). *The mind's new science*. New York: Basic Books.

Geertz, C. (1983). *Local knowledge: Further essays in interpretive anthropology*. New York: Basic Books.

Geertz, C. (1995). *After the fact*. Cambridge, Mass.: Harvard University Press.

Gelfand, D. E. and Kutzik, A. J. (Eds.). (1979). *Ethnicity and aging*. New York: Springer.

Genoni, L. and Erlanger, A. (1985). Landlichen Verhaltnissen. *Schweitz-Arch-Neurol-Psychiatr. 136*, 6, 105–108.

George, D. and Sanders, S. (1995). Reconstructing Tonto: Cultural formations and American Indians in 1990s television fiction. *Cultural Studies 9*, 3, 427–452.

Giat Roberto, L. (1991). Symbolic-experiential family therapy. In A. S. Gurman and D. P. Kniskern (Eds.), *Handbook of family therapy II* (pp. 444–478). New York: Brunner/Mazel.

Gleckman, A. D. and Streicher, P. J. (1990). The potential difficulties with Jewish intermarriage: Interventions and implications for the mental health counselor. *Journal of Mental Health Counseling 12*, 4, 480–494.

Globus, G. (1995). *The post-modern brain*. Amsterdam: Benjamins.

Goldfried, M. (1994). *Clinical behavior therapy*. New York: Wiley.

Goldman, E., Miller, R. and Lee, C. A. (1993). A family with HIV haemophilia. *AIDS-Care 5*, 1, 79–85.

Goldner, V. (1985). Feminism and family therapy. *Family Process 24*, 1, 31–47.

Gonzalez-Santin, E. and Lewis, A. (1989). *Defining entry level competencies for public child welfare workers serving Indian communities*. Tempe: Arizona State University, ASU School of Social Work, Office of American Indian Projects.

Gopaul-McNicol, S. (1997). *A multicultural, multimodal, multisystems approach to work-ing with culturally different families.* Westport, Conn.: Praeger.

Gottfried, S. (1993). *Biology today.* St. Louis: Mosby.

Greeley, A. M. (1969). *Why can't they be like us?* New York: Institute of Human Relations Press.

Grevious, C. (1985). The role of the family therapist with low-income black families. *Family Therapy 12,* 2, 115–122.

Guernina, Z. (1992). Counseling adolescents of immigrant parents: A transcultural approach. *Counseling Psychology Quarterly 5,* 3, 251–255.

Guernina, Z. (1993). Transcultural family therapy. *Counseling Psychology Quarterly 6,* 4, 365–370.

Guiao, I. Z. and Esparza, D. (1997). Family interventions with troubled Mexican American teens: An extrapolation from a review of the literature. *Residential Group Care and Treatment 18,* 191–207.

Guillemin, J. (Ed.). (1981). *Anthropological realities: Readings in the science of culture.* New Brunswick, N.J.: Transaction Books.

Gurman, A. S. and Kniskern, D. P. (Eds.). (1981). *Handbook of family therapy I.* New York: Brunner/Mazel.

Gurman, A. S. and Kniskern, D. P. (Eds.). (1991). *Handbook of family therapy II.* New York: Brunner/Mazel.

Gushue, G. (1993). Cultural identity development and family assessment: An inter-action model. *Counseling Psychologist 21,* 2, 487–513.

Gwaltney, J. L. (1981). Common sense and science: Urban core black observations. In D. A. Messerschmidt (Ed.), *Anthropologists at home in North America: Meth-ods and issues in the study of one's own society* (pp. 46–61). Cambridge: Cambridge University Press.

Haley, J. (1980). *Leaving home.* New York: McGraw-Hill.

Hall, E. T. (1990). *Understanding cultural differences.* Yarmouth, Maine: Intercultural Press.

Halpern, E. (1985). Training family therapists in Israel: The necessity of indigenous models. *American Journal of Family Therapy 13,* 1, 55–60.

Hampate Ba, A. (1995). The weaver and the blacksmith. *Parabola (fall),* 29–31.

Hampson, R. B. and Beavers, W. R. (1989). Family therapy in the People's Republic of China: An update. *Contemporary Family Therapy 11,* 4, 235–245.

Handel, G. (1967). *The psychosocial interior of the family.* Chicago: University of Chi-cago Press.

Hardy, K. and Laszloffy, T. A. (1992). Training racially sensitive family therapists: Context, content and contact. *Families in Society 73,* 6, 364–370.

Harris, M. (1983). *Cultural anthropology.* New York: Harper and Row.

Herrerias, C. (1988). Prevention of child abuse and neglect in the Hispanic com-munity: The madre parent education program. *Journal of Primary Prevention 9, 1–2,* 104–119.

Herz, F. M. and Rosen, E. J. (1982). Jewish families. In M. McGoldrick, J. K. Pearce and J. Giordano (Eds.), *Ethnicity and family therapy* (pp. 364–392). New York: Guilford.

Hill, H. M., Hawkins, S. R., Raposo, M. and Carr, P. (1995). Relationship between multiple exposures to violence and coping strategies among African American mothers. *Violence and Victims 10,* 1, 55–72.

Hines, P. M. and Boyd-Franklin, N. (1982). Black families. In M. McGoldrick, J. K. Pearce and J. Giordano (Eds.), *Ethnicity and family therapy* (pp. 84–107). New York: Guilford.

Hines, P. M., Garcia-Greco, N., McGoldrick, M., Almeida, R. and Weltman, S. (1992). Intergenerational relationships across cultures. *Families in Society 73*, 6, 323–338.

Hines, P. M., Richman, D., Maxim, K. and Hays, H. (1989). Multi-impact family therapy: An approach to working with multi-problem families. *Journal of Psychotherapy and the Family 6*, 1–2, 161–176.

Hippler, A. E. (1976). Shamans, curers and personality: Suggestions toward a theoretical model. In W. P. Lebra (Ed.), *Culture-bound syndromes, ethnopsychiatry and alternative therapies* (pp. 103–114). Honolulu: University of Hawaii Press.

Hodes, M. (1985). Family therapy and the problem of cultural relativism: A reply to Dr. Lau. *Journal of Family Therapy 7*, 3, 261–272.

Hodes, M. (1989). Annotation: Culture and family therapy. *Journal of Family Therapy 11*, 1, 117–128.

Hodkinson, K. (1984). *Muslim family law*. London: Croom Helm.

Hoffman, L. (1981). *Foundations of family therapy: A conceptual framework for systems change*. New York: Basic Books.

Holdcroft, D. (1978). *Words and deeds: Problems in the theory of speech acts*. Oxford: Clarendon.

Holzworth-Munroe, A. and Jacobson, N. S. (1991). Behavioral marital therapy. In A. S. Gurman and D. P. Kniskern (Eds.), *Handbook of family therapy II* (pp. 96–133). New York: Brunner/Mazel.

Hong, G. K. (1989). Application of cultural and environmental issues in family therapy with immigrant Chinese Americans. *Journal of Strategic and Systemic Therapies 8*, 14–21.

Hyden, L. C. (1995). The rhetoric of recovery and change. *Culture, Medicine and Psychiatry 19*, 73–90.

Ibrahim, F. A. and Schroeder, D. G. (1990). Cross-cultural couples counseling: A developmental, psychoeducational intervention. *Journal of Comparative Family Studies 21*, 2, 193–205.

Irvine, R. W. and Stevens, J. H. (1985). A historical perspective on black family research. In L. L. Abate (Ed.), *Handbook of family psychology and therapy, vol. 2* (pp. 663–695). Homewood, Ill.: The Dorsey Press.

Isomura, T., Fines, S. and Lin, T. Y. (1987). Two Japanese families: A cultural perspective. *Canadian Journal of Psychiatry 32*, 4, 282–286.

Ito, K. L. (1985). Ho'oponopono "To make it right": Hawaiian conflict resolution and metaphor in the construction of a family therapy. *Culture Medicine and Psychiatry 9*, 2, 201–217.

Jackson, S. (1988). Shadows and stories: Lessons from the waywang kulit for therapy with an Anglo-Indonesian family. *Australian and New Zealand Journal of Family Therapy 9*, 2, 71–78.

Jacobs, J. B. (1990). Names, naming and name calling in practice with families. *Families in Society 71*, 7, 415–421.

Jensen, P. S. and Shaw, J. (1993). Children as victims of war: Current knowledge and future research needs. *Journal of the American Academy of Child and Adolescent Psychiatry 32*, 4, 697–708.

Kalichman, S. C. (Ed.). (1994). Multicultural issues in clinical training. *The Child, Youth and Family Services Quarterly 17.*

Karrer, B. (1989). The sound of two hands clapping: Cultural interactions of the minority family and the therapist. *Journal of Psychotherapy and the Family 6, 1–2,* 209–237.

Kaslow, N. J., Celano, M. and Dreelin, E. D. (1995). A cultural perspective on family theory and therapy. *Cultural Psychiatry 18, 3,* 621–633.

Kaufman, E. (1986). A workable system of family therapy for drug dependence. *Journal of Psychoactive Drugs 18, 1,* 43–50.

Kaufman, E. and Borders, L. (1988). Ethnic family differences in adolescent substance use. *Journal of Chemical Dependency Treatment 1, 2,* 99–121.

Kavapalu, H. (1995). Power and personhood in Tonga. *Social Analysis 37,* 15–28.

Keitner, G. I., Ryan, C. E., Fodor, J. and Miller, I. W. (1990). A cross-cultural study of family functioning. *Contemporary Family Therapy 12, 5,* 439–454.

Kim, K. C., Hurh, W. M. and Kim, S. (1993). Generation differences in Korean immigrants' life conditions in the United States. *Sociological Perspectives 36, 2,* 257–270.

Kinzie, D., Teoh, J. and Tan, E. (1976). Native healers in malaysia. In W. P. Lebra (Ed.), *Culture-bound syndromes, ethnopsychiatry and alternative therapies* (pp. 103–114). Honolulu: University of Hawaii Press.

Kleinman, A. (1980). *Patients and healers in the context of culture.* Berkeley, University of California Press.

Kleinman, A. and Good, B. (1985). *Culture and depression: Studies in the anthropology and cross-cultural psychiatry of affect and disorder.* Berkeley: University of California Press.

Knox, D. H. (1986). Spirituality: A tool in the assessment and treatment of black alcoholics and their families. *Alcoholism Treatment Quarterly 2, 3–4,* 31–44.

Kobac, R. R. and Waters, D. B. (1984). Family therapy as a rate of passage: Play's the thing. *Family Process 23, 1,* 89–100.

Kochman, T. (1981). "Rapping" in the black ghetto. In J. Guillemin (Ed.), *Anthropological realities: Readings in the science of culture* (pp. 55–70). New Brunswick, N. J.: Transaction Books.

Kurtines, W. M. and Szapocznik, J. (1996). Family interaction patterns: Structural family therapy in the context of cultural diversity. In E. D. Hibbs and P. S. Jensen (Eds.), *Psychological treatment for child and adolescent disorders: Empirically based strategies for clinical practice* (pp. 671–697). Washington, D. C.: American Psychological Association.

Lappin, J. (1982). On becoming a culturally-conscious family therapist. In C. J. Falicov (Ed.). *Cultural perspectives in family therapy* (pp. 51–67). Rockville, Md.: Aspen Systems.

Larkey, L. K. and Hecht, M. L. (1995). A comparative study of African American and European American ethnic identities. *International Journal of Intercultural Relations 19, 4,* 483–504.

Larner, M. (1990). *Social support perspectives on programs for parents: Lessons from the Child Survival/Fair Start Home Visiting Programs.* Paper presented at the 98th annual convention of the American Psychological Association, Boston, Massachusetts, August 10–14.

Lashley, J. C. (1993). Informed therapy: Using ethnographic interviews in family therapy. *Dissertation Abstract International 54, 3*, 1108-A-1109-A.

Lau, A. (1992). Commentary on Messent and Wieselberg. *Journal of Family Therapy 14, 3*, 331–336.

Laureano, M. and Poliandro, E. (1991). Understanding cultural values of Latino male alcoholics and their families: A culture sensitive model. *Journal of Chemical Dependency Treatment 14, 1*, 137–155.

Lawson, W. B. (1986). Chronic mental illness and the black family: Mental health perspectives. *American Journal of Social Psychiatry 6, 1*, 57–61.

Lawson, E. J. and Thompson, A. (1995). Black men make sense of marital distress and divorce: An exploratory study. *Family Relations 44*, 211–218.

Lazarus, A. A. (1995). Different types of eclecticism and integration: Let's be aware of the dangers. *Journal of Psychotherapy Integration 5, 1*, 27–40.

Lebra, T. S. (1982). Self-reconstruction in Japanese religious psychotherapy. In A. J. Marsella and G. M. White (Eds.), *Cultural conception of mental health and therapy*. Dordrecht, Holland: D. Reidel.

Lebra, W. P. (Ed.). (1976). *Culture-bound syndromes, ethnopsychiatry and alternative therapies*. Honolulu: University of Hawaii Press.

Lee, D. H. (1988). Korean shamans: Role playing through trance possession. In R. Schechner and W. Appel (Eds.), *By means of performance*: Intercultural studies of theater and ritual (pp. 149–166). Cambridge: Cambridge University Press.

Lee, E. (1982). A social systems approach to assessment and treatment of Chinese American families. In M. McGoldrick, J. K. Pearce and J. Giordano (Eds.), *Ethnicity and family therapy* (pp. 527–549). New York: Guilford.

Lee, E. (1988). Cultural factors in working with Southeast Asian refugee adolescents. *Journal of Adolescence 11*, 167–179.

Lefley, H. P. (Ed). (1998). *Families coping with mental illness: The cultural context*. San Francisco: Jossey-Bass.

Lemon, S. D., Newfield, N. A. and Dobbins, J. E. (1993). Culturally sensitive family therapy in Appalachia. *Journal of Systemic Therapies 12, 4*, 8–26.

Leung, P. K. and Boehnlein, J. (1996). Vietnamese families. In M. McGoldrick, J. K. Pearce and J. Giordano (Eds.), *Ethnicity and family therapy* (2nd ed.). New York: Guilford.

Lewis, E. A. and Ford, B. (1990). The network utilization project: Incorporating traditional strengths of African-American families. *Social Work with Groups 13, 4*, 7–22.

Lieb, H. H. (1993). *Intergrational linguistics*. Amsterdam: Benjamins.

Lindblad-Goldberg, M., Dukes, J. L. and Lasley, J. H. (1988). Stress in black, low-income, single-parent families: Normative and dysfunctional patterns. *American Journal of Orthopsychiatry 58, 1*, 104–120.

Littlewood, R. and Dein, S. (1995). The effectiveness of words: Religion and healing among the Lubavitch of Stamford Hill. *Culture, Medicine and Psychiatry 19*, 339–383.

Lloyd, R. (1986). Black physicians' perceptions of the ability of marriage and family therapists to meet the needs of black middle-class families. *Dissertation Abstracts International 46, 7*, 2089-a.

Lock, M. (1995). Contesting the natural in Japan: Moral dilemmas and technologies of dying. *Culture, Medicine and Psychiatry 19, 1*, 1–38.

London, H. and Devore, W. (1988). Layers of understanding: Counseling ethnic minority families. *Family Relations 37, 3,* 310–314.

Long, K. A. (1986). Cultural considerations in the assessment and treatment of intrafamilial abuse. *American Journal of Orthopsychiatry 56, 1,* 131–136.

Luthar, S. and Quinlan, D. M. (1993). Parental images in two cultures: A study of women in India and America. *Journal of Cross-Cultural Psychology 24, 2,* 186–202.

Lutz, C. (1985). Depression and the translation of emotional worlds. In A. Kleinman and B. Good (Eds.), *Culture and depression: Studies in the anthropology of cross-cultural psychiatry of affect and disorder* (pp. 63–100). Berkeley: University of California Press.

Macintyre, M. (1995). Violent bodies and vicious exchanges—personification and objectification in the Massim. *Social Analysis 37,* 29–43.

MacKinnon, L. (1993). Systems in settings. The therapist as power broker. Australian and New Zealand Family Therapy Conference, Canberra, Australia, 1993. *Australian and New Zealand Journal of Family Therapy 14, 3,* 112–117.

Madanes, C. (1991). Strategic family therapy. In A. S. Gurnman and D. P. Kniskern (Eds.), *Handbook of family therapy II* (pp. 396–416). New York: Brunner/Mazel.

Mageo, J. M. (1995). The reconfiguring self. *American Anthropologist 97, 2,* 282–296.

Maharajh, H. D. and Bhugra, D. (1993). Brief family therapy with alcohol-dependent men in Trinidad and Tobago. *Acta Psychiatr Scand, 87, 6,* 422–426.

Mailick, M. D. and Vigilante, F. W. (1997). The family assessment wheel: A social constructionist perspective. *Families in Society 78,* 361–369.

Man Keung, H. (1989). Applying family therapy theories to Asian/Pacific Americans. *Contemporary Family Therapy 11, 1,* 61–68.

Martinez, J. (1991). Father-daughter incest in Spanish-speaking and Anglo families. *Dissertation Abstracts International 52, 3,* 1092-A.

Martinez, K. J. (1994). Cultural sensitivity in family therapy gone awry. *Hispanic Journal of Behavioral Sciences 16, 1,* 75–89.

Mazurova, A. and Rozin, M. V. (1991). Family conflicts of countercultural youth in the USSR and possible psychotherapeutic approaches. *The American Journal of Family Therapy 19, 1,* 47–53.

McGill, D. (1983). Cultural concepts for family therapy. In C. J. Falicov (Ed.), *Cultural perspectives in family therapy* (pp. 108–121). Rockville, Md.: Aspen Systems.

McGill, D. W. (1987). Language, cultural psychology and family therapy. Japanese example from an international perspective. *Contemporary Family Therapy 9, 4,* 283–293.

McGill, D. W. (1992). The cultural story in multicultural family therapy. *Families in Society 73, 6,* 339–349.

McGoldrick, M. (1982). Ethnicity and family therapy: An overview. In M. McGoldrick, J. K. Pearce and J. Giordano (Eds.), *Ethnicity and family therapy* (pp. 3–30). New York: Guilford.

McGoldrick, M. (Ed.). (1998). *Re-visioning family therapy: Race, culture and gender in clinical practice.* New York: Guilford.

McGoldrick, M., Pearce, J. K. and Giordano, J. (Eds.). (1982). *Ethnicity and family therapy.* New York: Guilford.

McGoldrick, M., Pearce, J. K. and Giordano, J. (Eds.). (1996). *Ethnicity and family therapy* (2nd ed.). New York: Guilford.

McGoldrick, M., Preto, N. G., Hines, P. M. and Lee, E. (1991). Ethnicity and family therapy. In A. S. Gurman and D. P. Kniskern (Eds.), *Handbook of family therapy II* (pp. 546–582). New York: Brunner/Mazel.

McGoldrick, M. and Rohrbaugh, M. (1987). Researching ethnic family stereotypes. *Family Process 26, 1*, 89–99.

Messent, P. (1992). Working with Bangladeshi families in the East End of London. *Journal of Family Therapy 14, 3*, 287–304.

Messerschmidt, D. A. (Ed.). (1981). *Anthropologists at home in North America: Methods and issues in the study of one's own society.* Cambridge: Cambridge University Press.

Miller, D. R. (1987). Shame/guilt proneness, symptoms and treatment satisfaction in Irish and Jewish families. *Dissertation Abstracts International 48, 4-B*, 1157.

Minuchin, S. (1974). *Families and family therapy.* Cambridge, Mass.: Harvard University Press.

Mitchell, G. and Cronson, H. (1987). The celebrity family: A clinical perspective. *The American Journal of Orthopsychiatry 58, 1*, 104–120.

Mohanan, D. J. (1993). Assessment of dementia patients and their families: An ecological—family-centered—approach. *Health and Social Work 18, 2*, 123–131.

Mondykowski, S. M. (1982). Polish families. In M. McGoldrick, J. K. Pearce and J. Giordano (Eds.), *Ethnicity and family therapy* (pp. 393–411). New York: Guilford.

Montalvo, B. and Gutierrez, M. (1983). A perspective for the use of the cultural dimension in family therapy. In C. J. Falicov (Ed.), *Cultural perspectives in family therapy* (pp. 15–2). Rockville, Md.: Aspen Systems.

Moos, R. and Moos, B. S. (1976). A typology of family social environment. *Family Process 15, 4*, 357–371.

Morley, P. and Wallis, R. (1978). *Culture and curing: Anthropological perspectives on traditional medical beliefs and practices.* Pittsburgh: University of Pittsburgh Press.

Moro, R. and Mazet, P. (1993). Construction d'un nouveau cadre therapeutique pour les familles migrantes [Development of a new therapeutic approach to migrant families]. *Ann-Med-Psychol-Paris 151, 2*, 87–92.

Morris, J. R. (1987). Family-of-origin and family therapy considerations with black families. *Family Therapy Collections 21*, 69–79.

Moskos, C. C., Jr. (1981). Growing up Greek in America. In J. Guillemin (Ed.), *Anthropological realities: Readings in the science of culture* (pp. 387–400). New Brunswick, N.J.: Transaction Books.

Mullender, A. (1990). The Ebony Project—Bicultural group work with transracial foster parents. *Social Work with Groups 13, 4*, 23–41.

Munroe, A. H. and Jacobson, N. S. (1991). Behavioral marital therapy. In A. S. Gurman and D. P. Kniskern (Eds.), *Handbook of family therapy* (pp. 96–133). New York: Brunner/Mazel.

Murdock, G. P. (1949). *Social structures.* New York: Macmillan.

Newfield, N. A., Kuehl, B. P., Joaning, H. P. and Quinn, W. H. (1990). A mini ethnography of the family therapy of adolescent drug abuse: The ambiguous experience. *Alcoholism Treatment Quarterly 17, 2*, 57–79.

Nomura, N., Noguchi, Y., Saito, S. and Tezuka, I. (1995). Family characteristics and dynamics in Japan and the United States: A preliminary report from the Family Environment Scale. *International Journal of Intercultural Relations 19, 1*, 59–86.

O'Brian, C. (1990). Family therapy with black families. *Journal of Family therapy 12, 1*, 3–16.

O'Connor, J. J. (1984). The resurrection of a magical reality: Treatment of functional migraine in a child. *Family Process 234*, 501–509.

O'Connor, J. J. and Hoorwitz, A. N. (1984). The bogeyman cometh: A strategic approach for difficult adolescents. *Family Process 23*, 237–249.

Olson, F. (1993). The development and impact of ritual in couple counseling. *Counseling and Values 38, 1*, 12–20.

Onnis, L., Gennaro, A. D., Cespa, G. A., Agostini, A., Chouby, A., Dentale, R. C. and Quinzi, P. (1994). Sculpting present and future: A systemic intervention mode applied to psychosomatic families. *Family Process 33*, 431–355.

Oswalt, W. H. (1972). *Other people, other customs. World ethnography and its history.* New York: Holt, Rinehart and Winston.

Papp, P. (1980). The Greek Chorus and other techniques of family therapy. *Family Process 19, 1*, 45–57.

Papp, P. (1982). Staging reciprocal metaphors in a couples group. *Family Process 21*, 453–467.

Pare, D. A. (1996). Culture and meaning: Expanding the metaphorical repertoire of family therapy. *Family Process 35*, 21–42.

Parry, A. (1991). Universe of stories. *Family Process 30*, 37–54.

Parthasarathy, A. (1989). *The symbolism of Hindu gods and rituals.* Bombay: Vedanta Life Institute.

Pearl, D. (1987). *A textbook on Muslim personal law.* London: Croom Helm.

Pedersen, P. B. (1997). *Culture-centered counseling interventions: Striving for accuracy.* Thousand Oaks, Calif.: Sage.

Penn, P. and Frankfurt, M. (1994). Creating a participant text: Writing, multiple voices, narrative multiplicity. *Family Process 33*, 217–231.

Piaget, J. (1971). Biology and knowledge. Edinburgh: Edinburgh University Press.

Pinderhughes, E. (1987). *Understanding race, ethnicity and power: The key of efficacy in clinical practice.* New York: Free Press.

Pinsoff, W. P. (1992). Commentary: Culture and psychotherapy integration. *Family Process 31*, 116–118.

Ponterotto, J. G. and Pedersen, P. B. (1993). *Preventing prejudice: A guide for counselors and educators.* New York: Fordham University.

Preli, R. and Bernard, J. M. (1993). Making multiculturalism relevant for majority culture graduate students. *Journal of Marital and Family Therapy 19, 1*, 5–16.

Purves, W. K. (1995). *Life: The science of biology* (4th ed.). Sutherland, Mass.: Sinauer Associates.

Quinn, W. H., Newfield, N. A. and Protinsky, H. O. (1985). Rites of passage in families with adolescents. *Family Process 24, 1*, 101–111.

Rabin, C. (1992). The cultural context in treating a lesbian couple: An Israeli experience. *Journal of Strategic and Systemic Therapies 11, 4*, 42–58.

Ramondo, N. (1991). Cultural issues in therapy: On the fringe. *The Australian and New Zealand Journal of Family Therapy 12, 2*, 69–78.

Ravich, R. (1992). Recent advances toward meta-psychology of human relationships. *Ann-Ist-Super Sanita 28*, 2, 161–167.

Reichelt, S. and Sveaass, N. (1994). Therapy with refugee families: What is a "good" conversation? *Family Process 33*, 247–262.

Reid, J. (1983). *Sorcerers and healing spirits: Continuity and change in Aboriginal medical system.* Canberra: Australian National University Press.

Richeport-Haley, M. (1997). Ethnicity in family therapy: A comparison of brief strategic therapy with culture-focused therapy. *American Journal of Family Therapy 26*, 77–90.

Richmond, Virginia P. (1991). *Non-verbal communication in interpersonal relations.* New York: Prentice-Hall.

Roberto, L. G. (1991). Symbolic-experiential family therapy. In A. S. Gurman and D. P. Kniskern (Eds.), *Handbook of family therapy II* (pp. 444–478). New York: Brunner/Mazel.

Roberts, H. H. (1991). The experiences of black families who are involuntarily involved in family therapy treatment. *Dissertation Abstracts International 51*, 10-B, 5039.

Roijen, S. (1991). Art therapy in transcultural family therapy. *Contemporary Family Therapy 13*, 6, 563–571.

Roizblatt, A. and Pilowsky, D. (1996). Forced migration and resettlement: Its impact on families and individuals. *Contemporary Family Therapy 18*, 513–521.

Rolland, J. S. (1987). Family illness paradigms: Evolution and significance. *Family Systems Medicine 15*, 4, 482–503.

Rosaldo, R. (1993). *Culture and truth: The remaking of social analysis.* Boston: Beacon Press.

Roth, N. F. (1987). *Working with fusion in lesbian couples.* Paper presented at the annual conference of the American Association for Marriage and Family Therapy, Orlando, Florida.

Rowe, P. and Beamish, P. M. (1992). *The African American and AIDS: Counseling issues and strategies.* Evaluative Report 142. Ohio: Geographic Sources.

Rubin, S. S. and Nasser, H. Z. (1993). Psychotherapy and supervision with a bereaved Muslim family: An intervention that almost failed. *Psychiatry: Interpersonal and Biological Processes 56*, 4, 338–348.

Sager, C. J. (1981). Couples therapy and marriage contracts. In A. S. Gurman and D. P. Kniskern (Eds.), *Handbook of family therapy I* (pp. 85–130), New York: Brinner/Mazel.

Santisteban, D. A., Szapocznik, J., Perez-Vidal, A. and Kurtines, W. M. (1996). Efficacy of intervention for engaging youth and families into treatment and some variables that may contribute to differential effectiveness. *Journal of Family Psychology 10*, 1, 35–44.

Saussure, F. de. (1959). *Course in general linguistics.* Translated from the French by W. Baskin. New York: Philosophical Library.

Scandariato, R. (1993). La therapie avec les families immigrees [Therapy with immigrant families], *Sante-Ment-Que 18*, 1, 125–142.

Schact, A. et al. (1989). Home-based therapy with American-Indian families. *American Indian and Alaska Native Mental Health Research 3*, 2, 27–42.

Schacht, A. J., Tafoya, N. and Mirabla, K. (1989). Home-based therapy with American Indian families. *American Indian Alaska Native Mental Health Research 3*, 2, 27–42.

Schensul, J. J. (1988). *Conceptual framework of child abuse in Latino communities*. Hispanic Health Council, Hartford, Conn.

Schieffelin, Edward L. (1985). The cultural analysis of depressive affect: An example from New Guinea. In A. Kleinman and B. Good (Eds.) *Culture and depression* (pp. 101–133). Berkeley: University of California Press.

Schlossberger, E. S. and Hecker, L. L. (1998). Reflections of Jewishness and its implications for family therapy. *American Journal of Family Therapy 26*, 129–146.

Schwartzman, J. (1982). Creativity, pathology and family structure. A cybernetic metaphor. *Family Process 21*, 1, 113–128.

Schwartzman, J. (1983). Family ethnography: A tool for clinicians. In C. J. Falicov (Ed.), *Cultural perspectives in family therapy* (pp. 137–149). Rockville, Md.: Aspen Systems.

Sciarra, D. and Ponterroto, J. (1991). Counseling the Hispanic bilingual family: Challenges to the therapeutic process. *Psychotherapy 28*, 3, 473–479.

Sebring, D. L. (1985). Considerations in counseling interracial children. *Journal of Non-White Concerns in Personnel and Guidance 13*, 1, 3–9.

Seedat, M. and Nell, V. (1990). Third World or one world: Mysticism, pragmatism and pain in family therapy in South Africa. *South African Journal of Instructional Psychology 117*, 4, 183–189.

Segal, L. (1991). Brief therapy: The MRI approach. In A. S. Gurman and D. P. Kniskern (Eds.), *Handbook of family therapy II* (pp. 171–199). New York: Brunner/Mazel.

Seltzer, W. J. (1985). Conversion disorder in childhood and adolescence: A familial/cultural approach. *Family Systems Medicine 3*, 3, 261–280.

Seltzer, W. J. and Seltzer, M. R. (1983). Material, myth and magic: A cultural approach to family therapy. *Family Process 22*, 3–14.

Serrano, J. A. (1985). La terapia con familias emigrantes. [Therapy with emigrant families]. *Psicopatologia 5*, 3, 255–263.

Shapiro, E. R. (1996). Family bereavement and cultural diversity: A social developmental perspective. *Family Process 35*, 313–332.

Simons, R. C. and Hughes, C. C., eds. (1985). *The culture-bound syndromes: Folk illnesses of psychiatric and anthropological interest*. Dordrecht: D. Reidel.

Singer, M. (1988). *Alcoholism, Impact on the Hispanic Child. Report no. 5*. Hartford, Conn.: Hispanic Health Council.

Sluzki, C. (1979). Migration and family conflict. *Family Process 18*, 4, 379–390.

Sluzki, C. E. (1992). Transformations: A blueprint for narrative changes in therapy. *Family Process 31*, 217–230.

Smith, D. (1996). Hungarian families. In M. McGoldrick, J. K. Pearce and J. Giordano (Eds.), *Ethnicity and family therapy* (2nd ed.). New York: Guilford.

Smith, P. B. and Bond, M. H. (1993). *Social psychology across cultures*. New York: Harvester Wheatsheaf.

Solomon, A. (1992). Clinical diagnosis among diverse populations: A multicultural perspective. *Families in Society 73*, 6, 371–377.

Spaights, E. (1990). The therapeutic implications of working with the black family. *Journal of Instructional Psychology 17*, 4, 183–189.

Spiegel, J. (1982). An ecological model of ethnic families. In M. McGoldrick, J. K. Pearce and J. Giordano (Eds.), *Ethnicity and family therapy* (pp. 31–51). New York: Guilford.

Stein, H. F. (1985). Therapist and family values in a cultural context. *Counseling and Values 30, 1,* 35–46.

Steinberger, C. B. (1989). Teenage depression: A cultural-interpersonal-intrapsychic perspective. *The Psychoanalytic Review 76, 1,* 1–18.

Strier, D. R. (1996). Coping strategies of immigrant parents: Directions for family therapy. *Family Process 35,* 363–376.

Sue, D. (1994). Incorporating cultural diversity in family therapy. *The Family Psychologist 10, 2,* 19–21.

Suttles, G. D. (1981). Anatomy of a Chicago slum. In J. Guillemin (Ed.), *Anthropological realities: Readings in the science of culture* (pp. 297–310). New Brunswick, N. J.: Transaction Books.

Suwanlert, S. (1976). Phii Pob, spirit possession in rural Thailand. In W. P. Lebra (Ed.), *Culture-bound syndromes, ethnopsychiatry and alternative therapies* (pp. 68–87). Honolulu: University of Hawaii Press.

Sykes, D. K. (1987). An approach to working with black youth in cross-cultural therapy. *Clinical Social Work Journal 15, 3,* 260–270.

Szapocznik, J. et al. (1986). Bicultural Effectiveness Training (BET). *Hispanic Journal of Behavioral Sciences 8, 4,* 303–330.

Szapocznik, J, Kurtines, W. M., Santisteban, D. A. and Rio, A. T. (1990). The interplay of advances among theory, research and application in treatment interventions aimed at behavior of children and adolescents. *Journal of Counseling and Clinical Psychology 56, 6,* 696–703.

Tafoya, T (1989). Circles and cedar: Native Americans and family therapy. In G. Saba, B. Karrer and K. Hardy (Eds.) *Minorities and family therapy* (pp. 71–98). New York: Haworth.

Tamasese, K. and Waldegrave, C. (1996). Cultural and gender accountability in the "just therapy" approach. In C. McLean, M. Carey and C. White (Eds.) *Men's ways of being: New directions in theory and psychology* (pp. 51–62). Boulder, Colo.: Westview Press.

Tamura, T. and Lau, A. (1992). Connectedness versus separateness: Applicability of family therapy to Japanese families. *Family Process 31, 4,* 319–340.

Thomas, V. G. (1990). Problems of dual-career black couples: Identification and implications for family interventions. *Journal of Multicultural Counseling and Development 18, 2,* 58–67.

Thrasher, S. and Anderson, G. (1988). The West Indian family: Treatment challenges. *Social Casework 69, 3,* 171–176.

Todd, T., Joanning, H., Enders, I. and Mutchler, I. (1990). Using ethnographic interviews to create a more cooperative client-therapist relationship. *Journal of Family Psychotherapy 1, 3,* 51–63.

Tomm, K., Suzuki, K. and Suzuki, K. (1990). The kan-nomushi: An inner externalization that enables compromise? *Australian and New Zealand Journal of Family Therapy 11, 2,* 104–105.

Triandis, H. C. and Berry, J. (Eds.). (1980). *Handbook of cross-cultural Psychology, Vol. 2.* Boston: Allyn and Bacon.

Tseng, W. (1976). Folk psychotherapy in Taiwan. In W. P. Lebra (Ed.), *Culture-*

bound syndromes ethnopsychiatry and alternative therapies (pp. 164–178). Honolulu: University of Hawaii Press.

Turner, J. E. (1991). Migrants and their therapists: A trans-context approach. *Family Process 30*, 4, 407–419.

Tyler, S. A. (1969). *Cognitive Anthropology*. New York: Holt, Rinehart and Winston.

Vazquez-Nuttall, E., Avila-Vivas, Z. and Morales-Barreto, G. (1984). Working with Latin American families. *Family Therapy Collections 9*, 74–90.

Verhoff, J., Chadiha, L., Veber, D. and Sutherland, L. (1993). Affects and interactions in newlyweds' narratives: Black and white couples compared. *Journal of Narrative and Life History 4*, 3, 361–370.

Waidron, J. A. et al. (1986). A children's divorce clinic: Analysis of 200 cases in Hawaii. *Journal of Divorce 9*, 3, 111–121.

Waldegrave, C. (1998). The challenges of culture to psychology and postmodern thinking. In M. McGoldrick (Ed.), *Re-visioning family therapy: Race, culture and gender in clinical practice* (pp. 404–413). New York: Guilford.

Wang, L. (1994). Marriage and family therapy with people from China. *Contemporary Family Therapy 16*, 1, 25–37.

Waters, D. B. (1986). Over the threshold. *Family Therapy Networker 10*, 4, 52.

Watson, M. F. (1998). African-American sibling relationships. In M. McGoldrick, (Ed.), *Re-visioning family therapy: Race, culture and gender in clinical practice* (pp. 282–294). New York: Guilford.

Watts-Jones, D (1992). Jamaican woman with a panic disorder. *Family Process 31*, 105–113.

Wieselberg, H. (1992). Family therapy and ultra-Orthodox Jewish families: A structural approach. *Journal of Family Therapy 14*, 3, 305–329.

Williams, S. E., and Wright, D. F. (1992). Empowerment: The strengths of black families revisited. *Journal of Multicultural Social Work 2*, 4, 23–36.

Willis, J. T. (1988). An effective counseling model for treating the black family. *Family Therapy 15*, 2, 185–194.

Wilson, I. and Stith, S. (1991). Culturally sensitive therapy with black clients. *Journal of Multicultural Counseling and Development 19*, 1, 32–43.

Winawer, H. and Wetzel, N. A. (1996). German families. In M. McGoldrick, J. K. Pearce and J. Giordano (Eds.), *Ethnicity and family therapy* (2nd ed.). New York: Guilford.

Woehrer, C. E. (1988). Ethnic families and the circumplex model. Integrating nuclear and extended family systems. *Journal of Psychotherapy and the Family 4*, 1–2, 199–237.

Wolf, M. (1981). *Child training and the Chinese family*. In J. Guillemin (Ed.), *Anthropological realities: Readings in the science of culture* (pp. 123–138). New Brunswick, N. J.: Transaction Books.

Wood, B. (1992). Do cultures clarify models or do models clarify cultures? *Family Process 31*, 2, 193–195.

Yaccarino, M. E. (1993). Using Minuchin's structural family therapy techniques with Italian American families. *Contemporary Family Therapy 15*, 6, 459–466.

Yahyaoui, A. (1988). Ethnopsychoanalytic family consultation and intercultural framework: Two-way speaking or the secret of Polichinelle. *Perspective Psychiatriques 27*, 13, 206–214.

Yalung, F. N. (1992). *A cross-cultural counseling framework for Asian parents of children with special needs based on the dynamics of the Filipino family.* MA Thesis. San Jose State University.

Zayas, L. H. and Palleja, J. (1988). Puerto Rican familism: Consideration for family therapy. *Family Relations 37*, 3, 260–264.

Zimmerman, J. L. and Dickerson, V. C. (1994). Using narrative metaphor: Implications for theory and clinical practice. *Family Process 33*, 233–245.

Ziter, M. L. P. (1987). Culturally-sensitive treatment of black alcoholic families. *Social Work 32*, 2, 131–135.

Zulueta, F. (1990). Bilingualism and family therapy. *Journal of Family Therapy 12*, 3, 255–265.

Index

159; let the family define its own
identity and respect it, 160; respect
the family's norms, values and customs, 159; share your own self and
life, xv, 162; try to create a common
cultural ground with the family, 160,
207; try to influence within the frame
of reference of the family's own culture, 163; use intermediaries, xv, 162.
See also therapeutic alliance in culturally competent family therapy

handicapped children, 224
history of the case, 144
homeostasis, 10, 16, 17–18, 24
honor and respect, 63, 73, 106, 115–16,
146
honor of the family, 59–60, 112, 128,
145, 147

illness and death, attitudes toward in
families, 64
images, 53–54, 58; as part of the family's self-concept, 53, 58
immigration, xi, xiii, 3–4, 6, 13, 16,
147, 216
individualism, 12, 13, 38, 58, 59, 148,
149
inducing an altered state of mind, 182–
83
industrialization, xiii, 6, 40
information processing, xi, 21, 25–28,
30, 33, 38, 42, 65, 83–117; family
programs, xii, 25–28, 83, 86–87; as a
framework for systematizing culturally competent family therapy, 25–28,
85–86; input and output, 25, 86;
memory, 86; metaprograms, 28
intermarriage, 6–7, 13, 216
intimacy, attitudes toward expressions
of, 62
intolerance, 4

kinship systems, 17

leaving home as a right or duty, 62
lesbian couples, 223

level of organization of the family, 45,
47–48, 66, 68; flexibility versus rigidity in division of labor and roles, 68;
flexibility versus rigidity of family
structure, 45, 47–48
lineage clans, 15–16
linguistics, xi, xv, 19, 21, 30

marriage: endogamous versus exogamous, 148; as a value, 58–59
membership of the family, 45–46, 48,
66
metaprograms for restoring simplicity,
28, 30, 103–6
military occupation, xiii
modern professional help, attitude toward, 81–82
multicultural families, xi
multiculturalism, 4, 6; current interest
in, 4
multisystemic therapy, theoretical language of, 21
Muslims, 7, 12
mutual responsibility among family
members, 60–61
myths, 7, 20, 53–54, 128, 147; as parts
of the family's self-concept, 53–54

narrative family therapy, 14, 20, 172–73
nudity and touch in the family, 68–69, 74

obligatory codes, 7–8, 15–16
ontological and epistemological premises, xii, 87–89
openness in family relations, 62

parsimony of an information-processing
system, 27; as a definitional trait of
simplicity, 27; loss of, 27; restored
and cannot be restored, 28
patrilineal, matrilineal, bilineal, and
double descent families, 15–16, 20,
46, 128
persecution, 40
presenting symptoms, as external manifestations of bugs, xiv, 29
prevalent trends, 7–8

About the Author

SHLOMO ARIEL, a licensed expert and supervisor of clinical psychology and marital and family therapy, is the co-director of the Integrative Psychotherapy Center in Ramat Gan, Israel. He is also the Coordinator of Research and Academic Development at the Israeli branch of Lesley College, Boston, Massachusetts, a member of the faculty of the Program for Advanced Studies in Integrative Psychotherapy at the Hebrew University in Jerusalem, Israel, and the chairperson of the Israeli Association of Psychotherapy Integration.

ISBN 0-313-31079-3

EAN

9 780313 310799

90000>

HARDCOVER BAR CODE